THE
WRECK
OF THE
NEVA

A full and Horrifying Account
of a most dreadful
SHIPWRECK

Of the Neva, Convict Ship,
Which sailed from Cork, for
New South Wales, in May
last, containing **241** Souls on
Board, consisting of **150** female Convicts, **9** free Women,
and **55** Children, all of whom
perished except **6**; and **9** of
the Crew; with an Account
of the dreadful Sufferings of
those who were saved, while
staying on a desert Island,
being altogether one of the
most heart-rending Accounts
of Human Suffering which
has occurred for a very long
Period.

Detail from a broadsheet announcing the wreck of the *Neva*.
Courtesy of Mitchell Library, State Library of NSW. ML An 7

THE
WRECK
OF THE
NEVA

THE HORRIFYING FATE OF A CONVICT SHIP
AND THE IRISH WOMEN ABOARD

CAL McCARTHY & KEVIN TODD

MERCIER PRESS
IRISH PUBLISHER – IRISH STORY

MERCIER PRESS

Cork

www.mercierpress.ie

© Cal McCarthy & Kevin Todd, 2013

ISBN: 978 1 85635 981 8

10 9 8 7 6 5 4 3 2 1

A CIP record for this title is available from the British Library

Printed and bound in the EU.

Contents

A map of Van Diemen's Land (now Tasmania) published in 1839. The inset shows the River Tamar with George Town and Launceston marked with circles. *Courtesy of Tasmanian Archive and Heritage Office, NS59/1/1 George Frankland's map of Tasmania.*

Introduction

King Island (sometimes called King's Island) is a small and seemingly inconsequential island lying just off the north-western coast of Tasmania (formerly Van Diemen's Land) in a shipping channel, about halfway between Tasmania and the mainland Australian state of Victoria. Today the island is home to about 1,700 people – a small but vibrant community built around the dairy, beef, fishing and tourism industries. Key to the development of tourism is the maritime history of the island and its reputation as one of the southern hemisphere's most notorious graveyards for shipping.

The northern end of the island is the site of the Cape Wickham lighthouse. Established in 1861, the lighthouse is the tallest in Australia. It stands at the southern side of 'The Eye of the Needle' – the eighty-four-kilometre-wide western entrance to Bass Strait. Shipping moving eastwards from the vastness of the Southern Ocean has to locate and navigate this comparatively tiny entrance before moving along the strait towards Sydney. The lighthouse was built in reaction to the wreck of an emigrant ship, the *Cataraqui*. Her voyage from Liverpool ended in tragedy when she was wrecked off King Island in 1845.

In the shadow of this lonely tower, a little plaque marks the

The Wreck of the *Neva*

location of seven bodies re-interred on the site after they were exposed by a bush fire. Many of their shipmates lay in close proximity whilst, for almost two centuries, restless seas crashed against the treacherous rocks and sandy shores beneath. These are the women of the *Neva*.

The lighthouse at Cape Wickham was established in 1861 and at 48 metres is the tallest in Australia. *Photo: Kevin Todd*

At approximately 5 a.m. on the morning of 13 May 1835, a three-masted barque called *Neva* was wrecked off Cape Wickham. The ship broke up upon hitting a reef and more than 200 souls were drowned. Mystery still shrouds the exact site of the wreck and the precise reason why the treacherous waters to the north of King Island claimed the ship. The loss of the *Neva* was one of the worst shipwrecks in Australian history. It was also one of the most peculiar.

Most of those who perished were not sailors, or pirates, or profiteers. They were not engaged in any spectacular naval manoeuvre or battle. They were not seeking out new continents or territories. They had not even set off for Australia by choice. They would not be mourned by the British Empire, for they were considered among its lowest forms of life: these unfortunate souls were Irish and female, and they were convicts. How was it that some 200 Irish women met their end beneath the raging waters of Australia's Bass Strait? Why did these women die almost 20,000 kilometres from the land of their birth and oceans away from their nearest and dearest?

This book will answer those questions, shedding light upon a mystery that has endured for almost 200 years. Over the eight decades of convict transportation from the British Isles to Australia, only five convict ships were wrecked. The *Neva* wreck resulted in a greater loss of life than any of the other four. It created quite a stir and newspapers in Australia, Ireland and Britain reported the events in a tragic and dramatic tone. No doubt all of this created conversation, which sometimes turned to inspiration.

A few years after the ship was lost, a pamphlet entitled *Full Particulars of the Dreadful Shipwreck of the Ship Tartar, Free Trader, With the Horrible Sufferings of Part of the Crew, Who were compelled to Eat each other to Support Existence* was published in Glasgow. The pamphlet told the story of a ship named *Tartar* being wrecked in Bass Strait during its passage from Cork to Sydney. It stated that the survivors were washed ashore on an uninhabited island some 145 kilometres from King Island. They attempted to reach King Island on a makeshift raft. However, they were stricken by hunger and forced to resort to cannibalism. The unfortunate victims were selected by lot. By the time it reached King Island, the raft was home to only two survivors: John M. Daniel, who returned to his native Galway, bringing with him the terrible story of the *Tartar*, and Captain Peck, master of the *Tartar*. The pamphlet claimed that Captain Peck died on King Island.

The pamphlet's story of the *Tartar* was fiction, but it was almost certainly based on the story of the *Neva*. It paid homage to the actual events by using the names of people, places, dates and ships that all featured in the *Neva*'s story. The true story was almost as dramatic as the fiction it inspired. Yet the hundred years following the wrecking of the *Neva* produced little literature related to the disaster itself. General texts such as George Dunderdale's *The Book of the Bush* and J. F. Layson's *Memorable Shipwrecks and Seafaring Adventures of the Nineteenth Century*, and periodicals such as *The Chronicles of the Sea*, examined the topic, but their accounts were brief and primarily based on eyewitness statements given to the *Neva* enquiry. In the twentieth century that brevity was not greatly expanded upon and the *Neva*'s story was usually framed in a wider context. Graeme Broxam and Michael Nash's excellent *Tasmanian Shipwrecks* recorded the reported details, whilst Charles Bateson's seminal *The Convict Ships, 1787–1868* devoted a section to the disaster. However, to date, the most searching examination of the circumstances surrounding the loss of the ship came in G. A. Mawer's exceptional *Most*

Perfectly Safe: The Convict Shipwreck Disasters of 1833–42. Mawer did not concentrate entirely on the *Neva*, but rather on all five convict shipwrecks. Nonetheless he presented a clear and compelling narrative of the *Neva*'s last days and advanced a credible theory for the location of the wreck.

This book builds on Mawer's work and is the product of a collaboration between two researchers located in different countries. It makes use of additional source material, resulting in a much more detailed narrative, which focuses not only on the ship and its tragic end, but also on the convicts and crew who sailed on her. It tells their story from Cork to King Island, and onward to colonial Australia. In addition, it details the authorities' reaction to the tragedy, and presents competing theories of what really happened to the *Neva*. It is written as a narrative, not as a historical study. To make the text fully accessible, we have provided some general information for those readers not intimately familiar with nineteenth-century Irish or Australian history. In constructing the more detailed story, we have sought to maintain the highest standards of scholarly research to ensure that much of the story we present is entirely, and verifiably, true. Whilst we also present what is probably true, and what might be true, we have taken great care to ensure that the reader is always able to distinguish between credible theory and irrefutable fact.

There are gaps in the *Neva* narrative. Much of the most relevant source material has been ravaged by time or destroyed by human action. The story's main characters are neither rich nor powerful, and thus they are not accessible through traditional archives. Where possible, we have used alternative sources, but some gaps remain. We cannot definitively comment on the emotions or psychological profiles of illiterate women who died nearly two centuries ago; we can only guess at such things. In that regard we are no more qualified than our readers. What follows is what we know and what might have been. The facts are absolute. The theories are based on those facts.

1

Ireland and Transportation

Human nature remains constant from age to age. Yet its outward manifestations (behaviour) are a direct result of its interaction with two major variables: place and time. Thus, before entering into the narrative of the *Neva*'s tragic tale, it is necessary to place that story in its correct context, the places and time in which its events occurred. Consequently, to understand why 150 women were forcibly removed from Ireland on a ship called *Neva*, one must understand that 1830s Ireland was a very different place to the Ireland of today.

Politically Ireland was ruled by Great Britain from the London parliament. Whilst Britain had had varying degrees of influence over Irish affairs for nearly seven centuries, the direct rule of the 1830s was comparatively new. It was the result of a violent assertion of their right to independence by a group of Irish rebels known as the United Irishmen. In the wake of the French and American revolutions, the United Irishmen struck for independence in 1798. Throughout that summer ferocious violence engulfed parts of Leinster and the north-east. Later that year small French forces attempted to support the Irish rebels and engaged British forces in Connaught and in Donegal. In the end, however, the disorganised rebellion was crushed and its leaders were executed. Nonetheless, small rebel forces continued to fight a disjointed guerrilla campaign in various parts of the countryside. In 1803 Robert Emmet attempted another large-scale rebellion. It, too, failed, and the United Irishmen's organisation was soon dissolved. However, the names of battles such as Vinegar Hill and Castlebar were etched into Irish folk memory. The parents of many of the women upon whose story we will dwell remembered these events, and as young girls these women were doubtlessly told of the very recent and bloody conflict between some Irish people and the British authorities who sought to rule them.

Those British authorities decided they could no longer tolerate a quasi-independent Irish parliament and began to organise its dissolution. In 1800 the Irish and British parliaments passed the Acts of Union, establishing a new nation known as the United Kingdom of Great Britain and Ireland. In effect the Irish parliament voted itself out of existence. This act of self-destruction was partly achieved by bribery. The new nation's flag, a combination of the flags of all of its constituent countries, was, and is, known as the 'Union Jack'. It incorporates the St Patrick's cross of Ireland, and still adorns one corner of the modern Australian flag.

All of this political manoeuvring was of little consequence

to the ordinary Irish people among whom the *Neva*'s convicts were reared. Most of them were Roman Catholics. Yet centuries of state-sponsored discrimination had ensured that most of Ireland's property was owned by Protestants. At that time voting rights were contingent upon the ownership of property, and since very few Catholics owned property, very few Catholics could vote. Those who were lucky enough to maintain the ownership of some property could do so, but they could not sit in the parliament.

A wealthy Irish Catholic, Daniel O'Connell, sought to overturn that restriction. He succeeded in being elected to the British parliament in 1828 and 1829, and his campaign, along with the pressure of British public opinion, led to the Catholic Relief Act of 1829, which allowed Roman Catholic property owners to sit in the British parliament. Again, this was of little consequence to the women who would sail on the *Neva*. They would not be running for parliament and their husbands and fathers did not have enough property to exercise a vote. In fact the women would have had to live to be more than 100 years of age if they were to exercise the franchise.

Of much more consequence to these ordinary Irish people was the issue of tithes and the way in which this manifested itself all around them. Catholic emancipation failed to remove the obligation of Irish Catholic farmers to pay a percentage of their productivity (a tithe) to the established Protestant church. This caused huge resentment in a country that was already alive with the folk memory of large-scale rebellions and the long and bitter campaign for emancipation. From 1831 Catholics resisted the collection of tithes in various ways, which often led to violent clashes with the British military sent to seize cattle in lieu of payment. The country was degenerating into chaos, and relations between the peasantry and the military had never been more strained. Thus, the *Neva's* convicts grew up in conditions in which continuous civil disobedience was regularly punctuated by spiralling violence. The 'law and order' imposed by an authority that many considered alien seemed to protect the rights of a minority at the expense of the overwhelming majority. It commanded little respect and presented its critics with much ammunition.

As respect for British laws diminished, the vacuum created was gradually filled by numerous secret societies. The 'Whiteboys' were the best known of these clandestine groups. They acquired their peculiar name from their practice of wearing white smocks when active during the hours of darkness. Over time all agrarian agitators were generally categorised as Whiteboys, regardless of the group to which they belonged. The Whiteboys attempted to rule the countryside in pursuit of a quasi-political agenda. In theory they opposed tithes, excessive rents, evictions and all the oppressive acts of a regime that governed the poor in the interests of the rich. However, in reality many Whiteboy groups served the interests of their members ahead of any communal cause, and some came to terrorise their communities as much as the red-coated troops of the British crown did. The Whiteboys contributed greatly to the breaking down of law and order and helped to propagate a negative image of Ireland in the minds of those who governed from Britain. For many British lawmakers, Ireland came to be seen as a lawless wasteland overrun by disloyal and untrustworthy subjects who were incapable of organising any kind of acceptable civilisation.

For people who grew up in an environment in which law and order were not respected, it was perhaps relatively easy to overlook those laws in order to better their own situation. Add poverty to this waning respect for the laws of a biased legislature and one begins to understand that nineteenth-century Ireland was a fertile breeding ground for criminality.

One of the primary causes of poverty was the system of land ownership. The people who toiled upon the Irish soil did not own the land they worked. They were tenant farmers; they rented their land from wealthy landowners. Many of these landowners lived in Britain and relied on agents to collect the rents due from their estates. Irish tenant farmers had to sustain their own families and pay as much rent as the landlord thought they could bear, and they had to do this on comparatively small parcels of land. In addition, the Irish tended to have large families. This was seen as a method of guaranteeing care in old age. However, large families came at a price: not only did tenant farmers have to support their children, but ultimately they had to provide those children with the means to support themselves. Typically this meant subdividing small holdings between many children, and so more and more Irish families lived off ever-decreasing plots. As the Irish population grew rapidly, occasional shortages of food became a problem. Further, the potato crop suffered varying degrees of failure in various parts of the country throughout the first three decades of the nineteenth century. Such failures brought intense hardship upon a population that was far too dependent on one food source. The potentially catastrophic consequences of a complete failure were obvious. However, by the time that failure came, the *Neva* had already gone.

The Industrial Revolution did not transform Ireland in the way that it transformed Britain. Most Irish urban centres still depended on the surrounding countryside to support their economic activity. Thus, if tenant farmers were struggling to produce any surplus to sell, this had a detrimental effect on the urban traders who bought and sold their goods. Then, in 1832, Irish towns suffered their most serious setback in generations: cholera arrived. Cholera is a life-threatening condition caused by bacteria that infect the small intestine. Its symptoms are persistent diarrhoea and vomiting, often accompanied by violent headaches and facial discolouration, leading to rapid dehydration. The time between presentation of the first symptoms and death can be as short as twenty-four hours. In the 1830s the afflicted were treated by a variety of methods, including blistering, bleeding and cupping; all of these methods were completely ineffective and merely added to the discomfort of the dying patient. The cholera bacterium is typically spread via infected food and drinking water. However, this was not fully understood when the disease made its first appearance in Dublin and Belfast in January 1832. Characteristically it first appeared at the major ports and by April had made its way to Cork. Although cholera swept the entire island, the disease was most severe in urban centres. It is estimated that the outbreak of 1832 took some 25,000 Irish lives.

With poverty, famine and disease prevalent in Ireland, some people were, unsurprisingly, forced to participate in crime. However, the punishments were severe: various forms of corporal punishment were commonplace and, up until the late eighteenth century, the death penalty had been regularly enforced for crimes against property. As the nineteenth century progressed, society began to find the severity of the death penalty distasteful; forfeiting one's life for the theft of an animal was no longer considered a fair exchange. Whilst hanging remained on the statute books, the frequency with which it was used declined as judges sought ways to avoid imposing the sentence. On some occasions, the judge – or even the prosecutor – deliberately undervalued stolen goods, so that the death penalty would not apply.[1] The justice system needed a way of punishing and deterring criminals without resorting to such extreme measures. The solution it found was transportation of the offender to a faraway colony.

Transportation of prisoners was not a new idea. As early as the 1650s Irish rebels were exiled to Jamaica and Barbados for resisting the armies of Oliver Cromwell. The seventeenth and eighteenth centuries had seen Britain export some 60,000 criminals to the Americas. However, having lost the War of American Independence in 1781, Britain could no longer dispose of convicts in that fashion and British prisons filled to the point of overflow. In 1776 'prison hulks' (old ships with their masts and rigging removed) were placed on the River Thames. These rotting, dilapidated structures were permanently anchored in various harbours to provide temporary accommodation for those under sentence of transportation.

As the hulks and prisons filled, it was obvious that the authorities needed to find a new destination for banished criminals. In 1770 Captain James Cook had mapped the eastern coastline of a new country located on the opposite side of the world. Today that country is known as Australia. In the years immediately following Cook's discovery, the British administration had shown little interest in this far-flung possession. However, with the Americas now lost, this new land seemed to the British a viable solution to the problem of prison overcrowding. The first transport ships sailed southwards in 1787. Four years later, on 16 April 1791, the *Queen* carried 133 men and 22 women from Cork harbour. They were the first convicts to sail from Ireland for the new colony of New South Wales. Over the following six decades some 40,000 more followed them southwards.

The terms of a transportation sentence were simple. Convicts were banished for a set period of time. Usually they were not permitted to return for seven or fourteen years. However, some were transported for life; this meant that they could never return to their homeland. Of course, in reality, those banished for any period seldom returned – they could not afford to do so. In his influential work on transportation A. G. L. Shaw estimated that approximately 5 per cent of all transported convicts returned to the United Kingdom.[2]

The emerging colony may have offered convicts far greater opportunities and a higher standard of living than their homeland could. In the colony, transported convicts were put to work for free settlers, some of whom were themselves former convicts. However, over time, convicts' good behaviour could secure them increasing degrees of freedom. Ultimately those who were not transported for life received certificates of freedom, which gave them back all of the rights that the prison system had taken away. Those serving life sentences were simply granted conditional pardons, the main condition being that they remain in Australia.

Between 1791 and 1853, 209 ships carried almost 40,000 convicts between Ireland and Australia. It is estimated that another 6,000 Irishmen departed from Britain.[3] Although, in the first half of the nineteenth century, Ireland held approximately 33 per cent of the United Kingdom's population, only 25 per cent of all transported convicts came directly from Ireland's shores. Given that some 5,000 convicts transported from Ireland were thought to be political offenders, it is quite clear that transportation of criminals was proportionately higher in Britain than in Ireland. This might have been the result of a lack of urban development in Ireland, and a consequentially lower rate of ordinary crime.[4]

Bateson's *The Convict Ships, 1787–1868* recorded the details of every convict voyage between the British Isles and Australia. The particulars of the Irish convict ships are extracted from Bateson's work and, along with some further noted detail, reproduced in Appendix I. The table in Appendix I does not include Bateson's data on convicts who were originally scheduled to sail on given ships but were subsequently 're-landed' at the port of departure when they were deemed unfit for the voyage. The re-landing of sickly convicts inevitably lowered the mortality rate. Over the entire period only 1.9 per cent of convicts departing from Irish ports died before they left the ship. Curiously the male mortality rate stood at approximately 1.6 per cent, whilst that of females was higher than 2.8 per cent.[5] There was little gender balance in the transportation system generally, and the number of men transported from Ireland was three times that of women.

Almost 9,000 women were transported directly from Ireland. However, that number does not tell the full story. L. L. Robson has estimated that approximately 47 per cent of the 25,000 women transported from the British Isles were Irish born. This is clear evidence that, even before the Famine, Irish women were already leaving Ireland in their droves. Those who did not leave Ireland itself were often forced to leave their birthplace; Deborah Oxley has calculated that 80 per cent of Irish female convicts offended in towns, although the great majority were born in the countryside.[6]

Most of the Irish convict voyages originated in the same harbour from which the *Neva* departed: Ireland's largest harbour located on the south coast, at Cork. In total, 116 of the 209 Irish convict voyages began in Cork; 87 in Dublin, 1 in Waterford, and a further 5 in unidentified Irish ports. Cork shipped more than 53 per cent of all the convicts, Dublin almost 44 per cent and other ports nearly 3 per cent. In the decade before the *Neva* sailed, sixty-two convict ships left Ireland in the middle of the peak period of transportation. The decade before that had seen only forty-one convict ships leave, whilst the decade following the *Neva*'s departure witnessed fifty-six convict ships depart. The final nine years of the transportation period saw just thirty ships depart from Ireland. This period coincided with that of the Great Famine, when, between 1845 and 1850, as many as one million Irish people died of starvation and disease, and a further one million emigrated. The final Irish convict ship left Kingstown (now Dun Laoghaire) on 2 June 1853, when the *Phoebe Dunbar* departed for Western Australia with 295 Irishmen aboard.

Convict ships did not depart Irish ports frequently or regularly. Thus, when a convict was sentenced to transportation, the sentence was not carried out instantly. Instead the prisoner was sent to a temporary prison to await the next available ship. Such temporary prisons were known as convict depots. They occupied various locations in Dublin and Cork throughout the period. From the 1820s male convict depots took the form of 'hulks' in Cork and Kingstown. Just a year after the *Neva*'s departure the hulks were abandoned in favour of onshore depots. From 1837 the onshore depots in three Dublin locations made that city the new centre of Irish transportation.[7] Given that 20 per cent of all transportation sentences were imposed in Dublin, and that the capital city occupied a more central location than Cork, it was the more cost-effective location for convict depots.[8] It took fourteen years for convict ships to return to Cork harbour, and by then Spike Island had opened as a temporary depot.

The Wreck of the *Neva*

In 1833 one of Ireland's two female convict depots was located in Kilmainham gaol. During a period that spanned three different centuries, the gloomy walls of that Dublin gaol bore witness to many of Irish history's most famously tragic tales. But one tale has not yet been told. Three decades after Kilmainham saw Robert Emmet reflect upon his epitaph, and almost a century before the founders of the Irish nation met their end in the haunting stonebreakers' yard, the dreary corridors of Ireland's most notorious prison were temporary home to a group of ordinary women whose story is truly extraordinary. That story began with a twenty-one-year-old Roscommon girl named Margaret Drury.

2

Kilmainham

On 26 September 1833 Margaret Drury passed through the gates of Kilmainham gaol, County Dublin, having travelled more than a hundred kilometres from the place of her first detention.[1] Her journey was probably a pensive one, as she reflected on the circumstances that put her on a path to the other side of the world. The hills and valleys of Drury's youth receded to the confines of her memory as each step took her further from everyone she had ever known. By the time she reached Kilmainham, on the western fringes of Dublin city, her world had already slipped from her grasp. Now, she was about to enter a gaol that later acquired the title 'Ireland's Bastille'.

Drury was a petite young woman, standing just 1.55 metres tall. She had black hair, grey eyes and a sallow complexion. As a member of the Church of Ireland, her upbringing was slightly more privileged than that of her Roman Catholic neighbours. She was partially literate, and one of her sisters had attained the distinguished position of housekeeper to the archbishop of Tuam. Originally from Corbally near Elphin, the Drury family had spread further afield. While three of Margaret's sisters remained in the vicinity of their home, a brother had settled elsewhere in the county and her mother and three other brothers resided in Dublin. Margaret herself had lived with her aunt, Elizabeth, who was married to shopkeeper Thomas Lloyd in Belturbet, County Cavan. It was whilst in Belturbet that the young woman had stolen a watch and seal from her uncle-in-law.

Drury may have felt that her theft would go undetected when she succeeded in selling the items to local basket boy Alexander Maxwell. However, luck deserted her when Maxwell attempted to sell the stolen goods to watchmaker Robert Wilson. Lloyd had alerted Wilson to the recent loss. Hence, when he recognised the items that Lloyd had described, the watchmaker had Maxwell arrested for the theft. Maxwell then deposed that Drury had sold the items to him. Consequently she was sentenced to seven years' transportation at the Cavan Assizes on 2 March 1833.[2]

As she passed beneath the five sculpted dragons that stood sentry above Kilmainham's sturdy doors, Drury's future was uncertain. Kilmainham gaol was an intimidating and foreboding sight for all who entered it for the first time. A historian of the gaol describes the prisoners' passage into the prison as follows:

Prisoners entering Kilmainham Gaol for the first time came through the front door. As they stepped from the gaol delivery cart, bound in irons, some hungry, dirty and diseased ... they huddled together in fear at the first sight of their awesome surroundings, watched always by a curious passing traffic who came to peer inquisitively. Well-endowed coaches and fours trotted past from the direction of the newly established North and South Circular Roads, or from the fashionable Phoenix Park nearby.[3]

Kilmainham gaol, Dublin. Although this wing of the prison has been slightly altered, this was the female exercise yard in the early 1830s. Women like Margaret Drury and Rose Ann Dunn probably exercised in this yard, before their departure for Cork.
Photo: Cal McCarthy.

The Wreck of the *Neva*

Margaret Drury entered Kilmainham along with four others who were convicted in Cavan. Of those four, only three would sail on the *Neva*. One was Rose Ann Dunn. Of fair complexion with blue eyes and black hair, Dunn was some two years younger than Drury and a little taller, at 1.57 metres. However, her background was somewhat different. Her father, Thomas Dunn, was a stone-cutter, and her family was Roman Catholic. It appears that her mother was already dead, but Dunn left two brothers and a sister behind her. Unlike Drury, she was illiterate. Dunn was a native of Kingscourt, County Cavan, and had been sentenced to seven years' transportation as far back as 1831, for 'vagrancy', an offence which had a peculiar meaning in Ireland. Whilst men were also convicted of vagrancy, the offence was more common among women. Frequently, women convicted of vagrancy, particularly repeat offenders, were habitual prostitutes, and it is likely that Dunn was a member of this profession. Many prostitutes ended up on convict ships and their interaction with crews had a significant impact on various voyages. By 26 September 1833 Dunn had travelled nearly a hundred kilometres from Kingscourt. She would never return.[4]

Inside the prison the women's clothes were removed, boiled and fumigated. They would be returned to them upon their release date. However, Drury and Dunn did not have a release date, so they swapped the clothes they had worn in Cavan county gaol for check frocks, colour coded for their status as prisoners awaiting transportation. They were then led along the narrow stone corridors of the west wing and placed in one of its cold, damp cells.[5]

Because the gaol doubled as a convict depot, extreme difficulties with overcrowding were frequent throughout the first half of the nineteenth century. Although one prisoner per cell was the desired quota under the Prisons Act of 1826, the Act also stipulated that where overcrowding rendered such an arrangement impossible, three prisoners should share a cell. Consequently, in an overcrowded Kilmainham, it is likely that Drury was lodged with two other women and, given their consecutive positions on the prison register, she probably shared her cell with Dunn. At this time, the prison's windows had no glass, and it was believed that the cold wind that howled through the corridors would assist in cleansing the convicts' souls.[6]

As Cavan's convicts lay in the blackness of Kilmainham for the first time, the hours may have passed sleeplessly as they listened to the stirrings of new companions all around them. Somewhere nearby, Mary Redmond shared the darkness with them. Found guilty of stealing spoons, she had already spent nearly two months behind Kilmainham's walls waiting for her sentence of transportation to begin.[7] Over the next two years Redmond would become closely acquainted with these Cavan women.

Two days later the group was augmented by four convicts from County Meath. At thirty years of age, Jane Farrell was the eldest. Her companions were Catherine Byrne (twenty-seven), Judith King (twenty-two) and Margaret Crane (twenty-two).[8] The crimes of which these Meath women were convicted are unknown – records of their cases were destroyed in 1922 when the shelling of the Four Courts marked the beginning of the Irish Civil War.

The drip feed of convicts into Kilmainham continued when Monaghan convicts Anne Stenson and Anne McCardle arrived on 28 September. Stenson was convicted of highway robbery, primarily motivated by her consumption of alcohol, and she was extremely lucky to avoid the death sentence. The *Newry Commercial Telegraph* described her arraignment as follows:

Anne Steenson [*sic*] for having feloniously and unlawfully robbed William McKenna of a purse containing in notes and silver £3, 7s. The prosecutor deposed that Mary Steenson [*sic*], one night, accompanied by a man named Slevin (who had since escaped) approached him on the street, put her hand on his breast and forcibly took away the money specified in the indictment; he was quite sober on the occasion and had no connection whatever with the prisoner; he lost more money that night, but afterwards got £2 of it from James McGurk, a publican. McGurk, who lives in Monaghan, was sent for and deposed that the catholic Curate of the parish gave him the £2, which had been found by some person on the street, and desired him to give it to the owner: that was all he knew of it. The prisoner, a woman of the town, said that if she did take the money, she was quite drunk and could not have known what she was doing. Guilty: the Judge said that as she had been guilty of highway robbery, he should pass sentence of death on her – nevertheless, he would recommend her to the mercy of transportation for (we believe) life.[9]

The next of the *Neva*'s eventual complement to arrive at Kilmainham was twenty-nine-year-old Jane Tims from County Kildare. She entered the prison on 30 September, the same day as thirty-two-year-old Anne McCormick from County Tyrone and twenty-year-old Bridget King from County Wexford.[10] The youthful King was one of the *Neva*'s most serious offenders, having been convicted of the manslaughter of her father-in-law at Oldcourt almost a year before her arrival in Kilmainham. The mysterious death of her elderly father-in-law was described thus:

Bridget King was indicted for the wilful murder of her father-in-law, Michael King, in the month of October last. It appeared that the prisoner lived with her father-in-law, a man about seventy years of age, with whom she was on bad terms; her husband was not then at home; the deceased had sent the prisoner to prepare dinner for persons he had digging potatoes, and who, in about an hour afterwards, followed in to see if dinner was ready, a short time after which the prisoner went to the field, clapping her hands and crying out murder, murder; the persons in the field went in and found the deceased lying on the floor, with his skull fractured, and several gashes on his face, and they found the apron the prisoner had worn in the field when sent in, lying on the settle bed, fresh washed, as well as a hatchet at the fire also, as if fresh washed. The prisoner's counsel endeavoured to show the impossibility of her being able to commit the murder, after which the Judge charged the jury, and they, after considerable deliberation, brought in a verdict of 'Manslaughter'.[11]

Unfortunately, further details of King's defence are unavailable. However, it seems obvious that her counsel succeeded in persuading the jury that she did not intend to kill when she struck the fatal blows. He did not, however, persuade them that King was unable to kill. Her infant son, Patrick, was most likely still at her breast and so accompanied her to prison and shared in her sentence of transportation.[12]

The 3 October saw the arrival of twenty-year-old Mary Williams from County Longford. In her wake came twenty-five-year-old Mary Smith from Queens County (now Laois). She was imprisoned in Maryborough for at least six months before her arrival at Kilmainham. Smith had been convicted of larceny and was sentenced to seven years' transportation at her trial the previous March.[13] On 4 October seven women arrived from County Armagh, and on 5 October they were followed by six from County Antrim.

Significant numbers were arriving at Kilmainham almost every day. Women who, like Margaret Drury and Rose Ann Dunn, had spent some three weeks in the Dublin gaol, may have interpreted the influx as a sign that plans for their transportation were well advanced. However, whilst their journey to Australia was about to begin, it did not proceed at nearly the pace they may have expected.

On 18 November fifty-four prisoners, including all of those named above, were moved across the city to Kingstown.[14] It was a journey of little more than fifteen kilometres. Kingstown was the site of a large artificial harbour just south of Dublin Bay constructed between two enormous piers. It had been known as Dunleary until it was renamed in honour of King George IV after his visit in 1821. One of the sights confronting the women at Kingstown was the dreaded convict hulk *Essex*. The *Essex* had originally been an American naval vessel, but was captured by the British in 1814. She was converted to a prison hulk and had been anchored off Kingstown's East Pier since 1824. The *Essex* was not, however, the women's destination; rather, aboard the convict transport *Erin*, they began a journey that took them to the southern city of Cork. With them were twenty-seven convicts who had been held under sentence of transportation in the city gaol at Newgate.[15] It is unlikely that any of them had been on board a ship before, and consequently it is likely that this voyage was their introduction to seafaring.

Over the following eight weeks they sailed through some of the most ferocious storms imaginable. Three nights before the *Erin* made it to the shelter of Cork's lower harbour, the waves were breaking over the quays at the harbour town of Cove (now Cobh). A steamer left the town that night, but had to return when she met the towering swells outside the harbour.[16] All along the coasts of England, Ireland, Scotland and Wales ships were laid to waste by these fierce storms. By mid-January almost 500 outward-bound ships lay in southern English ports from Falmouth to the Downs. Many of them had been detained since early November; intending passengers ran out of money and were reduced to selling jewellery and clothes to sustain themselves whilst waiting for the weather to clear.[17] The appalling weather conditions were described as follows:

> There has probably been no quarter of a year, in the memory of man, in which the loss of shipping has been so great as in the last. For nearly three months we have had perpetual storms, and those not partial in their devastations, but felt along all the coasts of England, Scotland, Ireland, as well as on both sides of the British channel, and on the shores of the German Ocean. It is not possible to form any very correct estimate of the number of ships lost, or of their value, and it is still more difficult to estimate the value of their cargoes … the destruction of property is frightful, though far less so than the loss of life with which it has been attended. We have heard it repeatedly stated that the total amount of tonnage destroyed is at least one hundred thousand tons.[18]

On the day that the *Erin* limped into Cork, a local newspaper commented that a large fleet of merchant vessels were 'beating into the harbour'.[19]

The frequent and heavy gales blew primarily from the west.[20] They howled across the decks of the *Erin* as she made her passage across the Irish Sea to the Isle of Man and Wales. We cannot say why she went to these places before she arrived at Cork, but it is likely that her course was altered by the storms. Such alterations were not uncommon when ships encountered 'contrary' winds. On one occasion a convict ship departing the south coast of England was blown all the way to Cork before she could continue her journey to the Australian colony.[21] Whilst it was common practice to allow convicts access to the upper decks, bad weather resulted in the withdrawal of that privilege, and it is likely that the women were seldom freed from beneath the deck. One can only imagine how rapidly the condition of the prison ship deteriorated, as the high seas took their toll upon this group of women at sea for the first time. The continuous heaving and rolling, coupled with the lack of light and the pungent smell of nauseous humanity, surely made for a terrifying voyage.

Finally, on 10 January 1834, the *Erin*'s crew sighted the lighthouse standing on the eastern side of Cork harbour's narrow entrance. A light had been located on the land of Edward Roche since 1817. Roche was a wealthy local landowner and lived in nearby Rochemount House. The point on which the first lighthouse was located, was (and still is) known locally as 'Roche's Point'. As she rounded the point, the prison brig passed between two formidable harbour forts guarding the entrance to the world's second-largest natural harbour. And if the crew found the guns staring down from Fort Camden and Fort Carlisle imposing, they had only to look forward to see the third of Cork harbour's awesome military forts atop Spike Island. At this time, Camden and Carlisle forts were not heavily garrisoned, but Spike Island's Fort Westmoreland was a bustling place, providing a temporary home to the various British military units passing through Cork harbour. The three harbour forts had been in various states of construction since

The Wreck of the *Neva*

the War of American Independence; however, the Napoleonic wars had been the catalyst for significant expansion of all three and for the addition of several Martello towers around the vast harbour.

Robert Lowe Stopford (1813–98) (attrib.), *The Cove of Cork,* *c.* 1850, lithographic print, published by Newman, 20 x 30 cm. This view is from the southern side of Great Island on the hills that comprise the modern town of Cobh. Haulbowline Naval Base is on the right and Spike Island is the largest island shown, with Roche's Point and the entrance to the harbour beyond. *Courtesy Port of Cork*

Now in the lower reaches of Cork harbour, the *Erin* turned to starboard, rounded Spike Island and moved toward the harbour's largest island, the aptly named Great Island. On the southern shore of Great Island was the little town of Cove. Cove also owed much of its existence to the military expansion of Cork harbour during the Napoleonic wars, when the settlement grew from little more than a fishing village to a vibrant harbour town. Merchant vessels and their naval convoys came and went from Cork's lower harbour at a tremendous rate. At one time it was claimed that '600 sail of merchant vessels' were anchored in front of Cove, whilst on another occasion '400 sail … left the harbour under convoy in one day'.[22] The battered *Erin* finally came to rest at Cove's waterfront, beneath the steep hillsides up which the settlement had expanded. She had spent some fifty-three days at sea. The Cork–Dublin route usually took three days.

The women were disembarked from the *Erin* and placed on board one of the smaller vessels used to navigate the confines of Cork city's narrow channels. All this activity occurred under the watchful eye of another of the harbour's heavily garrisoned islands, Haulbowline. With the women loaded, the smaller craft then slowly started up the River Lee. As Haulbowline Island slipped from their port-side view, it opened up a line of sight to one of Cork harbour's uglier curiosities, a hulk similar to the one they had seen in Kingstown. HMS *Surprize* was a converted naval frigate that had served as a male convict depot in Cork harbour since 1823. It was moored in the shallow waters between Monkstown and Ringaskiddy, a location considered 'the best adapted to the security of that Ship, and the safe custody of the Convicts who may be embarked on board her, and also as affording the least interruption to the Navigation of the port'. About one-third bigger than Kingstown's *Essex*, the *Surprize* was a temporary home to as many as 400 male convicts at a time. However, these men were hidden from the sight of passing traffic. The hulk's bulwarks were deliberately raised to prevent any communication between the men and those who passed by. Behind this timber screen, convicts often grew restless as they waited many months for transport shipping. Sporadic violence became a feature of life on the hulk, and even as the *Neva*'s convicts passed, the men aboard were described as 'disposed at that time to riot and turbulence'.[23] Leaving those restless men behind them, the female convicts continued their journey towards the city depot.

As it approached the city of Cork, the little transport turned to port and steered its way into the more southerly of two channels that surround a central island upon which most of the city was built. Then the craft probably passed beneath a bridge or two before finally docking. The convicts' feet first touched Cork soil somewhere south of the central island. As they alighted from their transport, it is likely that the convicts were formed up, with guards on all sides, before being marched along the quayside. As they moved further up the river, they could see the spire of a cathedral that stood on the slope of a steep hill, the site where St Finbarr had built his original monastic settlement some thirteen centuries before. They may also have noted the dull grey walls of a seventeenth-century fort rising from the face of the hill near the cathedral. This was Elizabeth Fort, and it had stood sentry over the city of Cork for more than two centuries. The buildings within the walls of the fort were abandoned by the military when they moved to a new barracks on the north side of the city in 1806.[24] Now, those same old buildings would imprison the women of the *Neva* for twelve more months. Overall, the Cork depot was considerably less crowded than many of the city and county gaols. Inspectors described its 'highly creditable state', and the women from the *Erin* probably appreciated its sparse population and stable situation.[25]

Elizabeth Fort (*top right*) overlooking the south channel of the River Lee, Cork. The *Neva* women were held here before being shipped downriver to join the *Neva* at the Cove of Cork (Cobh). *Photo: Cal McCarthy*

In May 1834 at least thirty-three of those who had made the *Erin*'s terrible journey to Cork boarded the steamer *Waterloo* and travelled back down to Cove. There, along with 142 others

The Wreck of the *Neva*

removed from Elizabeth Fort, they boarded the *Andromeda II* and set sail for New South Wales.[26] They were the lucky ones. Others – including Rose Ann Dunn, Margaret Drury, Anne Stenson and Bridget King – remained in Cork. Within the depot they were employed in needlework, washing, knitting, making convict clothing and bedding, pumping water, cooking and attending to the sick. Some of the eleven male convicts held in Elizabeth Fort were probably among the sick they attended to, as most of these men were too old or infirm to proceed to the colonies and were consequently removed from the hulk.[27] However, two were employed as handymen and might have been removed from the *Surprize* for that purpose. In August one of these men fell from the walls of the fort into a neighbouring vegetable patch during a botched attempt at escape. He broke both his legs and was probably placed under the care of some of the *Neva*'s women when returned to the depot's hospital.[28] When the excitement of the escape attempt subsided, the women's minds turned again to waiting. Whilst they waited, more of their eventual shipmates were gathering in Kilmainham.

3

The Second Shipment

On 24 April 1834 twenty-three-year-old Jane Williams entered Kilmainham. She was committed to the gaol to await trial on a charge of larceny.[1] She was the first of a gathering that eventually followed Margaret Drury and the others who had departed Kilmainham five months previously. Described as a 'rather decent looking' person, Williams carried with her the youngest girl to sail on the *Neva*, Mary Williams. Indeed, as she entered the prison, it is probable that Jane could already feel the baby moving within her.[2]

On 16 June Williams was tried at the Dublin Quarter Sessions, before Baron Foster. She was convicted of larceny, and although she must have been heavily and visibly pregnant, was sentenced to seven years' transportation. The *Dublin Evening Mail* was dispassionate and clinical in reporting the facts of her case and trial:

Jane Williams and Patrick Malone were indicted for stealing ten barrels of oats, the property of Mr John Chipsey. It was proved that in October last, Mr Chipsey had seen his corn made up; but in March, hearing that some of it was made away with by Jane Williams, who was in care of it, he had an investigation and discovered that there was a defalcation in the property. It appeared that Jane Williams had the corn removed to another barn, where it was disposed of by Malone.[3]

Malone attempted to mount a defence that 'having acted under the orders of Jane Williams, who had been in the habit of giving directions about the management of the farm, he could not be considered culpable'.[4] The court was not impressed, however, and ultimately Malone's guilt was established along with that of Williams. He was transported on board the *Hero*, and arrived in New South Wales on 31 August 1835.[5] Williams' fate was much more dramatic.

She returned to Kilmainham on the evening of 16 June and, as the months passed, watched the prison refill with those recently sentenced to transportation. As Kilmainham's dreary confines became seriously overcrowded, conditions cannot have been conducive to the good health of a woman in the later stages of pregnancy. Nonetheless, within the prison, Williams (prisoner number 216) had little option but to settle into a daily routine; the days of all Kilmainham's prisoners involved work, exercise, sleep and a diet consisting entirely of bread and milk. As a female prisoner, it is likely that Williams worked in the prison laundry. She might also have washed the cells or corridors.[6]

Her daughter, Mary, was born in the prison infirmary some time in August 1834. Jane began rearing the child in a prison cell – her duties were decreased whilst she cared for her infant daughter. Now, with her daughter for company, prisoner 216 witnessed an influx of prisoners who would share her extraordinary story.

The first to arrive was Dubliner Bridget McDonnell, who entered Kilmainham on 13 September 1834. On 15 October she was convicted of stealing banknotes and sentenced to seven years' transportation. By that time, Mary Gaffney, Catherine Molloy, Catherine Rahill and Jane Cruise had all arrived from County Cavan.[7] They were originally lodged at Kilmainham on 4 October. Mary McDermott from County Fermanagh arrived on the same day. McDermott was one of three brazen opportunists in attendance at an Enniskillen carnival. The following is an account of their trial:

Thomas McDermott, Mary McDermott and Rosanna Stevenson were indicted for stealing or having in their possession knowing to be stolen, a silver watch, seal keys, the property of Mr Denis Mulhern of Enniskillen.

D Mulhern – Who regarded the prisoners with becoming indignation, deposed to his having lost his watch with its appendages, in this town on the evening of the curious feat performed by the Black, of walking five miles [eight kilometres] backwards in an hour; that having waited upon Mr and Mrs McDermott and Miss Stevenson in company with a policeman, he politely requested the return of his property; but the maiden prisoner added insult to injury by asking Mr Mulhern with an impolite sneer 'if he was come to tell the time of day'. His search on this occasion having proved fruitless he afterwards followed the prisoners to Irvinestown, where the fugitive timeteller was discovered.

Mrs Mary Mullen deposed that the prisoners having come to her house looking for lodging and entertainment, she informed them that she had a bed and a half to let; her guests having ordered tea, toast and eggs, sat down to that excellent cheer, and retired afterwards to rest; having breakfasted in similar style next morning, Mrs McDermott unfortunately discovered that she had forgotten to bring her purse, and placed in the hands of her hostess a watch, when Mr McDermott and the two ladies walked out to enjoy the beauties of the neighbouring scenery and on their return again indulged themselves at Mrs McMullen's [*sic*] hospitable board: but early next morning the good landlady was shocked by a visit from the police who took the watch and the guests under their safeguard, and left Mrs McMullen to mourn the loss of her 'bed and board'.

The Policeman, who had made his visit at an unreasonably early hour, detected the three prisoners in one bed and as the watch was identified by Mr Mulhern, accommodated them with lodging without charge.

Mrs Mary McDermott was found guilty and sentenced to seven years transportation – the others were acquitted.[8]

As McDermott took her place among the other thieves at

Kilmainham, she may well have regretted her enthusiasm to pay for the lodgings of her husband and friend. It would seem that her possession of the watch, and her payment of same to the landlady at Irvinestown, was all that separated her sentence of transportation from her spouse's acquittal. It also appears that Rosanna Stevenson's taunting of their victim with her 'time of day' comment might have provided motivation for Mulhern as he rigorously sought the recovery of his watch and the apprehension of those who stole it. McDermott had approximately three months to contemplate her friend's sharp tongue and her husband's lack of chivalry before she left Ireland on her journey to the far side of the world.

Three days after McDermott crossed Kilmainham's threshold, twenty-six-year-old Jane Gaffney and twenty-four-year-old Anne Thomas arrived from Wicklow. On the same day, Margaret Hamilton (eighteen) and Jane Doyle (twenty) were brought from County Westmeath. Both were guilty of larceny and both were sentenced to seven years' transportation. Doyle's co-convicted was forty-six-year-old Thomas Doyle, possibly her father, who arrived in New South Wales on board the *Lady McNaghten* in 1835.[9] Doyle and Hamilton were accompanied to Kilmainham by thirty-one-year-old Bridget Lynn, whose crime is lost to history.[10]

The following day saw the arrival of forty-six-year-old Martha McClure from County Armagh. Described as 'an infamous character, and an old offender', McClure and a fifteen-year-old accomplice were convicted of breaking into a dwelling and stealing a quantity of linen yarn.[11] McClure had journeyed south to Dublin from County Armagh with fifty-year-old Sarah Gallagher, thirty-year-old Mary Smith and eighteen-year-old Mary Ann Hughes.[12]

Kilmainham was surely a particularly upsetting sight for nineteen-year-old Donegal woman Margaret McShee. Like many of those transported, McShee was an habitual offender, yet she was not a hardened criminal. Her trial in Ballyshannon had created a scene common in courthouses of the time, but this had done nothing to alleviate the permanence of an appalling sentence:

> Margaret McShee, a young woman, was convicted of having stolen articles of wearing apparel from a house in Bally-shannon, and, being an old offender, was sentenced to seven years' transportation. On receiving the sentence she raised the most frightful screams, which made it necessary to hurry her out of the dock.[13]

McShee's punishment was indeed severe. A sentence of transportation frequently resulted in heart-rending scenes. Although the sentence was most often of seven years' duration, the friends and family of an offender knew that their loved one probably would not return, and the convicts were mourned as if they had died. The offender herself probably felt that all of those she knew and loved had died on the very same day. Just a few months after McShee was dragged screaming from the Ballyshannon courthouse, the *Galway Advertiser* speculated that the grief caused by a sentence of transportation might well negate the need for the imposition of death sentences:

> We observed yesterday afternoon and evening, loud demonstrations of grief amongst a considerable number of poor people in the neighbourhood of the court house, on account of the sentencing of their relatives or friends to transportation. We are glad to see that this punishment, formerly thought so lightly of, is now coming to be regarded with so much dread, and to produce so wholesome and salutary an effect on the popular mind. More grief than we have witnessed, could not, we think, have been caused by a sentence of capital punishment. May we not hope that the general erection of tread mills and the growing dread of transportation, will soon induce our legislature to erase the punishment of death from the statute book? ... with the exception of a case of aggravated murder, we feel satisfied that a banishment for life, or a long period of solitary confinement or hard labour, would serve all the purposes of justice, and of the penal sanction of the law, far more effectually than death, and a thousand times more effectually than the heart hardening process of a public execution.[14]

The reaction of women like McShee, and the family she left behind, was enough to convince many that no death sentence could cause greater grief. Nonetheless, others seemed to bear their fate with greater fortitude and publicly expressed their anger at the system that sought to exile them. Two such women entered Kilmainham on the same day as McShee – eighteen-year-old Eleanor McMullan and twenty-year-old Mary Anne Stewart, two accomplices who were tried in County Down. Their hopes of freedom were raised, only to be dashed again, when their arraignment proceeded as follows:

> Elenor [*sic*] McMullan and Mary Anne Stewart, for stealing three yards of muslin, the property of Mr William John Davidson, at Newry, on 8th April instant. Prosecutor was not able to identify the muslin, and the prisoners were Acquitted. They were then put on trial, charged with stealing three yards of muslin, property of Mr E Bell, on same day. They were found Guilty. As they appeared to be strolling vagabonds, his worship sentenced them to transportation for 7 years – On receiving sentence, they cursed both Judge and Jury; and on being removed from the dock, they shouted out, 'H– thank you all – we'll be young girls coming home again'.[15]

McShee, McMullan and Stewart were three of seventeen women who arrived in Kilmainham on the same day. Sixteen of them would eventually sail on the *Neva*. McShee was from Donegal, three came from Kings County (now Offaly), one from County Monaghan and, in addition to McMullan and Stewart, ten more from County Down. Among the Down women were two known prostitutes: twenty-eight-year-old Mary Johnston and nineteen-year-old Anne Smith. Johnston and Smith had been arrested as part of a general round-up of prostitutes in Newry. Curiously, one of those tasked with taking the offenders into custody was himself the son of a brothel owner:

> Ellen Reilly, Mary Johnston, Margaret O'Hara, Elizabeth Seymour, Margaret Rellett, Mary Anne Atkinson, Anne Carey, Anne Smith, Mary Roxberry, Anne Curteis and Sarah Courtney, were severally, by presentment from the Grand Jury, given in charge to the Jury as vagrants, they being persons of bad character, and having no fixed place of abode.
>
> These actions arose in consequence of the Committee of the Newry Workhouse having appointed special constables, whom they authorised to take into custody all prostitutes they found on the streets at an unreasonable hour. One of the prisoners (O'Hara) brought a charge against the principal witness, named Brannigan, one of the 'specials,' whose mother, she said, kept a common brothel in Newry, *which he acknowledged!* His LORDSHIP said it would be a disgrace to the authorities of Newry – and most discreditable to the Workhouse Committee – if they allowed such a character to retain his present situation. In the case of Johnston and Smith, the Jury found in favour of the presentment – all the others were discharged.[16]

Johnston and Smith were subsequently convicted of vagrancy. They would be transported unless they could raise substantial sureties within six months.[17] Their sentence was a reasonably common one and yet, with the benefit of hindsight, it made little sense. If a vagrant was able to raise such substantial sureties, she probably would not have practised prostitution. Vagrants were seldom able to buy their freedom, so almost all of them were transported.

Several of the women who arrived on that same day were convicted thieves, including Catherine Kennedy, Ellen Magennis and Margaret Fulton.[18] Fulton was one of the *Neva*'s three eldest prisoners and was convicted of two separate thefts of shirts and shifts, in August 1833 and January 1834. She too was sentenced to seven years' transportation.[19]

On 10 October those already in the County Dublin gaol may have noted the arrival of nine convicts from County Antrim. Foremost among these was twenty-four-year-old Rose Ann Hyland (or Heyland, depending on the record). Born near Castlewellan, County Down, Hyland was described as a fresh-faced young woman with brown hair and blue eyes. Her parents were already dead and she had no siblings. Her closest relatives were her mother's surviving brothers and sisters. It seems that Hyland was a barmaid, as she resided with innkeepers in Castlewellan and later on High Street in Belfast. It was there that she was convicted of stealing money from Thomas Flack on 8 June 1834. Her co-accused, Bridget Kelly, was found 'not guilty' of the same crime.[20]

Hyland was accompanied to Kilmainham by five of her future shipmates: Jane McIlvenna, a thirty-three-year-old thief who had stolen a hat; Mary Jordan (thirty-nine), who was convicted of larceny; Mary Anne Develin, who had been in receipt of stolen goods; twenty-seven-year-old Mary McQuillan; and Esther Raw, whose conviction was the only one from three who were arraigned for stealing a cloak in Belfast.[21]

McQuillan was perhaps the most interesting of Hyland's companions. On 24 July 1834 she had been convicted of stealing a substantial sum of money from William John Mc-Coard during the previous May. Her trial revealed details of a prisoner greatly affected by alcohol consumption and the courage that it lent her. The trial was also peculiar in that the victim and the chief witness appeared to give slightly different accounts of the events that led to McQuillan's arrest. The *Belfast Commercial Chronicle* described her placement at the bar and subsequent trial as follows:

Mary McQuillan, for stealing, at Antrim on 26th May, a purse, and £16, 10s in money, the property of Wm John McCoard.

William John McCoard – Lost, on the 26th May last, some money; prisoner came up to him on the road, and took off his hat, and wanted money to drink; gave her a shilling to get quit of her; got his hat, and, on attempting to mount his horse, she took his hat a second time; he took out his purse, containing £16, 10s, to give her another shilling, when she snapped the purse, and ran off; searched for her with the Police, in Antrim, and found her under a bed; this occurred about 11 o'clock at night, near to Antrim; he was on his way from Belfast.

John Walker – On the night of 26th May met Mr McCoard coming out of Antrim with a woman hooked in his arm; he (Mr McC) returned in a few minutes, and said he was robbed; identified the prisoner as the woman; gave notice to the police, when he heard of the robbery, who the woman was.

James Wilder, Constable – Arrested prisoner on the night of 26th May; she was concealed under a bed; got only 2s on her person; McCoard was present and identified her.

James Erskine, Governor of the gaol – On the morning on 14th June got, from the matron of the gaol £3.

Margaret Orr – Is matron of the gaol; got a pound note from prisoner to change; found two more notes on searching another prisoner, and witness claimed them. Guilty; transported for seven years.[22]

The reader will immediately note some inconsistencies in the stories presented by McCoard and Walker. McCoard claimed he was on his way from Belfast to Antrim, yet Walker claimed to have met McCoard coming from Antrim. Walker mentioned that McCoard had McQuillan on his arm as he left Antrim town, yet McCoard claimed that she approached him on the road and made no mention of having her on his arm. In addition, McQuillan did not have any more than two shillings on her person when arrested on 26 May. It was only on 14 June that the matron where she had been detained presented £3 found on McQuillan and another prisoner. Had McQuillan succeeded in hiding this money when first arrested? Who owned the money found on McQuillan and the other prisoner? Had McQuillan been involved in some kind of romantic tryst or sexual act with McCoard? Or did she simply steal his money as he described? There is no way of knowing whether or not the newspaper gave an accurate account of the case. However, McQuillan was tried at an Assizes, and consequently before a jury. That jury was satisfied that she had stolen money from McCoard, which was enough reason for her to find herself entering Kilmainham gaol on 10 October 1834. There she waited among the ever-increasing numbers of women bound for the decks of the *Neva*.

The day after Hyland, McQuillan and the rest of the Antrim women had slept their first night in Dublin, Catherine Gormley and her ten-month-old child arrived from County Tyrone. With her came another of the *Neva*'s most senior convicts, sixty-year-old Mary Johnston.

For three Wexford women, 13 October was the unlucky date of their arrival at Kilmainham: twenty-two-year-old Judith Henning, twenty-four-year-old Mary Martin and twenty-four-year-old Anne Everington. When Everington had been sentenced to seven years' transportation at the Wexford Assizes in March, she may not have understood the permanency of such a sentence and was heard to remark, 'Thank God it's not twenty.' Her two-year-old child Mary Anne entered the prison with her.[23]

Still more arrived in Dublin. On 17 October forty-year-old Anne Regan and her ten-month-old daughter Bridget came from County Sligo. Although three others arrived with her, none of them travelled on the *Neva*.[24]

Just a few days before the convicts embarked for Cork,

the final few were committed to Kilmainham. The first of these was twenty-seven-year-old Mary Headon (sometimes Hayden) who came from County Carlow on 7 November. Along with John Headon and John Neill, she had been convicted of stealing sheets from the County Carlow Infirmary. Although the thieves had cut the mark of the infirmary from the stolen items, the sheets had subsequently been identified and witnesses had placed the accused at the scene of the theft. Their trial had revealed that the Headon family were habitual thieves of almost anything they could lay their hands on.[25] Mary Headon spent exactly one week in Dublin before journeying southwards.

The last of the *Neva*'s passengers arrived at Kilmainham on 11 November 1834. The first of these entered on the register was prisoner number 721, twenty-eight-year-old Anne Lynch from County Westmeath, and she was accompanied by fifty-year-old Margaret Shaw. Both were convicted of the theft of 'Oxford grey cloth and a piece of cotton' from a merchant in Kilbeggan. The Lynch and Shaw families shared a tenement in the town. They had been caught with the stolen cloth soon after the shopkeeper notified police of her suspicion that the Shaws or the Lynches had pilfered it. The merchant in question had good grounds for suspicion, for it seems that the families were notorious. That fact was demonstrated when they could not produce a single character witness during their trial:

The prisoners were then asked if they had any person to give them a character, but all to whom they referred said they were characters most dangerous to society, as they had been frequently committed for similar offences.

The Jury returned a verdict of Guilty against all the prisoners, and the Barrister in pronouncing sentence on them said:-

It was evident that a robbery had been committed, and that the prisoners at the bar were the perpetrators of that robbery there was no reason whatever to doubt; he was most willing, even now, to receive a character that might justify him in remitting, or mitigating, that sentence which the sternness of justice required; but instead of receiving such character from those to whom the prisoners applied, even the persons in whom they confided were obliged to rise in judgement against them. He was determined to make a public example, not so much for the purpose of punishing the offence, as to warn and prevent others of committing a similar outrage; and that the honest industrious people of Kilbeggan should not be robbed, or injured, with impunity. The sentence of the court on you Bernard Linch [sic], Robert Shaw, Mary [sic] Shaw, and Anne Linch [sic], is, that you be transported for seven years; you James Linch [sic] are to be confined for nine months, you are twice to be privately whipt, and the last month to be spent in solitary confinement; Mary Shaw, in consideration of your youth, you shall be separated from that mother who has shewed [sic] you so evil an example, you are to be confined for three months and then released from your prison.[26]

The Wreck of the *Neva*

It was because nobody was willing to say anything positive on behalf of Anne Lynch or Margaret Shaw that they found themselves aboard the *Neva*. In effect, they were shunned by their own community. For young Mary, however, the punishment must have seemed particularly severe. Her mother's habitual re-offending and bad character had ensured that a permanent separation would occur. It was probably on 10 November 1834 that she last saw her mother, leaving the Westmeath county gaol. By the time she emerged from that prison, her mother was already one week into her journey from Cork harbour, bound for New South Wales.

Margaret Shaw and Anne Lynch spent only three nights behind Kilmainham's gates. On the morning of 14 November they and their future shipmates were escorted under guard from the throbbing confines of the prison's constricted corridors and towards the city to the east. Mary Williams, Jane Williams' infant daughter, now took her first breath outside prison walls. Her mother had spent almost seven months in Kilmainham. Unlike the previous convicts who had made the trip to Kingstown, this group may not have made the entire journey by horse-drawn prison-car. Instead, they could have travelled on the newly opened railway from Dublin to Kingstown, as subsequent convicts certainly did.[27] This was Ireland's very first railway and had opened just one month previously. Whatever their method of arrival, the women were in Kingstown by the afternoon of 14 November and boarded the prison brig, the *Erin*. They were joined by those who had congregated at Newgate.[28]

One of the most interesting of the Newgate women was Esther Brady. Although Brady was forty-two years old, the *Dublin Evening Mail* described her as 'a tall, elderly, rather ill looking, pock-marked woman'. A habitual thief, Brady had pleaded guilty to the pilferage of a stone weight of starch from a Dublin store. Throwing herself on the mercy of the court, she felt it necessary to ensure that the recorder would not do her an injustice when taking account of her previous offences:

> The Recorder – Esther Brady, you have been now seven times before this Court.
>
> Prisoner, interrupting him and curtseying – Only six times your Lordship.
>
> Recorder – There is very little probability that the usual punishment inflicted by this court upon you for the various felonies of which you have been, from time to time, convicted, will have any effect in reclaiming you from your evil practices. The sentence of the court now is, that you be transported for seven years beyond the seas.[29]

Although they had the same surname, Esther Brady and her eighteen-year-old namesake, Catherine Brady, were of very different appearance. The youthful Catherine was described as 'a girl of rather prepossessing appearance' by the same newspaper.[30] Indeed, Catherine Brady's appearance caught the eye of a number of journalists. Another described her as 'rather a young well looking girl'.[31] However, looks could be deceiving, and Catherine Brady, just like Esther, was a thief – indeed her theft was on a much grander scale. The brazen crime of the *Neva*'s most extensively described beauty was reported as far away as County Tipperary, where the *Clonmel Advertiser* ran the following article, under its own headline:

EXTENSIVE HOUSE ROBBERY BY A SERVANT MAID – On Tuesday morning, at about six o'clock, a girl named Catherine Brady absconded from the house of Mr Henry Conyngham, 37 Lower Ormond quay, taking with her money and valuables to the amount of over £150. She had, it was supposed, by means of a false key, obtained entrance into the drawing room where a small desk was, in which were notes of the following value: – One for £50, one for £20, one for £10, and two single pounds, in all £82 in money, besides papers and other valuable articles. The desk which was taken away had the owner's name engraved on a brass plate on the cover. She also took a considerable quantity of jewellery, rings, brooches, &c, and wearing apparel belonging to Mrs Conyngham. The delinquent is rather a well looking young woman, with dark hair and eyes, good complexion, and tolerably genteel figure.[32]

Catherine Brady pleaded guilty to the theft when she appeared in court less than one month later. She was sentenced to seven years' transportation.[33]

The two Bradys journeyed from Newgate to Kingstown with several other women convicted in Dublin city. Among them was Anne Dunne, who had stolen £2 from 'a countryman' in a public house on South Earl Street.[34] Mary Strahan and Margaret Halloran were old offenders sentenced to seven years' transportation upon their umpteenth conviction for petty larceny.[35] Eliza Cotter received a similar sentence, having stolen 'several articles of plate' from the house of a Rev. Mr Burrows.[36]

These Dublin city thieves, and all of the women who had passed through Kilmainham, left Kingstown aboard the *Erin*. Their southward voyage was straightforward. Under the command of Captain Neal, the *Erin* sailed into the lower harbour at Cork during the night of 15–16 November 1834. She arrived less than two days after the women had embarked at Kingstown.[37]

Whilst boarding the smaller vessel to carry them upriver to Cork city, the women were once again in view of Haulbowline Island, then home to a few convalescent convicts who had survived the recent appearance of cholera on board the convict ship the *Lady Kennaway*. The ships' guards and their wives were quarantined on Spike Island. Meanwhile, the *Lady Kennaway* had been moved to a lower anchorage where the Atlantic winds would better ventilate her. Eventually, once she had been fumigated and whitewashed, she departed for New South Wales just three weeks before the *Erin*'s arrival.[38] This cholera drama had subsided, but as the women moved up river towards Cork city on the morning of 16 November, the air was alive with the harbour's latest controversy: rumours of a murder perpetrated by soldiers garrisoned on Spike Island had developed, but it was now apparent that there had been no murder, and it had been revealed that the alleged victim had presented herself to the authorities at Cove.[39]

On 16 November 1834 the last of the *Neva*'s Dublin contingent slept for the first time in the Cork convict depot. They remained there for some seven weeks, the objects of a huge logistical operation that was already well under way.

4

Logistics and Organisation

The logistics and organisation of each convict voyage were the result of a system that had evolved over four decades of experience in convict transportation. The system sought to ensure that all convicts were delivered safely, and in good health, to the furthest corner of the British Empire. It did not always work as well as intended, but, nonetheless, by 1834 many of its constituent parts were running smoothly. Two things that worked reasonably well were the ships used and the method by which they were procured.

When the first fleet left Britain for New South Wales in May 1787 it consisted of eleven ships. Two were owned and operated by the Royal Navy; privateers under contract to the government owned and operated the other nine. The practice of privateers' ships being operated under state guidance and control was maintained throughout the period of transportation. The process of engagement with those

The Wreck of the *Neva*

privateers began when the ships were first chartered and ended when their owners were paid – with reference to the number of convicts they had delivered and the state of the convicts' health when they arrived.

Ships were chartered when the Convict Department applied to the Treasury to provide it with shipping for a certain number of convicts on a given date. The Treasury then asked for a notice to be placed with Lloyd's, whereupon tenders were submitted by the various privateers. If more than the required number of ships tendered for the job, the ship (or ships) provided at the lowest price was selected for fulfilment of the contract. Before the *Neva* was selected, six different vessels tendered for the job: the *Neva*, the *Ann*, the *Enchantress*, the *William Bryan*, the *George III* and the *Lloyds*. The *William Bryan* was rejected because she could not carry a sufficient quantity of convicts. The *Enchantress*, the *George III* and the *Lloyds* were also rejected: although they charged less per ton than the *Neva* and the *Ann*, their excess tonnage made their charter more expensive. By curious coincidence, the *George III* soon found a watery grave when she was wrecked near Bruni Island (now Bruny Island), south-east of Van Diemen's Land, around four months later. She took some 130 souls with her and entered the annals of Australian lore when it was reported that the guards had fired their weapons at the panic-stricken convicts after the ship was crippled.[1]

With a weight of 331 tons, the *Neva* tendered a price of £4.12.6 per ton, which made her considerably more expensive than the *Ann*, which weighed in at 339 tons, but quoted a price of £3.17.0 per ton. However, price was not the only concern; the safety of the vessels had to be certified by the Admiralty. In 1835 a report by the Comptroller of Victualling and Transport Services within the Admiralty stated:

> It may here be proper to observe that all merchant vessels, whether required for Transports, Convict Ships, or for the conveyance of Public Stores, are invariably surveyed by the Resident Agent for Transports at Deptford, assisted by an experienced and skilful shipwright; and that no vessel is finally accepted and a contract entered into, until a satisfactory report has been received from that Officer.[2]

The *Ann*'s price made her the preferred choice. However, in line with common practice, the *Neva* would be surveyed as a potential substitute should the *Ann* be found unfit for service. At first it appeared that the *Neva* would not secure the contract, until fate intervened and ensured that the ill-fated vessel would shortly weigh anchor, bound for Cork. The Comptroller of Victualling and Transport Services subsequently explained the selection process:

> On the 23rd of October a report was received that the 'Ann'… built at Douglas in Nova Scotia in 1824 and having recently received new Wales, was fit for the service for which she had been tendered and was therefore accepted; but a report having been subsequently received on the 31st of October, signed by the Resident Agent and Inspecting Shipwright, stating 'that

on opening the Ship abaft for the purpose of putting on a Poop, the upper Transom was found to be rotten, as well as some of the timbers, and that they had reason to suppose that she was otherwise defective, the broker of the Ann was informed that under these circumstances, she could not be employed for the transportation of Convicts to Australia; and orders which had before been suspended, were then renewed for surveying the Neva'.[3]

Although the *Ann*'s owners attempted to sue the Admiralty for ruining their ship's character, their claim fell on deaf ears, and shipwrights at Deptford proceeded to inspect the *Neva*. On 1 November George Bayley certified her as 'fit for the service for which she had been tendered, provided the Owners caused the works pointed out on survey to be performed, as well as such others as might necessarily be required': the *Neva* had received a hesitant vote of confidence. Later, an MP pointed out that the ship had merely passed the same initial inspection as the *Ann*. However, unlike what had happened in the case of the *Ann*, when the *Neva* underwent the necessary alterations at Dawson's dock in Deptford no hidden problems were uncovered and she was certified by Lloyd's as a category AE1 vessel.[4] Such a certification implied that the ship was more than ten years old and, although still considered very sound and seaworthy, she had not been repaired to the standard of a new, or A1, vessel.[5]

The cost of convict voyages was a pressing issue, as those who objected to the operation of the transportation system continually counted its cost as one of its major flaws. Consequently, the machinery of state attempted to control costs tightly. In Ireland, the use of ships larger than those necessary to transport the desired number of convicts had become an issue, and in June 1834 James Meek of the Admiralty wrote to the then home secretary, Viscount Melbourne (for whom the Australian city was later named), to appraise him of the problem:

> It has frequently been found impracticable to engage a ship which shall have accommodation for the precise number (usually 200) for whom application for passage has been made by the Lords Commissioners of the Treasury and the consequence has been that vessels capable of conveying a larger number have been engaged, and thus a greater expense per head incurred than would be the case if some latitude were given for embarking a moderately increased number – say 20 or 30 upon the usual number of 200.[6]

Two days later the Home Office in London informed the lord lieutenant's office in Dublin of its recommendation that such flexibility be applied when future charters were obtained.[7]

Two years after the *Neva* sailed, a survey of the cost of shipping male convicts on board the *Heber* and the *Calcutta* revealed that more than £3,000 was spent on 'Provisions and Medical Comforts' for the 570 convicts who sailed on both vessels. More than £223 was spent on their bedding, and approximately £400 on their clothing. Curiously, some £22 was spent on the devotional books intended to liberate their souls, whilst close to £90 acquired the chains that would deny their bodies such liberty. In all, the expenses listed on this breakdown translated to a cost of £22 10s 2d per male convict transported.[8]

The 1837 report also revealed another curious quirk of the administrative system – the practice of withholding part payment. This practice evolved due to the appalling mortality rates on earlier voyages. Between 1800 and 1815 approximately one female convict died for every seventy-two who landed. By 1825 this rate had fallen considerably and 284 convicts were successfully landed for every one death in the preceding five years. However, by the time of the *Neva*'s sailing the death rate had increased again and only seventy-seven women were being landed for every death that occurred.[9] In an effort to reduce these mortality rates, it was decided that various parts of payment should be held back until the convicts had arrived and been inspected by the authorities in Australia. In June 1801 the Transport Commissioners ordered that the master's log and surgeon's journal should be submitted to the governor upon arrival in the colony. If the governor was satisfied that all appropriate care had been taken to ensure the good health of the convicts, he furnished a 'certificate of good conduct' to the gentlemen involved. Only when such certificates were produced did the Treasury release the remaining portion of payment to the contractor. By 1837, in the cases of the *Heber* and the *Calcutta*, half the cost of freight carried, the master's gratuity, the officer of the guard's pay, the surgeon's pay, gratuity and passage money, along with certain unspecified 'necessary money', were withheld until the certificates were produced. The contractors were due a total payment of £12,828 14s 6½d; however, £4,613 10s 5d of that payment was withheld until 'good conduct' was certified.[10]

The organisation of a convict voyage incurred several further significant expenses, which occurred before a single convict set foot on the contracted ship. Among these was the cost of congregating, at convict depots in Cork and Dublin, those under sentence of transportation. Prisoners were transferred under armed guard to these locations, upon the request of the lord lieutenant. The number and consequential cost of such a guard depended on the number of prisoners being moved. All of these costs were initially incurred by local constabularies. However, they were later recouped from the Treasury. On some occasions local constabularies claimed that they did not have the funds required to move prisoners under guard. In at least one such case, the lord lieutenant subsidised the cost of a guard, on condition that his office was repaid when the constabulary received its due from the Treasury.[11]

Yet another significant part in the organisation of convict shipments from Ireland was the frequent transfer of prisoners from Dublin to Cork. This operation was performed by smaller ships such as the *Erin*, which were contracted by the lord lieutenant's office, and their operators were paid a given rate per ton. In addition, the operators charged for any delay – beyond those of weather or wind – encountered at either port. In 1818 two vessels of 183 and 132 tons were chartered to move convicts from Dublin to Cork. Their owners charged a rate of sixteen shillings per ton, and a further fourteen shillings for any and every day they were delayed at either port, with an eight-day period of grace.[12]

By the 1830s male convicts were located in the harbours aboard the hulks, but the costs of conveying and escorting female convicts from land-based depots to harbours by horse-drawn prison-car, train or small vessel were substantial. By the time of the *Neva*'s departure in 1835, paddle steamers such as the *Comet* and the *Waterloo* were frequently used to carry convicts between Cork city and Cove.

The most important logistical alteration to the convict system came with the appointment of surgeon superintendents to convict ships in 1792. The surgeon superintendent was appointed by the Admiralty and was responsible for the health and supervision of convicts during the voyage. The ship's master was expected to defer to him on all matters relating to these. The need for such a position was made abundantly clear after health-related issues aboard earlier transports. Although the Napoleonic wars interfered with the system of transportation, and the few ships that sailed during that era often did so without a surgeon superintendent, the principle was established, and the presence of these naval officers greatly reduced convict mortality rates.[13]

The surgeon superintendent on the *Neva* was Dr John Stephenson. A native of Rathfriland, County Down, Stephenson was born within seventeen kilometres of convict Rose Hyland's home. He had almost twenty years' seafaring experience as well as considerable experience of the convict system. He had made his first convict voyage, from Dublin to New South Wales, aboard the *Guildford* in 1829. Curiously, the first convict ship he sailed on met the same fate as the *Neva*, when she was lost after leaving Singapore on the third leg of her return voyage.[14] In 1831 Stephenson made his second convict voyage, with the *Eleanor*, delivering all 133 of his convicts in perfect health. Stephenson's supervision of the *Eleanor*'s convicts was so thorough that local newspapers had described his charges as 'a most valuable body of men'.[15] However, in 1832 Stephenson's luck took a dramatic turn for the worse when he began his third convict voyage aboard the *Katherine Stewart Forbes*. When a cholera outbreak – the worst that occurred on any convict ship – forced her to put in at Plymouth, the commanding admiral accused Stephenson of improper conduct, making this charge on the basis that the Down man allowed the ship to put to sea without sufficient medicine.[16] The validity of this charge was never proven, but it did result in all convict ship's physicians having to ensure that increased medical stores were provided for their ships. Curiously, Stephenson's reports of the incident were also criticised for their excessive detail when the authorities forwarded a supply of standard medical forms and asked that he substitute them for his previous tomes. With the outbreak spreading from the Plymouth docks to the town of Woolwich, and others diverting blame in his direction, Stephenson may have felt that he had become a scapegoat for the navy and the convict service.

Whilst the affair doubtlessly left Stephenson fearful of ever encountering the dreaded disease again, he had the misfortune of a second such encounter the following year. On 12 March 1833 the convict transport *Waterloo* left the Thames estuary with the Irish doctor on board as her surgeon superintendent. On that very day one of her 213 convicts presented with the ominous symptoms of cholera. Over the next three days the *Waterloo* met heavy weather in the English Channel and was forced to anchor. When high seas tore her anchor from her, the captain had little option but to make his way back to the shelter of the Thames. By the time the ship returned to port, eight of her complement had contracted cholera and two of these cases had already resulted in death. On 27 March the *Waterloo* was moved to quarantine just off Portsmouth. There she remained until 8 April. By then Stephenson had dealt with thirty-eight cases of cholera and nine related deaths. The *Waterloo* finally made it to Port Jackson (now Sydney) on 3 August 1833.

Stephenson had had the misfortune of dealing with two severe cholera outbreaks on two separate ships, but his association with ill-fated convict ships did not end there. The *Waterloo* continued to ferry convicts to the colonies until she became the fifth and final convict shipwreck in 1842. Thus, the unlucky Irish surgeon sailed aboard five different convict ships; three were eventually wrecked, two whilst still in convict service.

By the end of 1834 Stephenson was back in England. He had secured his next appointment as surgeon superintendent of the *Neva* and had also announced his engagement. He hoped to marry his intended before the *Neva*'s departure and have her join him on his voyage to the colony. However, the rules of service prevented this from happening and he was forced to postpone his wedding until his return. Having secured the hand of the woman he loved, Stephenson promised that the *Neva*'s passage would be his final voyage. Upon his return he intended to remain on dry land with his new bride.[17]

In the weeks before the ship departed Stephenson busied himself with ensuring that the vessel was fit for the reception of convicts and that those convicts were fit for the long voyage. As part of that process he began to develop concerns about the convicts' clothing. This put him at the centre of an administrative row between the Irish Convict Department and the Home Office. However, Stephenson was not a politician and probably did not realise that his concerns were being used as part of an administrative power-play. On St Stephen's Day 1834 he wrote to the Admiralty:

A delay in the embarkation of the Convicts on board this ship occasioned by the non arrival of the Free Women gives me an opportunity of addressing you on the subject of the clothing issued for the use of the former class of persons. It appears that it has hitherto been the custom for the Irish Government to furnish clothing for the voyage to such convicts as may be sent from the country; but in the present instance, this … has been departed from, and the clothing supplied in England; in consequence of this the General Superintendent of convicts refuses to make any addition whatever, altho' for one or two articles there is an absolute necessity. I allude chiefly to caps: We have none for use during the voyage, and none will be supplied us here, although this article, in addition to a good stout straw bonnet are [*sic*] excellent preventative against either sun or rain, always formed part of the articles of dress given to the women on leaving the Penitentiary. The consequence of their refusal will be, that the women must go bareheaded all the voyage.[18]

Stephenson's specific concern regarding the women, sailing from the northern hemisphere's winter, through the searing sun of the tropics and into the autumn breezes of the southern hemisphere without any form of protection for their heads, was well founded. Should one woman catch a simple cold, it could lead to further complications, all of which would be magnified by the close confines of the convict ship. For Stephenson, convicts' clothing was a particularly sensitive issue, as he had previously complained that inadequate clothing had contributed to the poor health of convicts aboard the *Guildford* and the *Waterloo*.[19]

The General Superintendent of Convicts, Dr Edward Trevor, subsequently confirmed that he had refused Stephenson's request for bonnets, whilst also opining that the provision of clothing for Irish convicts should remain within the remit of the Irish Convict Department. On 28 December he wrote to the Home Office as follows:

I have the honour to acquaint you that by reference to the

list of stores forwarded from the Victualling Department for Female Convicts for Transportation to New South Wales on board the Ship *Neva*, I find clothing has been provided in England, and forwarded by that Ship for female Convicts on the voyage which has not heretofore been the practice, clothing for the voyage having been provided in Ireland, the materials of which clothing are attained by yearly contract and the dresses are made by female convicts at the Convict Depot at Cork, which renders employment for the Prisoners (a circumstance so desirable) and the articles at a very moderate rate, having compared the dresses sent from England with those prepared in Ireland the latter appears in every way much better calculated for the purpose, and the other of so slight a texture likely to produce disease more particularly at embarkment at this season of the year, or meeting with cold weather on the Voyage, of which circumstance the Surgeon Superintendent of the ship feels satisfied who has written to the Comptroller of the Admiralty to know if he would be permitted to exchange the clothing as I refused to issue a second suit for the voyage.

I here beg leave to enumerate the Articles heretofore supplied in Ireland for the voyage.

1 Linsey Woollen Jacket lined with strong cotton

2 Shifts

2 Linen Caps

1 Check apron

2 pair of stockings

2 handkerchiefs

1 Straw Bonnet

1 Pair of Shoes

1 Linen bag to hold spare Articles

I have further to observe that as no communication has been made except by the list of stores received a few days before the arrival of the *Neva* that clothing for the Voyage for female prisoners would be sent from England, the Clothing for that purpose was consequently in readiness for the arrival of that ship. I therefore submit that should it be so arranged that articles of clothing are to be provided in this country no deviation therefrom should be made without giving sufficient notice that such articles are to be provided in England with the view to prevent unnecessary expense.

Under the foregoing circumstances I humbly recommend that application shall be made for the prices charged for each article sent from England for the voyage, notwithstanding the clothing made in Ireland would be equal to two suits of that sent from England, the shoes provided in England would not last a week, the jacket … without lining, the outer petticoat of the same quality and no cap sent – I therefore send herewith the charge made in Ireland, as it would be very desirable to compare the cost of the dresses made in England, which I hope you will retain, that they may be compared accordingly and considered which should be the most fit for embarkation.

If suitable clothing such as is supplied in Ireland can be obtained at a cheaper rate in England, the merchants or tradesmen in this country can have no cause for complaint, the only objection would then remain depriving the prisoners of so much work – but if it shall appear the clothing can be obtained at a cheaper cost than in England, I humbly consider that the country where the articles are required should have the preference to supply them.[20]

Trevor's charge went on to outline the cost of procuring Irish-made clothing for each convict. He estimated that 18s 10½d would have clothed one Irish convict, and he challenged the authorities to find a cheaper rate in England. Trevor's confidence in his own cost base was probably derived from intimate knowledge of the cost-cutting procedure he had implemented since 1818. The yearly contracts referred to above ensured that no one supplier could be too confident of maintaining the contract, should their costs rise above those of their competitors.

Trevor's economy drives were as notorious as the doctor himself. He had been a physician in Kilmainham gaol and had effectively run the prison in the early years of the nineteenth century. He claimed to have foiled an escape attempt by Robert Emmet, and gathered intelligence on Emmet and his loyal employee Anne Devlin. Trevor considered the resolute Devlin a 'rebelly bitch' and had threatened to hang her if no executioner would take on the task. Her treatment whilst in Kilmainham was infamously brutal and Trevor had overseen it all. Such services rendered on behalf of the British crown had accelerated his career progression, and by 1818 the 'haunting spectre of the gaol' had been appointed general superintendent of convicts.[21] In that role he had earned himself a reputation as a difficult and frugal taskmaster. When first placed in charge of the Convict Department, in an effort to eliminate any unnecessary overcrowding or delay, he had overturned the decision of a ship's surgeon regarding the fitness of three female convicts for a voyage, thereby ensuring their transportation.[22]

On this occasion it appears that Trevor would not contemplate the cost of clothing the *Neva*'s women twice, and would 'make no addition whatsoever' to the inferior clothing sent from England. In the end, caps and bonnets were supplied from the stores at Cork on the direction of the Home Office.[23]

Stephenson also sought permission to swap the inferior English clothing for the superior product that Trevor could provide in Cork. However, the Admiralty refused that request. And so, as the objects of a huge bureaucratic machine, the women of the *Neva* sailed for the far side of the world in clothing that the ship's doctor had deemed inadequate for the voyage. On any other passage inadequate clothing may not have had severe consequences. However, on the *Neva*, it may have doomed some convicts to the worst sentence of all.

5

Cork

In the weeks following the arrival of the *Erin*'s second shipment at Cork, as the remainder of the *Neva*'s women congregated, the Cork women were already waiting in the depot. Among them was forty-seven-year-old Louisa Mellefont, 'a respectable looking woman' from the district of Skibbereen. Mellefont's case was a curious one, and goes a long way towards explaining the rather complicated system of land ownership and occupancy in nineteenth-century Ireland.

It seems that Mellefont had leased a parcel of land from a gentleman by the name of Whitney. However, Whitney did not own the land in question, but rented it from the owner (called the head landlord), Nicholas E. Cummins. Matters were further complicated by the fact that Mellefont had rented some of her parcel to several undertenants. The head landlord was unconcerned as to who paid him the head rent he expected for all of his land, so long as he received all of it. Thus, the tenants frequently paid their share of the head rent directly to Whitney's agent, who then transmitted it to

The Wreck of the *Neva*

Cummins. When Whitney changed his agent, Mellefont spotted an opportunity to make some money. When she went to the office of the new agent, she paid only six months' head rent, instead of the eighteen months' rent that was due. Upon being questioned she furnished the new agent with a receipt from his predecessor. Mellefont was convicted of forging the receipt in March 1833. The judge explained her punishment:

> The Jury have convicted you on the clearest testimony of the crime of forgery, the punishment for which, from its baneful consequences to society, was once the highest which the law knows as the life of the person who committed the offence was forfeited. The law has, however, mitigated the punishment, but in doing so it has left no discretion in the Court. The only sentence, therefore, which I can pass on you, is that you be transported for the term of your life.
>
> The prisoner bore this sentence with great firmness and the scene was particularly affecting, when a boy about 12 years of age, her son, rushed up to her, kissed her repeatedly, sobbed heavily, and frequently cried out, 'Oh Mother, are you to be Transported?'[1]

Mellefont bade farewell to the son she would never see again and returned to Cork county gaol. She was discharged from there on 8 November 1833, whereupon she made the short journey to the convict depot.

Almost twelve months later, on 17 October 1834, four more prisoners made that same journey from gaol to depot.

Twenty-year-old Margaret Kelliher and nineteen-year-old Mary Donovan were both convicted of theft in the spring of 1834 and transferred to the depot on 17 October. Transferred with them was thirty-year-old Mary Russell. On 20 September 1833 Russell had been committed to Cork county gaol under charge of 'stealing a piece of cloth'. She left a six-year-old boy outside the prison walls. Almost three months later, on 19 December, young John Russell was committed to the county gaol as a vagrant and was re-united with his mother. On 17 October 1834 his little feet plodded along the streets of Cork as he accompanied her, along with Kelliher and Donovan, to the convict depot.[2] He was part of an unofficial practice adopted by the authorities in Ireland that was best articulated by Superintendent Trevor when, in 1831, he had petitioned the lord lieutenant on behalf of five children then at Newgate in Dublin:

> I beg leave to acquaint you, that for these several years past, the regulation ordered to be pursued regarding the children of convicts to be embarked for N.S. Wales has been, that no children are to accompany their mothers except those at the breast, but as there are several not of that age as stated by the enclosed list of names, and whom I am informed have no friends to take care of them, and there being no place of refuge, for such persons, I feel it to be my duty to submit the same for your consideration, whether the children may be embarked with their mothers.[3]

The Wreck of the *Neva*

The lord lieutenant's office conferred its approval with the typical caveat that it 'be done without an improper infringement of the regulations'. Subsequently, at least one of the named children travelled on board the *Southworth*.[4] Trevor always sought to transport vagrant children with their mothers as it spared Irish ratepayers the expense of providing for additional orphans. Although he failed to produce written sanction, in 1822 Trevor insisted that verbal communication gave him the authority to place potential vagrants on convict ships with their mothers.[5] Those women who could leave their children with caring relatives, often did so.[6]

Less than one week after Russell's arrival at the depot a group of Limerick convicts entered it. When the *Andromeda II* sailed, seven months prior to the *Neva*'s departure, convicts from Limerick had arrived in the city, only to be shipped directly down the harbour to Cove. They never set foot in the convict depot at Cork.[7] The next departure of female convicts from Limerick occurred on 22 October 1834.[8] Having reached Cork, they entered the depot and began their wait for the *Neva*. Among them were twenty-eight-year-old Bridget Hayes, thirty-year-old Johanna Sweeney and their mother, sixty-year-old Johanna Galvin. Their crime was a nineteenth-century confidence trick that provides an interesting insight into the superstitious mindset that prevailed in the Irish countryside during that era. The *Limerick Chronicle*'s account of their activities was as follows:

Johanna Sweeny [*sic*], Bridget Hynes [*sic*], and Johanna

Galvin, were indicted for having stolen several silver coins, and many articles of wearing apparel, the property of a man named John Carthy.

Anastatia Carthy, a country woman, sworn – Remembered the eldest of the prisoners; Johanna Galvin coming to her house in January last; it was towards evening, and having told witness that she was from the Iron Mills in Tipperary, and a daughter of Mrs Jackson (a celebrated fairy woman and charm maker of the last age), she asked her for lodgings for the night. Having consented that she should remain, the prisoner then told her that her daughters, the two other prisoners, were on the road at a short distance, and witness having desired that they also should lodge with her for the night, the elder prisoner desired her to send for them as she was wholly unable to walk. They came and were not long in the house when they commenced putting their plans in operation. The eldest woman took a teacup, and having poured in some water placed therein a herb which she took from her pocket. The cup was laid on a shelf, and in some short time, when the prisoner went again to the cup, she appeared to be much concerned and called the witness to inspect the contents of the cup – the witness observed, that the water appeared as if tinged with blood. The woman, Galvin, then communed with the two younger women, when some mysterious signs and cabalistic words passed between them. The prisoner next asked the witness if anything ailed her daughter, who was present. The witness hesitated to tell her, but she observed it was useless to conceal the matter; and that she could do her a service if made acquainted with the fact. Witness then acknowledged that her daughter was afflicted by a swelling of the neck and throat when she caught cold! The old crone then at once affected to see the daughter's *berrin* [*sic*] in the cup and its bloody tinge – but she intimated that if proper means were used the calamity might still be averted. She went on conjuring them to affect this desirable object till the hen fell dead off the roost with the power of her charm – (laughter).

'Twas the fattest and strongest hen in the witness's house, and laid an egg that morning – (laughter). The next proceeding was to compose the philter which was to effect the restoration of her daughter from those ill favoured spirits which had nearly possessed her. A skillel [*sic*] was put upon the fire; water from the confluence of three steams was procured, poured into the skillet, placed over the fire, and *quan auf* of herbs having been added to the liquid the 'hell brota' was in the process of decoction, stirred by the old heldame [*sic*], attended by her daughters. Suddenly the hag stopped and declared that she could not proceed in the composition unless she had yellow money with a cross on it (a gold guinea) to aid her in the process. The witness assured her that she had none. 'Could she not procure it?' 'No.' 'What a pity; she could have the charm completed in a very short time indeed with such help; but in the absence of gold she would be enabled to do the cure with the aid of some white money (silver;) and with the assistance of more prayers.' The witness then persuaded her good man to give her a shilling which he happened to have in his pocket. This was put into the mess of herbs and the compound stirred; but it would not do without more *l'argent* – one shilling and six pence was then pulled from the stocking purse, or thrashbag [*sic*], and this was placed in the pot to boil. Still the mames [*sic*] of the spirit were not to be appeased by so slight an offering, more money still was wanted, none was in the house, and in this extremity the poor duped woman bethought herself of a neighbour who had the price of a new cloak, which was to be put in requisition to help the process of the prisoner's incantations. Ten shillings were obtained and the philter [*sic*] was on the point of completion when the old witch suddenly fell out upon the floor filled with inspiration, and in her trance called out 'the boy or the horse, the boy or the horse' and this she explained when recovered, that it had suddenly been revealed to her that the only son of the silly woman on whom she was practising, or her horse were to be carried off by the *fairies*. There was yet a remedy for this evil. In St Patrick's Church yard, near this city, there grew an herb, the only one in Limerick county which could avail, and this pulled with the paddle of a goose's foot and before sunrise, would prevent the loss of either man or beast. Well, of course the herb must be pulled and away they set, all three, the horse having been yoked for the purpose of bearing them to the church yard, and accompanied by the boy and girl who were to be rescued from the early grave. Previous to their setting out however, lest the night air should affect them, they begged the loan of all the disposable wearing apparel they could procure from the poor woman, giving of course a solemn promise to return in a hurry, and do service for the civilities which they had received. When they came near the church yard the prisoners left the car with strict instructions that the boy and girl should not seek to mar the charm by prying after them. It is unnecessary to say the trio did not return.[9]

The crime of these Limerick women was unusually cruel. They had deprived an ignorant woman of all her money along with much of her family's clothing. They had even watched her borrow money from a neighbour, before stealing that as well. Still not content with their haul, they stole a goose and a hen. They had done all of this by indirectly threatening her son and daughter with death. Such a crime could not be allowed to pass without severe punishment, and whilst he made no secret of his amusement, the judge was not lenient in his sentencing:

> John Carthy, sworn – Is husband to Anastatia; and his story was a queer one – (a laugh); for his own part he did not give in to the prisoners, 'till he saw the hen fall off the roost by their devilry – (much laughter); they desired that all the family should keep from the hen they struck dead as they had the power to place the malady of the daughter on the hen. – (Laughter.)
>
> The Chief Justice – Did they leave the hen after you when they left you?
>
> McCarthy [*sic*] – No, your honour, they carried it wid [*sic*] them. – (great laughter.)
>
> Chief Justice – So I thought. They did not want to leave you with such a diseased bird. – (Much laughter.)

McCarthy – My wife then said, my Lord, that they should have the best supper she had, and said she'd kill the goose for them – (laughter) – and then my Lord, they said they wanted the gooses's [*sic*] foot to pull the herb with.

Chief Justice – What; and did your wife part with you? – (Roars of laughter.)

McCarthy – No, your honour, 'twas only the goose she parted with. (Great laughter.) The herb was called *clochthoona-breena*. – (Laughter.)

The Jury without hesitation, found the ladies guilty of stealing the clothes, and the learned Chief Justice having lamented the credulity of the prosecutors, said he found he should be compelled to deprive the country of the medical aid of the prisoners, and directed that they should be each transported for seven years.[10]

Three Galvin sisters remained in their home on Mary Street in Limerick. Their father was dead and now their mother and two sisters awaited transportation. The family had lost much of its capacity to earn money by either legitimate or nefarious means. The girls who remained outside prison walls may have shared a similarly bad character, or may have been driven to a life of crime by the removal of half of their family unit. It was little wonder, therefore, that eighteen-year-old Ellen Galvin joined her mother and sisters in prison just two weeks after their conviction. This fresh-faced, brown-haired girl had been described as a vagrant and subsequently sentenced to seven years' transportation for larceny. She joined her mother and sisters on their journey to Cork in October 1834.[11] The youthful Ellen was free of marital ties, but her older sister Bridget was already a widow and carried an infant child with her. Bridget later bade farewell to her sisters and mother as they left the depot for the *Neva*; she and her child sailed on the *Roslin Castle*, which departed Cork some ten months later.[12]

Before the *Neva*'s departure, women from several other southern and western counties poured into Cork. There were three from County Tipperary, including Bridget Strang and her two children. Strang had been sentenced to transportation for life for stealing sheep.[13] Five more travelled from County Galway, among them twenty-six-year-old Margaret Doyle, who had been convicted of stealing the proceeds of a horse's sale from the pocket of the seller.[14] Seven women journeyed over the mountains from County Kerry. Among them was twenty-one-year-old Margaret Hassett. Convicted of 'stealing leather' in Killarney in June 1834, Hassett carried her three-year-old daughter Mary with her.[15] Companionship for Mary was provided by seven-year-old Honora Reilly. She was the daughter of Catherine Reilly, who was an accomplice of Hassett and several men, all of whom were transported.[16]

Perhaps the most interesting daughter of County Kerry who eventually boarded the *Neva* was Catherine Connor. Twenty-four-year-old Connor was sentenced to seven years' transportation in the summer of 1834. However, this was not her first brush with the law. The *Kerry Evening Post* described her case as follows:

Catherine Connor stood indicted for stealing a sheet, the property of Elizabeth Murphy, of Castleisland. The prisoner was convicted at a former quarter sessions, of various acts of thievery, sentenced to be transported for seven years, and for that purpose was removed to the hulk at Cove. On a favourable representation, however, to the Lord Lieutenant, she obtained a free pardon. On returning to Kerry, she stopped one night in Castleisland, at the house of the prosecutrix, and on her departure rewarded the poor woman's hospitality, by committing the larceny above mentioned. The sheet was found in her possession by Timothy Connell, a policeman. She was a perfect stranger to the prosecutrix. She was found guilty, and sentenced to be transported for seven years. On being sentenced she did not appear in the least concerned, and made no defence.[17]

Given the haste of her re-offending, and her apparent lack of concern at the sentence, it is worth considering that Connor may have welcomed her transportation. The grinding poverty in which many Irish people lived made transportation an attractive free passage to a new life for those who were willing to countenance the detention that came with it. Indeed, there were some who almost admitted as much. One of them was Connor's fellow Kerry woman Anne Hixon. Convicted of the theft of a cloak and a quilt, Hixon was sentenced to seven years' transportation. The twenty-two-year-old had left her home in Kerry at seventeen, and had since been living in 'vagrant immorality'. Having heard the sentence pronounced,

The Wreck of the *Neva*

Hixon had expressed the opinion that 'her family would not receive her back, and she thought she might as well leave the country first as last'. Hixon's five years of vagrant wandering had taken her as far as Waterford.[18] Her 'vagrant immorality' probably made her an acquaintance of Johanna Power, another young woman who had made her life in that town. Although described as being of 'decent, sedate appearance', Power was 'a notorious prostitute and thief'. She was convicted of vagrancy in June 1833 and sentenced to transportation, unless she could produce sureties of £5. She found no such surety and so, along with Hixon, was moved to Cork.[19]

Anne Hixon was not the only Kerry woman whose family would not welcome her return, and it seems that nineteen-year-old Mary Slattery had been similarly ostracised. Convicted in her native Tralee, Slattery's offence was the theft of £10 worth of silver spoons. Surprisingly, Slattery's father was supportive of his daughter's transportation and she was convicted upon his 'petition'. She seemed to have forgiven the father who had banished her, when she commented: 'I was ruining my father by continually stealing from him and he was obliged to adopt that way of removing me.'[20] Given the ease of Mary's forgiveness it is possible that the Slattery family had deliberately sought to provide her with the means of emigration. Either way, in early January 1835 she bade farewell to her home town of Tralee and began her journey towards the *Neva*. Slattery, Hassett, Reilly, Connor and two other Kerry convicts were shipped directly from the city of Cork to the lower harbour, without entering the depot. They would board the *Neva* on 4 January 1835.[21]

From 27 December 1834 the wind picked up and a southerly gale made the coast of Cork a dangerous place for inbound shipping.[22] The prisoners in Elizabeth Fort could hear the gale howling along the valley below. Through these winter winds and rain a few final passengers were en route to Cork. These passengers had done no wrong and merely sought to follow the loved ones gone before them. They were the *Neva*'s free settlers.

The *Neva* carried nine free women, and their twenty children, along with one grandchild. Cork's Johanna Sullivan was the only free woman who carried no children with her. Given her childless status and the prevalence of the Sullivan name in Cork, it is not possible to establish exactly why she was on the ship. However, it is quite likely that she followed in the footsteps of a husband who had been transported some seven years previously. Wexford's Mary Bulgers certainly fell into that category. She and her three children were to be reunited with their husband and father, Walter, a farm labourer who had been convicted of stealing a pig. He was transported on the *Marquis of Huntley* and had arrived in New South Wales in 1828. Joining Walter Bulgers on the *Marquis of Huntley* was James Hunt of Tipperary, a well sinker and miner by trade. He had been convicted of burglary in 1827. Hunt's wife, Mary, and their five children – Catherine, Margaret, Winifred, Johana and James – joined Bulgers' wife on the *Neva*. Mary Hunt's eldest daughter Catherine carried a grandchild whom James had never seen. After nearly seven years of separation, this Tipperary family hoped to reunite.[23]

The Wreck of the *Neva*

Others shared the Hunts' hope of joining loved ones: these included the wife and nine-year-old daughter of convicted highway robber Michael Hickey. Hickey's wife, Mary, had sought free passage to Australia soon after her husband's transportation aboard the *Borodino* in February 1828. However, her initial application had been refused because it was feared that her husband's recent arrival and ongoing sentence would not allow him to support his family. Colonial authorities did not want Mary and her child draining the colony's limited resources, so they remained in Ireland until Michael was in a position to support them. On 31 October 1832 Michael Hickey, having assisted his employer in the capture of two bushrangers, was deemed eligible to have his family shipped to New South Wales. By late 1834 Mary Hickey and her little daughter and namesake were bound for Cork.[24]

Another child moving south at that time was Michael Doyle from Westmeath. He hoped to meet the father he had never known, Martin Doyle, who was separated from his wife and infant child when convicted of arson in 1827. Doyle's incendiary activities were motivated by his membership of a local Whiteboy association. His wife, Rose, was one of three women who boarded the *Neva* in order to reunite with Whiteboy husbands.[25]

Of all the counties where Whiteboy organisations ruled the night, Longford was one of those where their grip was tightest. It was little wonder, therefore, that the wives of two Longford Whiteboys trod the decks of the *Neva*. Mary Ryan was one. In 1827 her husband, Bryan, was convicted of administering unlawful oaths. Just three months after his conviction, Mary had petitioned the lord lieutenant on her husband's behalf, claiming that he had been convicted upon malicious evidence 'arising from circumstances of personal enmity' and had not been given sufficient opportunity to defend himself. She described her own circumstances as deplorable and reminded the lord lieutenant that she was 'with an infant child and no means under Heaven towards our support'. Having attached a glowing character reference from the local Roman Catholic priest, Ryan went on to ask His Excellency to 'make such mitigation of the prisoner's sentence as Your Excellency in your wisdom and humanity may deem ... just'. He waited almost seven years to mitigate Ryan's sentence. Then, when their child, Elizabeth, was old enough and Bryan was freed from captivity, permission was granted for the couple to reunite.[26]

On the road from Longford, Mary Ryan might have joined Mary McCue. McCue's husband, William, was convicted of breaking and entering in February 1826. His case was typical of the kind of Whiteboy activity that the British administration found particularly shocking:

Sentence of death was pronounced on John Fury, Patrick Halpen, W. McCue and T. Mahon, for that they on the night of 8th of February last, attacked the house of P. Mullen at Kilmackinlin, County Longford, assaulted him and his wife Anne, demanded arms, agreeably to the horrid system of intimidation practiced by other lawless depredators, they

were also convicted of menacing them with death if they did
not leave the Kingdom in 8 days.[27]

In the cases of McCue and Mahon, the death sentence was
commuted and both were transported in 1827.[28] Whiteboys
condemned to death were frequently reprieved.[29] By 1834
McCue had finished his confinement and was sufficiently well
behaved to receive his wife, along with John, the nine-year-
old son he had not seen since the boy's infancy.

The final woman to reach the depot was almost certainly
Jane McLoughlin from County Mayo. Four daughters and
four sons, aged between eight and twenty-three, travelled
with her. Although it is impossible to say for certain, it would
appear that McLoughlin was married to a man named Edward
who was transported aboard the *Asia I* in 1824.[30] A local
gentleman, John Gardiner of Farmhill, then petitioned the
government on the McLoughlin family's behalf. The surviving
correspondence between Gardiner and the authorities reveals
that the McLoughlins were known locally by Jane's maiden
name, O'Hara. The family was described as 'people of excellent
character though in the most destitute circumstances'. On 27
December 1834 Gardiner informed them that the government
would grant them free passage to New South Wales. The
McLoughlin family took only two days to say goodbye to their
lives in Mayo before departing for Cork on 29 December.
Gardiner informed the authorities that 'they are poor and must
walk to Cork and very much fear they will find it impossible
to reach Cork by the fifth of next month, but will very soon

afterwards'.[31] He had underestimated Jane McLoughlin's determination. She managed to guide her family along 250 kilometres of unfamiliar roadway, through the limited daylight of December and January, and into the southern city by the morning of 5 January.[32]

Upon reaching the gates of Elizabeth Fort, the Mc-Loughlins might have felt that their journey from poverty to a new world of opportunity was about to begin. However, fate dealt the family another blow. Jane's two eldest sons, Patrick (twenty-three) and Owen (twenty-one), were too old to travel on a female convict ship. As per regulations they were parted from their family.[33] As their mother, two younger brothers, and four sisters were left to the care of Edward Trevor's convict system, they probably walked back through the gate onto the busy streets of Cork city.

6

Farewell to Ireland

With a new year just dawning, and the recent gales abating, the convicts in Cork were making final preparations for their departure. They probably received their last visit from the 'Ladies Committee for Visiting Females in Prison'. The membership of such committees commonly consisted of wealthy and charitable women who wanted to teach morality and assist in reforming those less fortunate than themselves.

A further sign of imminent departure was the visit of John Stephenson. Like all surgeons of the time, Stephenson would have visited the women in order to make a medical inspection before receiving them on the *Neva*. Any he found unfit would not leave the depot.[1] It is also likely that he addressed his charges at this point. To the poverty-stricken and poorly educated convicts, he may have seemed intimidating. Stephenson was a naval officer and he dressed as such. Some surgeons favoured long, rambling addresses emphasising morality and reform. However, Stephenson's diaries from his previous voyages indicate that he was much more concerned with physical health than spiritual well-being. His remarks to the women were likely to have emphasised the necessity of cleanliness and order aboard the ship. Stephenson no doubt informed his new charges that they would shortly be departing the depot to join him at Cove, a trip they made within days.

The morning of 5 January 1835 saw the *Neva*'s convicts released from the depot. Under armed guard the women and children were escorted down the steep hill that led from the fort and onto the quays below. Moving along the southern bank of the south channel, they passed the city's South Gate Bridge. A hundred metres further downstream a glance to their left revealed a statue of George II, prominently sited on the opposite bank. The statue was a vivid reminder that Cork city owed much of its former prosperity and economic expansion to the provisioning of British garrisons at home and abroad.

On that January morning the *Neva*'s women were probably marched some 300 or 400 metres along the quayside to a point just east of a handsome limestone crossing known as Parliament Bridge. It was here that they boarded the *Comet* steamer. The last recorded sighting of these women was made by a journalist from the *Cork Evening Herald*. Having witnessed their departure, he wrote:

This morning the *Comet* Steamer left the quay for Cove, with 148 Female Convicts; 20 Free Settlers, and 34 children. They were embarked on board the *Neva* Convict ship, which sails in a day or two. The females looked very well, and were

comfortably clothed – this may be expected from the excellent
regulations and discipline of the Governor of the Depot.[2]

From the *Comet*'s crowded deck the women watched as Ireland retreated to the quiet alcoves of ever-fading memory.
From city to country, between poverty and wealth, this journey
downriver saw all of Ireland's contrasts pass them by. Cork
city's streets were home to approximately 100,000 people. They
toiled in distilleries, iron foundries, steel mills, copper smiths,
tanyards, breweries, paper mills, glass houses, weavers, candle
manufacturers, banks, cloth processors, markets and shops.[3] A
hill above the city was the site of the United Kingdom's largest
butter market, and butter from Cork was exported to the four
corners of the British Empire. That morning, the sounds of
the city's bustling industry drifted through the cold January
air, reminding the women that few of Cork's inhabitants
would stop to dwell on their departure.

Soon they passed beneath Cork's newest bridge. Built in
1830, the bridge consisted of two contra-flow drawbridges,
each of which could be raised for shipping. The reason for
this elaborate structure was the construction of a new corn
market, which they could see on their starboard side. By 1835
the corn market was exporting approximately 200,000 barrels
of corn annually. Just ten years after these convicts passed it by,
this level of exports was one of the causes of major suffering
during the Irish Famine.

A few hundred metres downstream they reached the
point where the two river channels converged before flowing

onward through the marshes east of the city. On their port side they could surely hear the clanking and banging of working shipyards echoing through the cold morning air. On the wooded slopes north of these shipyards the wives of Cork's 'Merchant Princes' probably sipped their morning tea in the elegant drawing rooms of Cork's most ostentatious residences. Slipping beneath the gaze of these stylish dwellings, the *Comet* soon passed Cork Corporation's banqueting hall at Blackrock Castle. Here the channel widened and they surely tasted the tang of Lough Mahon's salty air.

George Mounsey Wheatley Atkinson, *Paddle Steamer Entering the Port of Cork,* 1842, oil on canvas, 61 x 100 cm. Note the convergence of the south and north channels of the River Lee. *Courtesy of the Crawford Art Gallery, Cork. Cat. No.773-P*

At this point the *Comet* probably picked up speed and the mothers may have sought to shelter their children from the January wind. Little boys like John Russell were surely caught up in all the excitement if they watched the smaller boats that ferried ballast from Little Island's limestone quarries to the ships waiting around the harbour. In the fields around the lough, tenant farmers may well have seen the *Comet* from the half-doors of their tiny thatched cottages.

Exiting Lough Mahon, the *Comet* entered the narrow channel that carried her between Great Island's western shore and the little village of Passage. Now the ships the *Comet* passed were larger. This was where bulky cargo was broken up to be ferried upstream to the city by smaller craft. Passage's shipyards could build and repair the largest ships, and one of the vessels under repair in the harbour that morning was the *Albion*. She had lost her boats, bulwarks and part of her deck load whilst shipping timber from Miramichi to Bristol. Now, she stood as a frightening reminder of the sea's unpredictable violence.

Beyond Passage, the narrow channel opened out to the vastness of the lower harbour. All around the *Comet* the grandiose masts of globe-traversing craft reached skywards. Like the *Albion*, the *Cyrus* had just crossed the Atlantic with a load of Canadian timber. She was taking on provisions before continuing her voyage to Liverpool. The *Judith and Hester* was also bound for Liverpool, whilst the *Miner and Fox* awaited her departure for Swansea. The *Barclay* would soon be Belfast bound with a cargo of wine, and the *Tiwell* was loading provisions for London. Meanwhile the British navy's presence was marked by the troop ship HMS *Romney*. All the while the colliers came and went, and steamers such as the *Victory* and the *William IV* tended their routes on the Irish Sea.[4]

In the midst of all this activity, a convict ship lay awaiting her human cargo. She stood 31.8 metres long and 8.32 metres wide, and her three towering masts formed an ominous silhouette against the sky. On her stern appeared a name that would soon feature on the pages of newspapers across the British Empire: *Neva*.

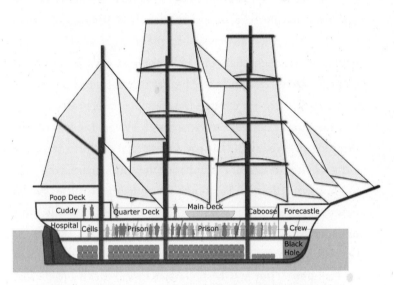

Probable configuration of the *Neva*. Built in Hull, England, in 1813; approximately 31.8 metres long, 8.32 metres wide and 1.95 metres between the decks. *Image: Kevin Todd.*

By the time she arrived in Cork, the *Neva* was already twenty-one years old. She had been built in Hull in 1813 and named in honour of the River Neva, which flows from Lake Ladoga in north-western Russia through St Petersburg and on to the Baltic Sea.[5] The river is a major shipping channel and it was in this vicinity that the *Neva* first saw service. Engaged as a merchant vessel, she spent her first winters traversing the icy waters of the Baltic region and occasionally journeying to the sunnier West Indies. On one such journey she first saw Cork harbour. Troops from the Royal Irish Regiment were aboard when the *Neva* transited the harbour on her way from Jamaica to Portsmouth in 1816.[6] By 1826 her hull timbers had deteriorated to a point that required significant repair, and this task was undertaken in the same year. The repairs complete, between 1828 and 1832 she had voyaged to North and South America and the Mediterranean region.[7]

In 1833 the *Neva* entered the convict service, carrying 170 convicts from Plymouth to New South Wales. The first of two deaths connected with that voyage was that of thirty-six-year-old Patrick Honrahan, a member of the ship's guard, who died of cholera before the *Neva*'s departure from Deptford on 20 June 1833. The first convict to die on the *Neva* was fifty-six-year-old Samuel Wright. He died on 9 November 1833 some hours after he 'fell from his seat in the Prison in a state of insensibility'.[8] The first Irish convict to sail on the *Neva* also sailed in 1833. He was twenty-one-year-old James Murphy from Armagh. Murphy was convicted of highway robbery at Warwick Assizes in 1832, and by the night of 29 July 1833 he was locked safely beneath the *Neva*'s decks.[9]

The ship had been radically overhauled to meet the partially standardised format of convict ships at that time. A new deck was added by planking over the beams above the cargo hold, thereby creating the three decks (floors) of a standard convict ship. In addition, a poop deck was added to the stern of the ship. Essentially, the construction of a poop meant that a little cabin had been added to the rear. This cabin, known as the cuddy, typically provided accommodation for the officers of the ship, the commander of the guard and the ship's surgeon. Female convict ships carried no guard or guard commander. Thus, the *Neva's* cuddy provided lodgings only for the ship's officers and surgeon. The roof of the cuddy formed the poop deck, which provided a raised platform from where the helmsman could steer the ship. The most rearward of the *Neva's* three masts – the mizzen mast – was also located towards the front of the poop deck.

In front of the cuddy stood a little area of the main deck, known as the quarterdeck. On male convict ships the quarterdeck was barricaded from the rest of the main deck, and was sealed off from the convicts. Cannon sometimes sat behind the barricade. These were loaded with grape shot and could sweep the deck with their deadly projectiles, should the convicts become unruly. On female convict ships, however, no such barricade was considered necessary. If the cannon remained from *Neva's* previous voyage, they were no longer loaded, and sat silently on the quarterdeck pointing towards the bow of the ship. On the *Neva*, the quarterdeck was probably amalgamated with the main deck, allowing the women an area approximately 18.3 metres long and no more than 8.2 metres wide in which to exercise. Towards the front of the main deck the longboat occupied some of that area. This large rowing boat was typically used to ferry crew ashore from the ship's outer anchorages. In front of the longboat and just behind the bow of the ship was the caboose – the area where food was cooked. The fires required for this were sheltered from the worst of the turbulent weather by a raised structure, known as the forecastle, on the bow. This forecastle was the poor relation of the cuddy and usually housed the ordinary seamen. However, the *Neva*'s forecastle was home to the bathing tub, where convicts bathed in rotation during the voyage.[10]

At either end of the main deck, two crude staircases emerged from the holes that formed the fore and main hatches. These hatches bore a metal grating which was used to keep convicts above or below, depending on the officer's wishes. At the foot of these staircases was the 'tween deck, where the women slept on both sides of the ship, in little berths, about 1.8 metres square. Each berth had two levels (similar to the bunk-bed concept) and four women lay on each. There was little headroom in the berths, as the 'tween deck was just 1.96 metres high. The *Neva*'s free women and their children probably slept towards the rear of the prison and may have been partially separated from the convicts. The walls around the berths were whitewashed, as was considered most hygienic at the time.

The sleeping berths occupied about the same area as the main and quarterdecks directly above them. Furthest forward on the 'tween deck, a small compartment usually housed the surgeon's hospital. This forward location was home to convict ships' hospitals for two reasons. First, the surgeon, who was obliged to make daily inspections of the prison, could not avoid doing so. Every day, upon descending from any of the hatches, he found himself in the prison or walking through part of it to get to the hospital. Second, it was thought that the sick should not be kept too close to the ship's guard. That guard was usually quartered at the rear of the 'tween deck, ensuring that convicts slept between the guardsmen and the hospital. However, by 1835 the location of ships' hospitals had changed. The pitching and rolling of a ship made the forward compartment an extremely uncomfortable location, so hospitals were moved to the rear.[11] On female convict ships this was easy to arrange as the guard's compartment was vacant. Thus, the compartment that had housed the *Neva*'s guard in 1833 had probably been converted to a hospital by 1835. Another part of that same compartment probably housed the ship's punishment cells. It is likely that the forward compartment was used as accommodation for the crew, who were removed from the forecastle to facilitate its role as a bath house for the women aboard.[12]

The treatment of seamen was not heavily regulated and their shipboard quarters were even more cramped and squalid than those of the prisoners. One contemporary sailor described sleeping among coils of rigging and spare sails, as no berths were built for the sailors. He also wrote of returning to the crew quarters after a ferocious storm had lashed the decks:

Soon all was snug aloft and we were again allowed to go below. This I did not consider much of a favour, for the confusion of everything below, and that inexpressible sickening smell, caused by the shake up of the bilge water in the hold, made the steerage but an indifferent refuge from the cold, wet decks. I had often read of the nautical experiences of others, but I felt as though there could be none worse than mine, for in addition to every other evil, I could not but remember that this was the first night of a two year voyage. When we were on deck we were much better off, for we were continually ordered about by the officer, who said that it was good for us to be in motion. Yet anything was better than the horrible state of things below. I remember very well going to the hatchway and putting my head down, when I was oppressed by nausea, and always being relieved immediately. It was as good as an emetic.[13]

By 1835 typical convict voyages lasted about four months. The months would pass slowly for a crew quartered in squalid conditions beneath the decks.

The lowest of the *Neva*'s three decks served as her cargo hold. Here the provisions for the longest voyages were stored. At the very front of the cargo hold, beneath the bow of the ship, a little cubbyhole formed a coal store. On other ships this 'black hole' had a double function, serving as a solitary cell for convicts who misbehaved. However, the *Neva*'s women were spared the torture of this gloomy space, as it seems that their 'black hole' occupied the same deck as the prison.[14]

In December 1834, just before the *Neva* left for Cork, all her copper fittings were replaced and she was thoroughly overhauled for the second time.[15] She was now considered a very sturdy and seaworthy craft. However, should tragedy befall her, four small boats on her main deck could be launched in an attempt to save those aboard. One was the longboat; another was the captain's gig. This little boat hung beneath davits on the ship's port side and typically served as a taxi for the captain. The *Neva*'s third potential lifeboat was known as the pinnace and was usually used as a tender for the larger vessel. However, on the *Neva* the pinnace saw little use and was filled with spare parts for the ship's rigging. The final lifeboat was the cutter, which probably hung from davits on the starboard side.

The *Neva*'s master was Captain Benjamin Hutchins Peck. Three years after the *Neva*'s sailing, Charles Dickens would immortalise Peck's home place of Bermondsey in the novel *Oliver Twist*. However, by 1835 Peck had long since departed that growing London slum and carved out a living on the high seas. He had previously captained the transport ship *Sylvia*, serving on her from 1829 to 1833 and voyaging to Bermuda, the Americas and the Mediterranean. Peck then made the *Neva*'s first convict voyage in 1833. Historian Charles Bateson has pointed out that the masters of convict ships 'were tough unlettered men risen from the foc's'le in the harsh school of the sea' and consequently 'placed scant value on convict comfort'.[16] Peck may have fallen into that category. Nonetheless, after his first convict voyage with the *Neva*, the Admiralty were satisfied with the certificate given to him by the governor of New South Wales, and they awarded him the standard gratuity.[17] Although his authority in seafaring matters was absolute, Peck was expected to defer to Stephenson on matters relating to the health and supervision of the convicts.

Whilst Peck and Stephenson were the *Neva*'s most senior officers, they could do little without their crew, consisting of twenty-five men serving directly under Peck. The first mate was Joseph Bennett, who had been with the *Neva* for some time and had seen her opened up for repairs in 1833. Bennett served as a conduit between Peck and his crew, ensuring that the captain's orders were carried out. At the head of that crew was second mate William H. Laws. Laws had a higher wage than that of a seaman, but with the additional money came additional responsibility and few of the benefits that officers enjoyed. He was expected to work with the men and exercise authority over them. He was not one of them, but was not really considered an officer either. Laws shared this strange no-man's land between officers and crew with the third and fourth mates, Charles Hagman and John May. The presence of four mates ensured that at least one was on deck for each of the ship's watches.

Three other members of the ship's crew had highly specific tasks: steward Henry Hollis, carpenter Edwin Forbes and cook Anthony Edwards. Their interactions with the ordinary seamen would characterise the nature of the *Neva*'s voyage. As steward, Hollis was really Peck's personal assistant and attended to the needs of his captain. Edwards not only fed the crew, but could also grant them little indulgences such as permission to dry their wet clothing near his fires. As ship's carpenter, Forbes busied himself with the *Neva*'s routine maintenance. All three worked all day and slept at night, unless 'all hands' were called to the deck.

The two ship's boys, Joseph Firrell and Thomas Quinn, stood at the bottom of the *Neva*'s chain of command, whilst sixteen ordinary seamen served directly above them. One, Robert Bullard, had joined the *Neva* at Deptford on 2 December 1834. He was an experienced sailor and had served on several other ships. Thomas Sharp had also joined the ship at Deptford, but his experience does not seem to have equalled Bullard's. Perhaps the final crew member to come aboard was William Hine, a man of considerable seafaring experience, who joined the ship at Cove.[18] Although their names were recorded (and are reproduced in Appendix IV), we know little else of the other men who completed the *Neva*'s crew. Like the crews of most ships of the age, these men were likely to have been a collection of nomadic wanderers who had left their homes for a life on the sea. They did not have any significant ties to any place, and they reserved their affections for a limited number of people. They were used to living almost exclusively among other men, and to the activities that were then defined as masculine. A sailor worked hard whilst at sea and many of them were known to play hard during their short sojourns on dry land. Charles Bateson has described them thus:

The men, recruited from the waterside taverns by unscru-pulous crimps and living aboard the ship under conditions of squalor and hardship, were tough and quarrelsome. Their indiscipline was notorious and desertions were frequent. Extant muster lists of incoming convict ships indicate that many arrived with two or three short of their complement of men and boys, due to deaths by disease or accident during the passage and to desertions before sailing or at ports of call … an examination of 22 muster lists of vessels which reached Australia in 1829–30 … shows that nine were deficient one or more men.[19]

Like the women with whom they shared the ship, the *Neva*'s crew were societal outcasts with different values to those in the land-based world they left behind. These kindred spirits first became acquainted in Cork's lower harbour.

By the afternoon of 5 January 1835 the *Neva* had received all of her convicts. Over the next three days those women who still had relatives who were close enough, or cared enough, would say their last goodbyes. The relatives were rowed out to the *Neva* and allowed on board at Stephenson's discretion. He had certainly allowed the relatives of departing convicts to come aboard the *Waterloo*, and there is no reason to believe that he abandoned that practice when appointed to the *Neva*.[20] Such parting scenes were doubtlessly filled with regret for convicts and their families. One surgeon commented on the 'mental despondency under which they laboured on reflecting that they were taking a final leave of their country and friends under such degrading circumstances'.[21] The degradation was added to by the curious onlookers who rowed out to see the ship's unfortunate cargo.[22]

A favourable wind blew across the harbour from the north-east on 6 January.[23] However, the *Neva* could not depart until she had taken on her full complement. Whilst she waited for some of the free women assigned to her, the women on deck saw some new ships arrive in the harbour: one, *William Wallace*, was bound for Rio de Janeiro, and another, *Marino*, had just shipped timber from Polar Island. When, on 7 January, the wind changed to a south-easterly direction, the convicts had to wait a little longer.[24] On 8 January the wind moved back to the north. Luckily for two intended voyagers, free woman Mary Hammond and her daughter, it was decided at this point that the ship had waited long enough. By the time they arrived from County Meath, the *Neva* was already gone. Their tardiness probably saved their lives.[25]

There is no way of knowing the exact time at which the *Neva* weighed anchor and started down the harbour. However, the tides allow us to make an educated guess. On 8 January ebb (or outward-bound) tides ran from Cork harbour until approximately 5 a.m., and again between 11 a.m. and 5.15 p.m.[26] Sailing ships could be towed out of a harbour by rowing boat or steamer; however, captains tended to favour ebb tides. Mary Slattery was later under the impression that the ship left Cork on 7 January.[27] This implies that Peck got under way early on the morning of 8 January, during the hours that Slattery may have considered night-time. Thus, it is likely that he departed on the first ebb tide and had cleared the harbour by 5 a.m. By the time that dawn broke over Roche's Point, the *Neva* had already departed.

7

The Voyage

By the beginning of 1835 convict voyages were not as arduous as they had once been. Where the first fleet had taken 252 days to reach the far side of the world, by the 1830s the *Neva* could expect to make that voyage in fewer than 123 days. Nevertheless, four months of confinement in a vessel that could not prevent uncomfortable proximity to each other was unlikely to be a pleasing prospect. Margaret Drury, Rose Ann Dunn and the others who had made the *Erin*'s nightmare voyage to Cork in 1833 were probably best prepared for the uncomfortable days ahead. However, the *Neva*'s voyage would take at least twice as long as the *Erin*'s.

There was nothing rigidly uniform about convict ship routines. Guidelines issued by the authorities were quite vague.[1] They informed the surgeon of his obligations to the convicts, but left the method by which he discharged these obligations to his own discretion. Like all surgeons, Stephenson was obliged to write a journal for each of his convict voyages. Unfortunately his *Neva* journal has long since disintegrated somewhere at the bottom of Bass Strait. However, all four of the journals from his previous voyages survive; they, along with those of the surgeons of several other female convict ships, have been used to construct a narrative of life aboard the *Neva*.

Shortly before boarding, or on the ship itself, the women were divided into messes of eight. Each mess was assigned to one berth. Free women were kept apart from prisoners insofar as was possible, and Stephenson also endeavoured to keep family groups together. Each mess was given drinking vessels and wooden platters. These were marked with the number of the mess to which they belonged. Messes were also assigned a 'mess head' or 'matron' from among their members. These matrons were given charge over their mess when the surgeon was absent. They had several distinct responsibilities. One surgeon directed his convicts to give the matron:

> … the most implicit obedience, she being held responsible for the correct demeanour of her messmates, cleanliness of their persons and drawing all their rations; has also to give me information from time to time of irregularities, which she might observe, and any means under which might in the most remote degree endanger the quiet of the prison.[2]

Stephenson appointed his matrons with reference to reports of the convicts' behaviour received from the governor of the Cork depot. An appointment as matron could be rewarding, and a matron might show some favouritism to herself and her closest friends. However, the appointment was not without disadvantages. A matron's power made her the target of mistrust and hostility, and among a group of criminals it was never wise to place a target on one's back.

In the days that followed, Stephenson probably formed 'divisions' from groups of messes. On the *Guildford* he had formed two divisions of a hundred men each.[3] It is quite likely that he operated a similar scheme on the *Neva*. The main purpose of this division was to enable the surgeon to supervise activities that could not be undertaken by everybody together, but still had to be performed by large numbers at the same time. On the *Guildford* Stephenson had allowed each of his two divisions two days to bathe and wash their clothes. However, when the ship reached colder areas he reduced this to one day per division. As the *Neva* sailed from northern winter to southern autumn he probably allowed each of his divisions only one day each to wash their clothes and themselves. Thus, one division of twelve or thirteen messes was rotated through the forecastle for bathing on a given day of every week. On the same day, the same division would wash their clothing. Some surgeons selected special washerwomen from each mess in rotation who would wash the clothing for the entire division.[4]

On the six days on which the women were not tasked with washing, their routine was as dull and boring as it had been in prison. In the mornings they were released from the prison deck. Cooks were the first prisoners to breathe the fresh morning air, making their way to the upper deck just before dawn. Stephenson appointed two or three cooks from among the women. They were responsible for preparing food for all convicts and for the timely lighting of necessary fires, using minimal fuel. The convict cooks probably worked under the supervision of crew cook Anthony Edwards. Each morning, this little group might have been the only *Neva* convicts that saw the sun rising over a vast foreign ocean. To a group of nineteenth-century Irish women such a sight was rare and eerily silent. A contemporary sailor described the dawn at sea as follows:

> Much has been said of the sun-rise at sea; but it will not compare with the sun-rise on shore. It wants the accompaniments of the song of birds, the awakening hum of men and the glancing of the first beams upon trees, hills, spires, and house-tops, to give it life and spirit. But though the actual rise of the sun at sea is not so beautiful, yet nothing will compare with the breaking of day upon the wide ocean.
>
> There is something in the first grey streaks stretching along the eastern horizon and throwing an indistinct light upon the deep, which combines with the boundlessness and unknown depth of the sea around you, and gives one a feeling of loneliness, of dread, and of melancholy foreboding, which nothing else in nature can give. This gradually passes away as the light grows brighter, and when the sun comes up, the ordinary monotonous sea day begins.[5]

About half an hour after sunrise, the matrons were brought up to supervise the stowing of bedding. Each woman was issued bedding emblazoned with her on-board number. Every morning she would come on deck and present this to the matron, who had it stowed away appropriately. Stephenson could inspect the bedding, if he so desired, and would have been wise to make regular inspections, as bedding could be a prized possession. On one voyage a convict was punished for stealing the bedding of another to make a pinafore for her child.[6]

About an hour and a half after dawn a breakfast of gruel was served. This, along with other meals, was typically consumed between the berths of the prison deck.[7] Each mess received its share via the matron. The matrons also procured tea and sugar from the ship's steward. The convict diet was quite reasonable, and for Irish prisoners who had frequently experienced hunger, a guaranteed supply of three meals daily was certainly welcome:

> The rations are both good and abundant, three-quarters of a pound of biscuit being the daily allowance of bread, while each day the convict sits down to either beef, pork or plum pudding, having pea soup four times a week, and a pot of gruel every morning, with sugar or butter in it. Vinegar is issued to the messes weekly, and as soon as the ship has been three weeks at sea, each man is served with one ounce of lime juice and the same of sugar daily, to guard against scurvy; while two gallons of good Spanish red wine, and one hundred and forty gallons of water are put on board for issuing to each likewise, three to four gills of wine weekly, and three quarts of water daily, being the general allowance.[8]

The passage quoted above describes the diet on a male convict ship, but the diet for women was very similar, although portions were probably revised downwards to adjust for the gender of the convicts. In 1837 the provisioning of Irish convict ships would become the source of some controversy when authorities in Sydney complained that Irish convicts were arriving in poor health. There was some suspicion that inspected ships' stores were sold and subsequently replaced with inferior produce. However, there is no evidence to suggest that the provisioning of Irish ships was considered inadequate before the arrival of the *Heber* and the *Calcutta* in 1837.[9]

The system of food distribution caused some controversy aboard the *Neva*. For the first three weeks some of the women found the food insufficient. Peck was responsible for victualling the convicts and crew, but Stephenson acted as the navy's overseer.[10] He was to ensure that the captain issued sufficient rations, and to attend at the opening of every cask or container to inspect the quality of the food. During each meal a portion was sent to him so that he could ensure it was cooked correctly.[11] Thus, one would expect that Stephenson was the first person to whom the women should have complained when rations seemed short and that Stephenson would then have attempted to resolve the issue with Peck. Whatever the chain of command, the *Neva*'s rationing issue was resolved when the captain 'took the duty of issuing the provisions upon himself'.[12]

After breakfast most of the women were sent to the upper deck unless the weather was particularly wet or stormy.

However, two from each mess stayed below to clean the prison.[13] In many cases the method by which the prison deck was scrubbed was that of 'dry holystoning' – the sprinkling of sand on the deck and its subsequent scouring with small smooth pieces of freestone. Some surgeons allowed female convicts to scrub the decks with damp cloths as it was considered that dry holystoning was an impracticable task for women.[14] Stephenson had not employed the holystoning method aboard the *Guildford*, instead using 'brushes and the smallest possible quantity of water'; it is unlikely that he departed from that method on the *Neva*. However, the use of water created a lingering dampness which was combined with the perspiration of closely confined prisoners. Surgeons who were convinced – as Stephenson was – that poor ventilation facilitated the spread of disease, always sought to avoid such dampness. After the prison deck was scrubbed to his satisfaction, Stephenson would not allow anybody below until it was perfectly dry. On days when the weather created dampness below, he had the decks cleaned by scraping and he always kept a number of convicts 'on duty to remove any accidental wet or dirt'.[15]

Whilst the prison was cleaned, another woman from each mess was tasked with washing the breakfast utensils. Shortly afterwards the matrons received their mess's dinner rations, which were placed in containers numbered by mess and brought to the cooks for preparation.

Stephenson had been specifically instructed to 'admit the convicts on deck as much as possible'.[16] On a previous voyage he ensured that 'the prison doors were open from sun rise to sun set and the prisoners allowed to get up and down as they chose'.[17] In inclement weather, however, they were denied this pleasure and forced to stay below in the overwhelming humidity of the 'tween deck. A day beneath the deck was particularly unpleasant in the tropics, when the poorly ventilated prison became a giant oven of confined humanity.

On such days temperatures beneath the deck soared and convicts competed to breathe the increasingly stale air. The stifling heat was somewhat alleviated by the provision of windsails above the prison hatches. These were canvas funnels designed to divert the breeze downward and into the areas beneath the main deck. Ship's surgeons' constant obsession with ventilation meant that they frequently urged their masters to fit these devices. Stephenson had specifically complained about the lack of fresh air afforded to convicts when rain had confined them below during the voyages of the *Guildford* and the *Katherine Stewart Forbes*.[18] Thus, he almost certainly favoured the fitting of windsails. However, the windsail had one major flaw: failure to operate when most urgently required. On occasion convict ships could lie becalmed on a still tropical ocean, whilst the windsails failed to offer any solution to the suffocating heat affecting all below deck.

When the ocean was not still, high seas could add to the pungent odour prevailing beneath the deck. Such seas often spilled through the portholes and hatchways, flooding the prison with seawater. In particularly angry seas this water could even smash the timbers supporting convict bedding. Whilst water was baled out, it always left a pungent smell behind it.[19]

Although the *Neva* encountered 'some bad weather between the cape and St Paul's', her final voyage was later described as 'a fair weather passage'.[20] Therefore the convicts spent most of their final days on the upper deck, but their time was not passed entirely in leisure. It was considered 'desirable to keep the minds of the convicts as constantly and usefully employed as possible'.[21] Female convicts were usually engaged in sewing and needlework, and supplies were provided for those specific purposes.[22] In theory, the surgeon superintendent was supposed to attend to their educational needs by schooling each division for a period every day, so those who were illiterate could learn basic literacy during the long passage. However, convicts did not seem to understand the potential benefits of formal education, as one ship's surgeon reported:

> I found much difficulty in keeping the children at school, for such was the mistaken kindness of their mothers, that they would come and take them away, for fear that instruction should make them sick ... The young women were taught in the fore prison and tho' not always studious acquired the rudiments of education most rapidly when they were so.[23]

Some convicts had received enough education to assist the surgeon in his endeavours. Another surgeon wrote:

Having observed the inattention of the Mothers of the respective children in teaching them to whom I had issued cards and Books which many had destroyed I appointed as the General schoolmistress to the children – Rose Richey – as well as to those adults who were inclined to be taught – [those who] rejected education served out needles and thread.[24]

Thus, on some ships education was optional, but some form of labour was compulsory on all.

Stephenson never mentioned his method of providing schooling on any of his previous voyages. Consequently, it is likely that he did not have a rigid educational regime and allowed participation on a voluntary basis. It is certain that the fruits of any on-board schooling were minimal as it was subsequently evident that half of the *Neva*'s convict survivors were entirely illiterate.[25] It is possible that some of the women still spoke Gaelic as a first language. However, by the late 1820s and early 1830s a convict's inability to speak English was an unusual occurrence.[26] Thus, Stephenson's attempts to educate were not significantly hindered by a language barrier.

Dinner was served at 12.30 or 1 p.m. About an hour later the convicts received their wine allowance. The moderate consumption of wine was considered nutritionally and medicinally beneficial. However, serving alcohol on convict ships was a troublesome task. Problems occurred when the convicts overindulged, having stored up several days or weeks of wine rations. This led to boisterous, rowdy and even violent behaviour. However, as intolerable as these behaviours were, they were not the most undesirable consequences of alcohol consumption.

On female convict ships the crew could store their wine to tempt more promiscuous women into their company.[27] This caused particular problems as surgeons were specifically instructed to ensure that there was no unnecessary contact between the crew and the prisoners. Even the basic layout of the ship meant that interaction between the *Neva*'s convicts and crew was naturally limited. Two of the three masts were positioned on, or behind, the forward part of the quarterdeck, meaning that the crew only had to go to the main deck when working on the foremast. Whilst this natural division curtailed contact between crew and convicts, it could not eliminate it. For that reason, both convicts and crew were forbidden any form of 'improper intercourse'.[28]

However, such regulations were made in the confines of a London office and in reality were not rigidly adhered to. Along with other convict ships, the *Neva* carried a sizeable portion of prostitutes. There is much evidence to suggest that crews on other ships frequently made use of convict prostitutes. Commenting on the enforcement of gender segregation one surgeon later opined that 'the truly pitiable surgeon who has hitherto endeavoured strictly to enforce the orders … has certainly most justly entitled himself to the full honour of Catholic canonisation on his landing'.[29] These impractical regulations were so widely ignored that on some ships a practice developed whereby a seaman took a kind of concubine wife for the duration of the voyage. Fifteen years before the *Neva*'s voyage, the *Janus* was at the centre of controversy when many of the female convicts she had carried from Cork were pregnant when they reached Sydney.[30] After the female convict ship the *Amphitrite* was wrecked off Boulogne in August 1833, boatswain John Owen testified that female convicts had had the freedom of the ship:

> The Doctor let them go where they liked, he never took any notice if they did not make a riot. The doctor had the sole management of them; never heard him expostulate, advise, or in any way converse with them. There was no attempt at restraint, instruction, or government of any kind ... There was no reward or encouragement for good conduct. No attempt to keep them employed.[31]

Owen claimed that he had occasionally resorted to dousing the women with buckets of water so that they kept their distance from the crew. By 1838 an enquiry into alleged improper intercourse aboard the *John Renwick* concluded that the crew 'confined this mischief to as small an amount as could be expected considering the difficulty attendant thereon'.[32] It is clear that contact between the crew and the convicts occurred on ships that sailed before and after the *Neva*'s voyage, and the authorities tolerated a certain amount of it.

Whether or not such things were allowed to happen on the *Neva* really depended upon Stephenson and, to a lesser extent, Peck. Probably somewhere on the ocean beyond Cove, convict Margaret Drury formed a relationship with seaman Peter Robinson. This is evidence that Stephenson may not have rigidly enforced gender segregation. Even in the unlikely event that Stephenson did try to practise an unnecessarily disciplined regime, it seems that he was confined to his bed with dysentery some days before the ship met her fate.[33] With the supervising surgeon no longer able to attend to his duties, it is a possibility that discipline was allowed to lapse, and even if Drury and Robinson's relationship had already begun, Stephenson's period of illness was likely a time of its blossoming. Several of the *Neva*'s survivors insisted that there had been no intercourse between convicts and crew; however, their denials are hardly surprising. It is unlikely that these survivors would make an admission that would defame their character or result in punishment.

The issuance of lime or lemon juice to convicts probably caused less bother than that of wine. Where concerned surgeons insisted that the wine allowance was consumed in their presence to prevent storage, they delegated the serving of lemon juice to their matrons. This beverage, used to prevent scurvy, was served every evening approximately three hours after dinner. About one hour after the serving of lemon juice, the matrons received their mess's beef or pork allowances for the following day. The meat was then washed and placed in the steep tub.[34] Convicts were then allowed to cook their own suppers from the rations provided.[35] Afterwards they would remain on deck until the surgeon decided to lock them below for the night. Some surgeons would send them below earlier than others, but on previous voyages Stephenson had not imprisoned convicts until sunset.[36]

Thus, evening time on the *Neva* probably saw the women on deck enjoying a few hours of leisure before sunset. Free of any formal duty, their attentions inevitably turned to other pastimes. Convicts frequently tore pages from the Bibles issued to them to manufacture makeshift playing cards. Although all forms of gambling were prohibited, some surgeons may well have tolerated this comparatively minor evil. They may also have tolerated a certain amount of singing, dancing and other merriment. Some suggested that the toleration of such activities actually made for the delivery of healthier convicts.[37] Stephenson never expressed any concern about convict pastimes in any of his surviving journals, so it is likely that the *Neva*'s women found their evenings the most enjoyable part of their day.

During those evenings the women had time to watch the vastness of the world through which they passed. They probably saw some other ships as the *Neva* sailed through the busy shipping channels south of the British Isles. As the vessel steered her course further south, the sight of other ships would have been increasingly rare, until she approached settlements such as St Jago island in the Cape Verdes and the Cape of Good Hope at the southern tip of Africa. The ships of foreign navies might show their colours and, if they did so, Peck would have returned the courtesy.[38] Merchant ships that sighted each other on open seas sometimes came alongside and exchanged reports of each other's situation. Surgeons were specifically instructed 'to avail ... of every opportunity during the voyage of reporting ... the progress of the ship'.[39] Thus, the *Neva*'s convicts quite likely witnessed Stephenson provide some United Kingdom-bound captain with a report of the ship's progress.

On the numerous days when the *Neva*'s complement had no sight of human beings beyond the decks of their ship, nature was their only reminder that the living world had not abandoned them. It is likely that they noted the presence of sharks, whales and turtles in the waters around them, whilst schools of dolphin were also known to accompany lone ships traversing the ocean. The *Neva*'s children and their mothers probably gazed in awe whilst such exotic creatures darted through the waters beneath them.[40] No doubt the children laughed and played as children always do, and as the weeks rolled by their surroundings were probably a source of endless amusement.

As the sun set, Stephenson began the process of imprisoning his charges below the deck. Whilst matrons were expected to take charge of their messes, the more timid prisoners still slept among a group of self-supervising convicts. There is little doubt that in the darkness items were stolen, threats made and retribution distributed with the cruelty that criminals were used to experiencing.[41] Owen stated that he had observed 'very little kindness among the prisoners' on board the *Amphitrite*. Indeed he remarked that 'the language and behaviour of some of the women was outrageous and disgusting beyond anything the men had ever seen'.[42]

Some of the convict women had learned to survive in the most hostile of environments. Part of that survival depended upon their expecting the worst from those around them. The streets and prisons from which they had come had taught them to offend before they were offended against. In their midst the free women did their best to survive, whilst the *Neva*'s children watched sunnier dispositions vanish when darkness descended on the 'tween deck. To sustain the health of all of his convicts, however, Stephenson had to ensure the women knew that quarrelsome behaviour had consequences in the form of a number of unpleasant punishments.

By the 1830s punishments on convict ships were not nearly as severe as they had formerly been. Even on male convict ships, surgeons seldom resorted to the use of the cat-o'-nine-tails whip. Indeed many showed pride in their ability to discipline convicts without having recourse to such barbarism. On a female convict ship that sailed seven years after the *Neva*, the surgeon recorded punishments as follows:

> Punishment consisted in being confined to 'the box' on bread and water, wearing handcuffs, with a distance chain, to being placed in the after hatchway with the ladder up on bread and water, and for fighting the two are handcuffed with a distance chain, together for a day or two when noisy or troublesome in their berth, immediately removing them, stopping them some … and doubling if repetition occurred, minor offences, by sweeping the decks every two hours above and below, throughout the day.[43]

The 'box' was a small, upright, coffin-like structure that stood on the deck. It was too narrow for its occupants to sit in, and thus they had to stand for hours at a time. The taller women had to bow their heads to fit into its confines and even the smallest could not move a muscle once locked inside. There is no evidence that this structure was used on the *Neva*, but it was in use on several contemporary female convict ships. The phrase 'stopping them some' related to the common practice whereby an offender's rations were shortened, or her lemon juice withdrawn. Of course such measures could have a severe impact upon the health of the offending convict, and consequently the surgeon had to be extremely careful in administering these punishments.

There were occasions when a more severe punishment was required, typically to deal with repeat offenders. Some surgeons used heavy wooden collars to inhibit the mobility of their more troublesome charges.[44] However, the collar was an uncomfortable and torturous device. By the time that the *Neva* sailed, the device was not widely employed and there is no evidence to suggest that Stephenson ever resorted to its use. However, we know that he did resort to the use of confinement. Convicts were confined in punishment cells for hours, or days, depending on the nature of their offence. Whilst inattentiveness to personal hygiene could incur such punishment, it did not frequently do so. It seems that the more common offences on a convict ship were those that came most naturally to many of her occupants, for example the theft of various items of food and clothing.[45] However, one historian has noted that 'whereas the key disturbance on male ships related to theft, disorder on female ships was characterised in terms of ... recalcitrant behaviour'.[46] The behaviour of the *Neva*'s convicts was not in any way unusual. One of the crew subsequently commented that 'the prisoners whose conduct was deserving had always the kindest treatment ... they were punished in various ways if they deserved it'.[47]

When it came to ensuring acceptable standards of behaviour, some surgeons sought to combine the carrot with the stick. The carrot reflected the Christian values prevalent in the nineteenth century. Surgeons were duty bound to 'read the Church Service to the convicts every Sunday'; the church referred to was the Church of England.[48] Thus, the *Neva*'s convicts were assembled on deck every Sunday whilst Stephenson read them the service of a faith to which most of them did not belong. He was also required to preach a sermon of his choice. Many surgeons used that opportunity to address the morality of behaviours with which they had become concerned. On the *John Bull* Surgeon Superintendent William Elyard punished the women who were repeatedly drunk in the company of seamen, but he also read sermons on chastity and intemperance.[49] The sermons preached were often pre-approved scripts written by Church of England clergymen and presented to the surgeons before they left the British Isles. Stephenson's surviving journals do not provide any detail regarding his observance of the Sabbath. However, his insistence that the men aboard the *Guildford* appeared at muster clean-shaven and in clean clothes, every Sunday and Thursday, is evidence that the Sabbath had a status that most other days did not.[50]

The Wreck of the *Neva*

The musters that Stephenson referred to aboard the *Guildford* were supposed to occur every day. Each prisoner's name was called and they stood in line for inspection by the surgeon. Some surgeons mustered prisoners as they came on deck each morning, others as they went below in the evening. The strictest surgeons mustered their prisoners twice a day. However, there is some evidence that Stephenson did not operate a strict rotation of musters on his ships. He may have mustered prisoners on Sundays and Thursdays, but what about the remaining five days? On the *Katherine Stewart Forbes* a number of prisoners had exhibited the symptoms of cholera for two days prior to their presentation in the hospital; one of them had 'kept to his birth [*sic*] without making complaint'.[51] Stephenson had not noticed their declining health. One of the muster's primary purposes was to allow surgeons to inspect the health and cleanliness of their charges. Thus, on the *Katherine Stewart Forbes*, even if Stephenson held regular musters, his inspections were not as thorough as they might have been.

Stephenson may not have been the most thoroughly regimented surgeon, but his journals reveal a man who was extremely careful in the administration of medical treatment to the sick. He had a scientific mind and always sought out patterns or irregularities that might assist fellow professionals in understanding, curing and preventing disease. He was also a humane man and could display great empathy. He had once described one of his cholera patients as exhibiting 'as perfect a picture of human suffering as it has ever been my fate to witness'.[52]

By comparison with Stephenson's voyages on the *Katherine Stewart Forbes* and the *Waterloo*, the *Neva*'s voyage was a very healthy one. Nonetheless he must have had some medical issues to deal with, and many of them were doubtlessly the routine complaints of convict ships. Illness was common during the early part of a voyage; one contemporary ship's surgeon speculated that 'change in diet, in the habits of life, as regards to exercise, sea sickness, depression and anxiety of mind arising from their situation … all tend to predispose the body to disease'.[53] The most common of these afflictions were headaches, febrile affection, constipation, foul tongue and diarrhoea. The last condition was most common among children and could become life-threatening. The others were commonly treated by the administration of an emetic followed by a brisk purgative, and the symptoms usually passed after two to three days.[54]

Seasickness tended to subside when the convicts found their sea legs after the opening days of the voyage, but could re-emerge whenever high seas and poor weather were encountered. We know that the *Neva* encountered such seas after rounding the Cape of Good Hope and for those who had not previously experienced such turbulence that part of the voyage was surely frightening. One surgeon described the fear that spread among the women he supervised, when their ship encountered stormy seas: 'At ½ 11 pm it blowing hard a sea struck the ship on the starboard side which so alarmed the convicts that they cried out to be let on deck but that of course could not be complied with.'[55] Thus, when a ship was at its most vulnerable, pitching and rolling upon the whims of Mother Nature, those locked beneath its deck were left in mental anguish imagining the extent of its peril.

Perhaps the most devastating illnesses suffered by female convicts were of the mental variety and there is some evidence that stress-induced conditions were prevalent. Ship's surgeons continually complained that female convicts were difficult to control and prone to fits of hysteria. In 1822 James Hall of the *Mary Anne* noted:

> I observed many complicated ailments among the women and have often been perplexed in devising a rational principle of care. The symptoms can be alarming; not simple fits of hysteria but rather more a commotion within the nervous system originating from a reciprocal action, as it seemed, of the Uterine system and Mind. I found very few females menstruate regularly; and learned that the uterine secretion generally ceases while the female convicts lie in Newgate and in other jails. Hence from the suppression of this periodical secretion arises many disturbances in the female system.[56]

Historian Gerald Stone has suggested that some of the symptoms described by Hall are related to amenorrhoea, caused by many different factors of which stress is thought to be one.[57] The *Neva*'s convicts suffered their share of stress as they were wrenched from their families and friends and came to realise that they would never see them again. Some, like Louisa Mellefont, had left their children behind. Anxiety at such separation was, on its own, enough to affect their mental health seriously.

Somewhere on the *Neva*'s journey the cries of a newborn infant echoed through the confines of the ship's lower decks. The gender and identity of the child born on the *Neva* remains a mystery. However, it is known that the infant perished in Bass Strait soon after its birth. During their 125 days at sea, the women also watched three people die, one of them a child. These three probably died in the ship's hospital, as anybody who contracted a serious or contagious illness was transferred there. Whilst the ill were in the hospital, it is probable that Stephenson appointed their mess matrons to safeguard their property.[58] In the hospital, they were nursed by attendants appointed from among the convicts.[59] It is likely that Stephenson allowed the sick child's mother to act as nurse and thus she watched as her child breathed its last.[60] The cause of death was not recorded, neither was it recorded for the crew member and the convict who also died on the voyage. We know that Stephenson succumbed to dysentery during the voyage, so it is possible that the three deaths were caused by this condition.

As the surgeon grappled with his rudimentary medicines, his patients' pain was probably evident to the convict nurses who attended them. As news of their illness circulated among the women, the final result was evident for all to see. Their passing was probably marked by a sombre service followed by a burial at sea. In 1842 the second officer of the *Garland Grove* convict ship witnessed one such burial off the Cape Verdes, and wrote the following account:

The Wreck of the *Neva*

Hereabouts occurred our first funeral. It was that of a poor woman who died the night before. 6 o'clock in the evening the ship was hove to, the body brought to the lee gangway, placed on a grating in the presence of most of the women. And the ship's crew covered it with the Union Jack for a pall, it was a solemn and affecting sight. The burial service was read by the commander and I officiated as Clerk. When we came to 'we therefore commit her body to the deep, to be surrendered into corruption, looking for the resurrection of the body when the sea shall give up her dead' and 'the life of the world to come, through our Lord, Jesus Christ', the body was launched into the deep, a universal shudder came over all present.[61]

The *Neva*'s women stood on the decks of a tiny ship in the midst of a vast ocean. They depended entirely upon Peck and Stephenson to guide them through the perils of the southern autumn's lengthening nights. Now, as they watched those bodies slide beneath the seas, they certainly had cause to reflect upon the fragility of human life. Death had cast its shadow over the *Neva* and the superstitious may have felt its presence linger.

8

The Wreck

Peck was making steady progress; as the days came and went, the women sensed that they were drawing ever closer to the colony where they would live out the remainder of their days. It was April when the *Neva* reached the Cape of Good Hope. However, unlike many masters of convict vessels, Peck did not think it necessary to put in there for fresh supplies. Instead, his haste became apparent as he pushed on for his final destination. At this point one would expect that he may have come into conflict with the surgeon. Stephenson was convinced that the *Eleanor*'s delaying at the Cape to take on an abundance of fresh supplies in 1831 was part of the reason that that ship's convicts reached New South Wales in exceptional health.[1] Within a month, Stephenson was definitely in his sick bed.[2] If his illness had already afflicted him when the *Neva* reached the Cape, Peck may have proceeded without the surgeon's input.

Peck divided his crew into two watches. Typically these were called the 'larboard' and 'starboard' watches, but on the *Neva* the larboard watch was referred to as the 'first' watch.

The Wreck of the *Neva*

First mate Joseph Bennett took command of one and second mate William H. Laws was charged with the other. These watches alternated their deck duty in rotations of four hours each. This being the case, one would expect that the day was divided into six four-hour watches. However, most merchant masters divided the watch of 4 p.m. to 8 p.m. into two 'dog watches', each lasting two hours. This meant that a typical twenty-four-hour day had seven watches instead of six; the odd number ensured that the same watches were not on deck at precisely the same hours of every day.[3]

For the crew of the ship, keeping the *Neva* moving forwards was not always easy, since the vessel was dependent upon the power of the wind. The ship was easy to sail when a wind came up behind the sails and happened to propel them in precisely the direction that Peck wanted to move. However, that seldom happened; when the wind did not blow exactly as required, the sailors had to adjust the sails accordingly. In simple terms the *Neva*'s sails reacted to the wind in two different ways. When the vessel sailed with the wind behind her (downwind), the crew arranged the sails so that they were pushed forward (the term for this is drag) by the wind blowing from behind. When the ship sailed into the wind, the crew set the sails in such a way that she was pulled forward (the term for this is lift) by the wind blowing from in front. Aeroplanes fly by using the same basic principle of lift. The wind flows quickly around the front of the sail (or top of the wing) and quite slowly at the back of the sail (or bottom of the wing). This creates a difference in pressure between the front and back of the sail (or top and bottom of the wing), and that differential draws the sail forwards (or the wing upwards): the ship moves from the high pressure behind the sail to the low pressure in front of the sail, thus making progress forwards. Nonetheless, the sailing ship could only sail at an angle into the wind. If she faced the wind dead on, the wind would not flow around the sail, but run headlong into it, blowing it back, and stopping the ship's forward motion. Sailing at angles into the wind is known as 'tacking'. The process of tacking involves changing direction periodically in order that a sail-powered vessel zigzags across the path of the wind, thereby correcting the angular course it had previously steered. Sailing ship's masters and mates were ever vigilant for changes in wind speed and direction, in case these changes made it necessary for them to alter the arrangement of their ship's sails, and they issued their orders to the crew accordingly.

A crew's work was never done. Masters could not afford to tolerate idleness among the crew as it led to ill-discipline, and ill-discipline could lead to inefficiency or, in the worst of cases, mutiny. In 1797 a mutiny had occurred on board the female convict ship the *Lady Shore*. With the co-operation of some convicts, the crew of that ship cast their officers off and sailed the ship and her convicts to Uruguay. The incident served to remind the officers of convict ships that the risk of mutiny was ever present. In 1817 the master of the *Chapman* was so fearful of mutiny that he had several convicts shot. In 1821 the captain of the *John Bull* had cause to reprimand his second mate, Mr Wise, for behaving inappropriately around the female convicts. The ship's surgeon ordered all convicts below 'in consequence of ... [their] showing a disposition to intercede on the quarter deck to give assistance to Mr Wise'. Later, the convicts were overheard discussing the *Lady Shore* mutiny. After consultation with the captain, the surgeon agreed that the convicts should be confined to the prison, and only matrons and cooks allowed on deck, until any chance of mutiny had passed.[4]

Whilst there is no evidence that Peck or Stephenson ever had specific cause to fear mutiny, they knew that it was a possibility. For that reason, Stephenson kept the minds of the convicts occupied and Peck ensured that his crew were always busy. A contemporary American sailor, Richard Henry Dana, later described the constant nature of a crew's duties in his classic memoir *Two Years Before the Mast*:

> In the first place, then, the discipline of the ship requires every man to be at work on something when he is on deck, except at night and on Sundays. Except at these times you will never see a man, on board a well ordered vessel, standing idle on deck, sitting down, or leaning over the side. It is the officers' duty to keep every one at work, even if there is nothing to be done but scrape the rust from the chain cables. In no state prison are the convicts more regularly set to work, and more closely watched. No conversation is allowed among the crew at their duty, and though they frequently do talk when aloft, or when near one another, yet they always stop when an officer is nigh.[5]

The crew's duties revolved around keeping the ship operating at maximum efficiency. A three-masted barque such as the *Neva* encountered significant natural forces all day, every day. Her crew, therefore, had to ensure that all her sails and rigging, along with her hull, were always in good repair. This involved hanging new rigging and sail cloth on a continual basis, and installing particular fittings that reduced any chaffing of the rigging. The crew were frequently expected to construct new fittings from basic materials strewn around the ship.

The officers commanded the crew to sail the course that they plotted. That course depended on their navigation, the most important component of navigation being the establishment of the ship's current location. The officers used a number of methods to determine this. Peck's primary method of discerning the position of his ship involved use of a chronometer, and the *Neva* had two of these on board. A chronometer was an extremely accurate clock, different to other clocks in that it was capable of maintaining accuracy without being disturbed by the sea's motion. Before departing the Thames estuary for Cork, Peck had probably set his chronometer by observing the newly installed time ball at Greenwich observatory. This ball dropped (and still drops) at precisely 1 p.m. every day to allow ships departing London to set their chronometers to Greenwich Mean Time. With this exact time being kept by both of the *Neva*'s chronometers, Peck could calculate his longitude at any point on the earth's surface by comparing the time difference on his chronometer with local noon as determined by the sun's highest position in the sky. He could then use the angle of the sun at that time to establish the *Neva*'s latitude. The whole system depended entirely upon the chronometer's accuracy, which was supposed to be checked by taking regular lunar observations. The angle between the moon and the various stars that surround it were laid out on set tables for navigators to consult. At given Greenwich Mean Times the moon would form a given angle with another celestial body. Therefore, by making accurate lunar observations, Peck should have been able to adjust any error in his chronometers before using them to establish longitude at noon the following day.

The *Neva* reached St Paul's Island in the Southern Ocean on 26 April 1835. Here it seems the captain took advantage of the fine weather, hove to for a few hours and obtained fresh provisions from the locals.[6] Given that the island was a barren and desolate spot, populated only by sealers for brief periods, it is unlikely that the provisions were of an elaborate nature. Nonetheless, the captain took on whatever was available and also noted that both chronometers had maintained their accuracy.[7] A few days before 12 May, the crew bent a new set of sails, and at some time between 26 April and 12 May the final lunar observation was taken to establish the accuracy of the chronometers. Subsequently none of the crew could say precisely when this event occurred, and Peck never even mentioned its occurrence. Nonetheless, on the night of 12 May, Peck was fully confident that he knew precisely where he and his ship were located.

Peck claimed that his last calculation of the *Neva*'s position occurred on the afternoon of 12 May. Considering that his

logbook went down with the ship, the captain later recalled
his co-ordinates with remarkable precision:

> On the twelfth day of May at noon we had good observations,
> the weather being fine the longitude by chronometer was
> 141°57' E. Latitude 39°37' S. by meridian altitude of the sun.
> I ordered the ship to be steered E.N.E. which allowing three
> quarters of a point easterly variation, would carry the ship
> fourteen miles [twenty-three kilometres] to the Northward
> off the Northern part of the Harbinger Reef ...[8]

Thus, by 12 May 1835 the *Neva* was bearing down on the
infamous ship's graveyard that is Bass Strait. On the night
of 12 May, Peck attempted to enter the strait by steering the
Neva into the eighty-four-kilometre-wide passage north of
King Island and south of present-day Victoria. To assist him
in steering a safe course on his voyage Peck carried James
Horsburgh's *India Directory*. However, it appears that the
captain chose to ignore Horsburgh's warning regarding Bass
Strait:

> Bass' Straits should be approached with caution by ships
> coming from the westward, if not certain of their latitude,
> which ought to be correctly ascertained before they reach
> longitude 143½°E: and the strait ought not to be entered in
> the night, unless the land has been previously seen, or both
> the latitude and longitude be known by observation. The
> parallel of 39° or 39°20'S according as the wind may incline,

is the best track for passing between King Island and Cape Otway; and a sight of either, or preferably of both, will point out the true situation.[9]

As twilight dimmed the skies above his ship, Peck should have had this warning ringing in his ears. He had not seen any land, and although he was sure that his chronometers had given him an accurate reading, he did not take any lunar observations to double-check their accuracy or his position. Instead he ordered that a close watch be kept for the land he knew was nearby. The crew were on the lookout for land from 12 p.m., although Peck did not expect to see it that night.[10] The *Neva's* survivors were the only witnesses to the drama that unfolded over the next twenty-four hours. The following narrative is based on their testimony. Questions as to the accuracy of that testimony are dealt with in subsequent chapters.

It was a calm, moonlit night, with only a very slight haze visible on the distant horizon. Occasional clouds obscured the moon, but it always re-emerged and shone favourably on the decks of the ship beneath. As the *Neva* clipped over the ocean waves, propelled by a fresh westerly breeze, there was nothing to indicate that this was anything other than a routine night on board a convict ship. At 8 p.m. Robert Bullard took up his position as one of two lookouts on the forecastle. He reported nothing extraordinary and returned below deck when his watch ended at midnight. As Bullard went below, Joseph Bennett emerged to take the next watch. He spoke to Peck before the captain went below. He was ordered to maintain a strict lookout for land, although Peck did not expect to sight it, having plotted a course some thirty-two kilometres to the north of King Island. Between 1 a.m. and 2 a.m. the wind freshened and Bennett ordered the topsails double reefed and the jib and mainsail set. Essentially this allowed him to stabilise the ship whilst taking advantage of the slightly stronger wind. Thomas Sharp watched this manoeuvre from the poop deck where he had the wheel. He then held the *Neva*'s course steady for approximately thirty more minutes. Then, at 2 a.m., somebody sighted a dark silhouette looming from the distant horizon and Sharp heard the traditional cry of 'land ahoy' echo across the decks. The land was distant, but first mate Bennett had his orders and immediately went below to alert Peck. The captain then quickly returned to the upper deck. He had not expected to see land that night so he must have registered his surprise. Nonetheless, he did not order any soundings taken nor did he order any lunar observations, but he remained on deck. Bennett had already ordered that the ship be 'hauled to the wind', which allowed the *Neva* to track the land on her starboard bow as she sailed to the north.

At 3.30 a.m. all hands were ordered up to trim the sails and allow the *Neva* to travel at greater speed. This order indicated a certain confidence returning to Peck just ninety minutes after an unexpected sighting of land. Robert Bullard completed his part in this task and then returned below decks to await the beginning of his watch. At 4 a.m. he returned to the upper deck accompanied by William Hine. Bullard began his duty as lookout on the starboard bow. Fourth mate John May took up watch atop the forecastle, whilst William Wright carefully scrutinised the ocean from the starboard gangway.

Thomas Sharp ended his watch at 4 a.m. and went below deck. He intended lying down, but something kept him awake. At 5 a.m. he heard Robert Bullard's voice cry out on the deck above him. If Sharp heard Bullard's cry, then any of the prisoners who lay awake below deck must have heard it too. They would have noticed the urgency in his voice, as he made the most terrifying call that any seafarer could ever make and which no seafarer ever wanted to hear.

'Breakers ahead,' Bullard shouted. The helm was instantly ordered 'hard a-starboard'. Thomas Sharp 'immediately jumped on deck' and joined his comrades as they awaited the *Neva*'s response to the helmsman's hurried manoeuvre. The ship began to turn. By now the seamen could see the breakers drawing ever closer to the bow as the *Neva* bore down on the submerged rocks that pitched those frothy warnings towards the surface. Men probably leaned over her side, straining to see if she could avoid the impending contact. Perched on top of the forecastle, John May had a clear view of the breakers. As the ship slowly came about, May would have seen the breakers disappearing beneath the bow and towards the port side. He and the rest of the crew hoped that the ship could somehow continue its turn and squeak past, or over, the treacherous rocks. Nobody could do anything other than wait and pray. Then, with a ferocious crack, the sound of splintering timbers split the night. Just as the *Neva* was clearing the danger zone, her rudder was ripped from the hull when she collided with the last of the rocks. The ship itself was not damaged, but was now drifting directionless among the rocks. It was 5 a.m. on 13 May 1835.

The force of the collision and the noise of a rudder being ripped from a 331-ton ship was more than enough to wake anybody who had slept through the panic that had accompanied the sighting of breakers. Having lost her rudder, the *Neva* was completely at the mercy of the wind. The crew attempted to re-align the sails and establish some semblance of control. However, they could not complete this task with sufficient speed; as the sails filled the ship swung to port and was dashed broadside against the rocks. As she struck, the sea washed over the upper deck, but it was beneath the waterline that she sustained fatal damage. The hull was compromised and the ship started to fill with water. The tide that swept across her decks was matched by a panic that moved with equal ferocity.

Some hours earlier Rose Hyland was confined to the black hole for an unknown offence. On the morning of 13 May she lay sleeping with two other offenders. The ship's collision with the reef woke her. Within minutes water was pouring into the punishment cell. Cut off from the rest of the prisoners, Hyland knew that she and her cellmates had to escape the black hole if they were to have any chance of survival. With panic summoning every ounce of their survival instinct, Hyland and one of her cellmates managed to break open the cell door and enter the main prison. The locks on the black hole were not always what they should have been, and surgeons on other ships had complained of prisoners releasing themselves from confinement.[11] Hyland found that all the other prisoners had made their way to the main deck. Accounts of how the prisoners did this vary. Most agree that the women flooded onto the upper deck when the middle of the ship was raised on the rocks, and the prison's stanchions gave way. However, one prisoner claimed that Peck released them as soon as the ship struck the reef, and that he extended this courtesy to Hyland and the others who occupied the black hole. In contrast Hyland claimed that when she entered the main prison, Peck withdrew the ladder in an attempt to keep her below. If he did so, then his attempt was in vain, as the indestructible Hyland somehow made her way to the upper deck. Upon reaching it, she and her two companions joined in the general panic.

By now the crew had cut away the rigging to allow two masts to fall over the side. They were no longer at the mercy of the winds and the ship's fate was now in the hands of the waves that continued to pound her against the reef. Each motion put more stress on the hull; it was only a matter of time before the *Neva* would break apart. By now all who sailed on her were fully aware that she carried only four small boats. It was obvious that these would not be sufficient to save everybody on board. Nonetheless, the crew began to launch the boats. They first turned their attention to the gig, which hung from davits on the *Neva*'s port side. As the ship was listing in that direction, the gig hung clear of the hull and should have presented the least difficulty in launching. However, luck was against the *Neva* and her crew; when they went to launch the little craft a davit broke, the gig swung from one of her ends and was quickly smashed against the hull of the ship.

With one potential lifeboat broken, the crew now turned their attention to the pinnace. The spare parts and rigging stowed within it were quickly discarded and the men carried the boat to the bulwarks on the port side. This vessel was successfully launched, but the officers' choice of the pinnace's complement did not appeal to those left behind. Peck was in the boat along with Stephenson, his nurse, Thomas Sharp and one other man. When the women saw the boat hit the water with the *Neva*'s most senior officers and only three others aboard, they rushed to fill the empty space. Their desperation capsized the little boat and all who were in her were pitched into sea. Peck and Sharp swam back to the wreck. It is possible that a third member of the crew also regained the ship. Stephenson and his nurse perished beneath the waves.

Peck and Bennett then attempted to launch the longboat. This time they made every effort to prevent too many from crowding into the boat before she was launched. Nonetheless, Robert Bullard formed the opinion that she carried too many people when launched from the gangway. This destabilised her and the surf capsized her: the third of the *Neva*'s four potential lifeboats was lost. Of the ten or twelve men and some women (Peck's estimate) who succeeded in boarding the longboat, only Peck and Bennett made it back to the *Neva*. Once again, her most senior officers had sought to desert the ship.

The Wreck of the *Neva*

Rose Hyland made her way towards the stern of the ship where most of the women were congregated in abject terror. She noted that some of them were in the cuddy. It was alleged that they were so drunk they couldn't help themselves, and that they were still drinking! She made her way onto the poop deck from where Bennett had just removed the cutter to the quarterdeck below. He and some of the crew were attempting to launch the last of the *Neva*'s potential lifeboats as Hyland looked on from above. Directly beneath her feet the women in the cuddy allegedly continued their drinking, whilst several others descended into fits of hysterical crying. As Bennett prepared the cutter, the *Neva* remained wedged on the reef. Every wave that crashed against her hull pushed her harder against the rocks. Finally the ship gave way and began to break apart. As Hyland stood on the poop deck, it gave way beneath her and collapsed in on the cuddy, crushing the women huddled inside. Hyland managed to cling to part of the poop's wreckage as she drifted off on the ocean waves.

Rose Ann Dunn was in the cuddy when the poop deck collapsed. She was lucky enough to avoid being crushed and managed to crawl out of a hole. Then, like the rest of the *Neva*'s lucky survivors, she clung to part of the wreckage and drifted away. Up to 100 survivors initially clung to various parts of the broken ship. However, the waves soon loosened their grip and most of them were left at the ocean's mercy.

First mate Bennett found that the women were trying to follow his lead. He moved from one piece of wreckage to another and, each time, panic-stricken women followed him, endangering all of their lives by overloading the timbers to which Bennett clung. Eventually he rested upon a piece to which four others were attached and slowly drifted towards the looming shoreline. Along the way he had rescued Ellen Galvin from the depths. Now, with daylight firmly established, they were carried to an unknown shore.

Somewhere in their vicinity Peck was clinging to a substantial part of the *Neva*'s main deck. Approximately twenty others managed to hold on to the same piece. As they watched the shore move ever closer, this little group may have dared to hope that they had somehow survived the ordeal. However, fate had another blow to deal them. The forward part of the deck to which they desperately clung still had the heel of the foremast embedded in it. Thus, as the shore came tantalisingly closer, the mast struck bottom and the wreckage was quickly consumed by the breaking surf. All but three were washed off and drowned. Once again, Peck was one of the lucky ones. He managed to survive the pounding surf and swam about 400 metres to the shore. He left convict Ann Cullen clinging to the wreckage behind him. Upon reaching the shoreline, he immediately noted that Cullen had not made it. As fatigued as he must have been, he somehow summoned the strength to swim back to her assistance. He brought the stricken woman to shore and then set about organising the survivors.

Further out to sea Robert Bullard and another of the crew had somehow fashioned a lifeline from various parts of the strewn rigging. This line gave some of the women something to hold on to as they drifted towards the shore. Meanwhile,

The Wreck of the *Neva*

as the wreckage to which Rose Hyland still held fast drifted landwards, she encountered Thomas Sharp. Sharp, at least one woman and several crew members occupied a separate piece of the wreck. Hyland decided that there was greater safety in numbers and attempted to join the seamen. However, as she tried to transfer her weight from one part of the wreck to another, she fell from the timbers on two separate occasions. Each time Sharp pulled her from the depths and placed her back by his side. As they drifted nearer the shore, he jumped from the wreckage and waded towards the island, carrying with him an unknown 'boy'. He soon returned for Hyland, and subsequently carried a third person to the shore. The survivors of the *Neva* had landed on King Island.

9

King Island

In 1835 King Island was little more than an uninhabited wilderness. At its longest point the island was some sixty-five kilometres from north to south, whilst at its widest point it spanned about twenty-six kilometres. Peck and his dishevelled band had just stumbled ashore on the northern part of the island. Sandy beaches stretched out on both sides of them, occasionally interspersed by treacherous rocks.

King Island was first sighted by Europeans just thirty-eight years before Peck was washed ashore. From 1801 a flourishing sealing industry grew around the island's abundant population of seals. However, by the time that the *Neva*'s survivors washed up on its shore most of the sealers had departed, having decimated the seal population. King Island was at this time the permanent home to just one sealer, the few aborigines he cohabited with, and a mysterious aboriginal woman known only as 'the Ranger'.

In 1827 surveyor G. W. Barnard made six traverses across the island, mapping its terrain and noting the seal remains that littered its beaches. Barnard also noted that the seas around the island made it difficult to select secure anchorages for ships. He could only recommend that they stick to the leeward side and stated that a channel between King Island and the much smaller New Year Island, off its north-west coast, offered the most sheltered option for visiting ships. Peck's group were located some twenty kilometres from this point. The interior was not easily traversed, and whilst speculating about the potential escape of men from any proposed penal settlement, Barnard had noted:

> Prisoners absconding from the Settlement must have considerable intelligence should they attempt to cross or penetrate the Islands, as the scrubs are so thick that without a com-pass [*sic*] (that not very available) or favourable weather, they would otherwise inevitably be lost and perish miserably. It will be seen by my descriptive Map, that it took me three days going 8 to 12 hours per day with the aid of a compass and men under command and direction and rarely seeing animals of any kind, except a few Birds.[1]

On the evening of 13 May 1835 the *Neva*'s survivors had to survive their first few hours in these inhospitable surroundings. They had just emerged from water that was probably no warmer than 11–14°C. No doubt they were tired, cold and extremely frightened. The survivors needed leadership. Peck did his best to provide it.

The master found that twenty-one others had made the

shore in his vicinity. There were twelve convict women and ten of the crew, including Bennett, Bullard, Sharp and Hine. Peck found part of a puncheon of rum washed ashore and, hoping that the spirit might stave off the deadly effects of the cold water that had soaked them to their skins, he ordered that each individual be served a dram. He then discarded the remainder of the rum and ordered that everybody retreat into the bush behind the shoreline. There, as the evening darkened the sky, this little band tried to settle down to rest. Peck and Bennett knew they had made King Island. Nobody knew whether the island could support them, or whether they would leave it alive.[2]

When Peck opened his eyes on the morning of 14 May he was greeted by an unpleasant sight. No more than ten or twelve yards from where he lay, he could see three women face down in the sand. Upon closer inspection, his worst fears were confirmed: they were dead. Joined by other members of the group, Peck moved further along the shore, where he found another corpse lying next to two women in the final moments of their lives. Both Peck and Bennett noted that a rum cask lay near this group. However, Bennett conceded that the likely causes of death were cold and exhaustion. They had not yet spent their first twenty-four hours on the island, and already their survivor group had been reduced from twenty-two to sixteen. Before that day was out, the full horror of the death toll would become more apparent.

One of the ship's boys – either Joseph Firrell or Thomas Quinn (we cannot say which) – had made it ashore. However, it soon became painfully obvious that the youth would not survive; by evening, the boy joined the six women who had already perished.[3] Their bodies were buried, and the group set about foraging for food. Luckily they found two casks of flour, some beef and some more rum, all washed ashore from the wreck. There was no shortage of rum washed up along the shores of King Island. William Hine later stated: 'Whilst we were on the island we had as much rum as we liked by going to fetch it.' Unfortunately the survivors could not live on a diet of rum. Peck therefore had to be careful to ration the beef and flour so that it would last as long as possible. Ellen Galvin later testified that he had served out the food in equal quantities and was cautious in serving the spirits.

For some days these few survivors foraged for whatever they could find among the wreckage that littered the nearby shore. They succeeded in fashioning some crude tents from various articles of sail, rigging and timbers that had once belonged to their ship. With the interior of the island presenting navigational obstacles, Peck and his band constructed their tents near the shoreline. These structures provided sufficient shelter from the cruel winter wind of the exposed coastline. Indeed they were sturdy enough to survive two winters and still stood on the island in 1837.[4]

Having brought some semblance of order to his dishevelled band, Peck set about ascertaining whether any others were washed ashore. He later stated that the delay in seeking out survivors or bodies was caused by his band's need to recover from fatigue.[5] However, it is quite clear that he spent a number of days organising his own camp before he went in search

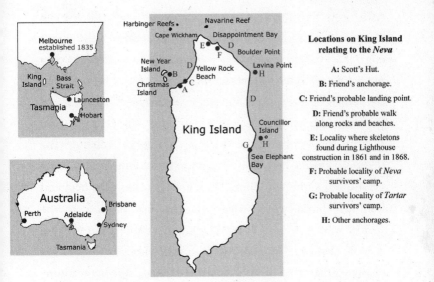

Map of King Island showing locations relating to the *Neva*.
Image: Kevin Todd.

of others. His negligence of any duty of care to those who were not washed up in his vicinity was never questioned, but it is likely that this cost some unfortunate women their lives. The clothing that Stephenson had deemed inadequate for the voyage was certainly inadequate now and while Peck organised the survival of his own group, there were quite probably others who lay dying of hypothermia. It was an undefined period of 'some days' before the captain went looking for them.

Peck took two men and moved in one direction, whilst Bennett took two more the other way. As they trudged along the sands and clambered over the rocks, they probably hoped that they would find some of their shipmates alive. Instead, with only the sounds of the crashing surf and calling birds around them, the horizon began to reveal darkened silhouettes contrasted with the lonesome rocks and yellow sands. As they moved closer they discovered that these lifeless masses were the bodies of those with whom they had shared the *Neva* just days ago. Many were horribly mutilated – it was assumed that these were the victims of the poop deck's collapse.[6] The forlorn survivors had little option but to bury them in shallow graves along the shoreline. Peck and Bennett later claimed that they buried ninety-five bodies in that fashion. In the 1860s, bushfires near Cape Wickham revealed the charred remains of several skeletons which were thought to be those of the women that Peck and Bennett buried along the shore. Some of them were subsequently re-interred in the shadow of the newly built Cape Wickham lighthouse.[7]

Although the surviving women did not participate in the burial of their shipmates, the few days that the men combed the beach revealed that there were no other survivors. Limerick-born thief Ellen Galvin now knew that the mother and sister with whom she had travelled were certainly dead. They had conned an innocent and superstitious woman out of all she had and for that crime they ultimately forfeited their own lives. The 'rather decent looking' Jane Williams and her infant daughter Mary were both dead. Jane McLoughlin and her six children were gone, whilst oceans still separated her two boys in Ireland from their convict father. Mary Russell and the son who had probably held her hand as they walked the streets between Cork's gaol and depot were both dead.

It is unlikely that any of the children made it to shore alive. They probably died in their mothers' arms, crying fearfully as the sea consumed them. None of the survivors specifically mentioned burying children, neither did they mention the names of any of those they had buried. Slightly more than half of the bodies were not recovered by Peck and Bennett. It is likely that bodies continued to wash up along various parts of the island's shoreline into early July.[8]

Only fifteen shipmates remained alive. Along with Ellen Galvin, there were the convicts Rose Hyland, Mary Slattery, Ann Cullen, and Margaret Drury and her companion of two voyages, Rose Ann Dunn. The surviving crew members were Bennett, Peck, Bullard, Sharp, Hine, Charles Willson, Henry Calthorpe, William Kidney and Peter Robinson, who appeared to be growing increasingly close to Margaret Drury. The dead having been buried, these fifteen once again turned to living.

With the interior presenting navigational obstacles, Peck and his band made their home in the tents they had pitched near the shoreline. There they were surrounded by various forms of wildlife with which they were entirely unfamiliar. Birds of alien shapes, sizes and colours flocked around their little settlement, among them King Island's black swans. Without guns, however, they could not hope to sample the meat of these exotic species. Luckily they managed to avoid any fatal encounters with the hundreds of poisonous snakes that thrived in the area. A particular species native to King Island is the King Island tiger snake, which lives among the rocks, dunes and coastal grasslands of the island. It is one of Australia's most dangerous snakes.

Whilst unfamiliar reptiles were a concealed threat, the crustaceans that shared their habitat proved useful during those early days on the island. Over the next two weeks the survivors supplemented their diet with a few morsels of shell-fish they found among the rocks. However, it was difficult to gather significant quantities of food and the group were constantly on the edge of hunger. Barnard had remarked that the bush of the interior provided much cover 'but no subsistence'. He found that the coast was the only part of the island that could sustain human life, but without guns or dogs even those who dwelt there would have to subsist on a diet of gull eggs. The *Neva*'s little group badly needed guns or dogs. In that regard their luck was finally about to change.

Although the survivors may have thought they were alone on the island, they were not. Some fifty-one kilometres from Peck's position a small cutter, the *Tartar*, had been wrecked some weeks before and her crew stranded on the island ever since. Whilst out foraging for food they observed the *Neva*'s wreckage being carried in on the tide and followed its trail to Peck's location. About two weeks after the *Neva*'s survivors first pitched their tents, they probably noted two strangers advancing along the beach and grew excited at the prospect of rescue, but it was immediately apparent when first contact was made that the *Tartar*'s survivors were in no position to rescue anybody. However, they did bring something of which Peck's band was in urgent need: the means to make fire. The *Tartar*'s crew had succeeded in lighting fires and were able to transfer cinder to the *Neva* camp.[9] They also brought some good news about the island's other inhabitants and their access to food.

One of these inhabitants was the Ranger. She had probably been brought to King Island by a sealer some decades previously. Tasmanian aboriginal women were skilled hunters and were often employed by foreign sealers. Some of them were traded by their tribes; others were abducted and enslaved by sealers. However, since the Ranger had come to King Island she had habitually shied away from contact with white men.[10] She had a hut near the south-west point of the island, but she travelled all of its length and breadth. Around the time that the *Neva* was lost, she too may have noted the wreckage coming ashore. If she did, then she probably helped herself to supplies, as she did with wreckage from a later wreck.[11] However, the Ranger had no contact with the *Neva*'s survivors. Their salvation came in the form of the island's other inhabitants.

The *Tartar* had been carrying a passenger to his home on King Island, a sealer named John Scott.[12] Later described as a 'fine venerable looking man', Scott was a former convict. By May 1835 he had attained conditional freedom in the form of a 'ticket of leave' – an indulgence granted by the lieutenant governor whereby a convict could seek employment outside the convict system, but only within a specific geographical area.[13] Scott had an encampment on the island and lived there with his aboriginal spouse, Mary. The couple had several children. An older aboriginal whom they called Maria also formed part of their group. His family were described as

The Wreck of the *Neva*

'objects of great interest' and his children as 'half caste'. Their lifestyle was strictly taboo in polite colonial society. Yet Scott was an educated and literate man; he loved his children and, although they were far removed from the society that frowned upon them, he sought to provide them with an education. By 1840 he had taught his son Tom to read, as evidenced by the child's reading of Bible passages. This little family made their home in the north-west quarter of King Island at a point called Yellow Rock. From there they extracted their living by hunting and farming. The women were particularly adept at hunting wallaby.[14]

The *Tartar*'s crewmen told the *Neva*'s survivors of Scott's presence. Finally they knew that they were not alone and that the island supported human life. The morning after their meeting with the *Tartar* sailors they set off in search of Scott. When eventually they found him, with his mixed-race family, they may have regarded him in an unfavourable light. Nonetheless, this group of white people had little option but to turn to the family for help. Luckily Scott had much more sympathy for them than the British and Irish colonists had for his spouse's race. He shared what little he had by providing them with dogs. From that day on the survivors knew they could eat wallaby meat. They did not remain with Scott at Yellow Rock, returning instead to their own encampment, or perhaps to a separate encampment occupied by the *Tartar* survivors. The men from the *Tartar* joined with them in late May or early June, with the heart of winter approaching. Whilst they knew that their food supply was more secure, contemplation of the months ahead surely fuelled their anxiety. They could only hope that rescue would come soon.

Some two weeks later, on 15 June, Charles Friend was sailing the sloop *Sarah Ann* north-west out of Launceston, Van Diemen's Land. He was bound for the whaling station at Port Fairy on the Australian mainland to provision some workers he had located there.[15] His course took him past the eastern shore of King Island, and as he tracked the shore-line northwards, Friend noticed smoke billowing from fires on the northern shore. They seemed to be signalling fires and the experienced seafarer immediately suspected that a wreck had occurred near the island.[16] He decided to investigate and sailed the *Sarah Ann* along the northern shore before turning southward towards New Year Island and the smaller Christmas Island adjacent to it.

Upon anchoring south of New Year Island, Friend 'obtained information that a Female convict ship had been stranded and that the survivors were in a distressed state on shore'.[17] As he was in the vicinity of John Scott's hut at Yellow Rock, it is assumed that this information was attained from the Scott family. Friend rowed ashore, landing an estimated eight kilometres from his anchorage. He subsequently stated that this manoeuvre was completed at great risk to himself – it seems that the infamous swells of Bass Strait made his journey particularly difficult. Once safely landed he proceeded north-wards along the shoreline towards the smoke that he had seen. As he moved he came upon a substantial amount of wreckage littering the coastline. Friend claimed that he walked 'thirty-five miles' (fifty-six kilometres) before he found the survivors 'in a most distressful state subsisting upon some flour which had washed on shore and a few wallabys'.[18] Upon finding the *Neva*'s survivors he also found those of the *Tartar*, confirming that she too was lost. This news was indeed distressing, for Friend was the *Tartar*'s owner!

No doubt the marooned convicts hoped that Friend could lead them from the island back to civilisation and a stable supply of food. Peck shared that hope and with Friend he began planning the rescue. However, Friend's people at Port Fairy 'were in want'. Thus they decided that the two of them would sail to the mainland in the *Sarah Ann*.[19] There, Peck would report the wreck and then return to King Island with another vessel for the rescue of the survivors. However, once again, Mother Nature had other ideas.

Leaving Bennett in charge of the camp, Peck, Friend and one of Friend's men set out for the *Sarah Ann* that evening. They walked through the night, reaching the vessel the following morning. They intended to sail immediately. However, winds were unfavourable and they decided to return to the encampment. Whilst they were pulling ashore from the *Sarah Ann*, the wind continued to blow hard, and Friend was thrown into the surf when the little boat beached on the way to shore. The boat was rescued, but Friend sustained slight injuries from his ordeal.

Having brought supplementary provisions ashore with them, they decided not to haul the supplies across the island. Instead, they left them at Scott's hut on the western shore and then struck out for the survivors' encampment again. There they remained the following day, before setting out for the *Sarah Ann* once again on 21 June. This time winds were more favourable, and the sloop put to sea, setting course for Port Fairy.[20] All went well until the *Sarah Ann* came within about forty-five kilometres of the mainland. Then, the wind came up from the north-west, completely at odds with the course Friend was attempting to navigate. Eventually, under severe pressure from a rising gale, he and Peck decided to turn the ship around and head back for King Island.

Back on the island the food situation was critical. After Peck's departure, Bennett dispatched William Kidney, Peter Robinson and Margaret Drury to the far side of the island in search of the food landed at Scott's cabin. Those left at camp probably noted the strong north-west wind that came up across the strait. They were no doubt aware that this jeopardised the *Sarah Ann*'s passage to Port Fairy. Their hopes that Peck and Friend would successfully reach the mainland were dashed when, on the morning of 24 June, the *Sarah Ann* once again hove into view.[21] This time Friend anchored her just in front of the encampment. Food was now running low on both the island and the *Sarah Ann*. By anchoring at this point, Friend was taking a risk. The wind was still blowing hard from the north-west, but there was little option other than attempting rescue. The *Sarah Ann*'s whale boat was launched. Whilst the heavy surf broke around them, Friend and company began an inward journey. From the shore the survivors could see the little boat each time it crested a wave; then they would watch it plunge from sight as it fell between the heaving peaks once again. These few women had just survived the worst convict shipwreck in history. They would soon be asked to place their lives at the mercy of the sea for a second time. Not all of them were happy to do so.

Rose Hyland was a survivor. She had escaped the black hole, survived the collapse of the poop, and been rescued from drowning twice on the way to shore. However, it is likely that all of these experiences had made her a nervous sailor. When the tide eventually flung Friend's little boat on the shore in front of her, she reacted as one may expect a traumatised and fearful criminal would. If fear motivated Hyland's behaviour, then Bennett did not share or understand her fear. Indeed his statement to the subsequent enquiry hints that three of the women rescued were not unreservedly grateful to the crew who had secured their rescue. It seems that some tension may have existed between Bennett and some of those with whom he shared King Island. That tension boiled over into full-blown hostility when he attempted to remove Rose Hyland from the security of dry land:

Since the wreck of the vessel, the conduct of three of the women has been good, two others indifferent, and one named Rose Hyland conducted herself very badly. The evening we left King Island, this woman behaved herself most violently, taking a Gun which she said was loaded and threatening to shoot Mr Friend and myself, and with great imprecations wishing the boat that took us to the *Sarah Ann* might sink.

We were obliged to pinion her, but when we got her into the boat, she continued to unloose herself, and in going through the surf she jumped overboard. We returned at great risk and secured her again, and were then obliged to tie her down in the bottom of the boat. Her language and conduct were extremely violent.[22]

For her part Hyland did little to explain her behaviour. She simply blamed it on rum consumption: 'As far as related to my own conduct on the morning of leaving the island I only left the boat to go back for some shirts, having had a little rum which had got into my head.'[23]

Drunk or sober, Hyland left the island tied down in the bottom of a boat. The survivors were bound for George Town in northern Van Diemen's Land. They reached their destination on 26 June 1835, more than six weeks after they first landed on King Island.

Peter Robinson, William Kidney and Margaret Drury were still on the other side of the island when the *Sarah Ann* left. It is unlikely that they saw the vessel go. Whether or not they knew it, their shipmates had left them with only the Scott family for company. Drury and Robinson had almost certainly grown closer and were probably glad of the time alone. These were Margaret Drury's last few days of freedom. On 29 June the government cutter *Shamrock* was dispatched to King Island to rescue these three remaining survivors and secure any government property that could be salvaged. Drury had left Dublin on the *Erin* in November 1833. Almost two years

The Wreck of the *Neva*

later, the *Shamrock* would deliver her to her final destination. She would one day return to Bass Strait, but was not granted her freedom for a further five years.

By August 1835 King Island had seen the last of the *Neva* survivors. John Scott, his family and the Ranger again had the island to themselves. Scott lived out his days on King Island. However, those days were not as numerous as he desired, and some eight years later the elderly sealer became another victim of the stormy seas around the island. When Scott observed a ship called *Rebecca* anchoring offshore, he and his entire family went out to her in search of writing materials, with which he hoped to continue his children's education. They secured the supplies, but on their return journey a violent squall came from nowhere and capsized Scott's boat before he could take down the sail. He and his infant child were drowned; however, Mary, Maria and the remainder of the family made it back to shore. The squall was so violent and so sudden that it also wrecked the *Rebecca*. Like the *Neva*'s survivors before them, the *Rebecca*'s crew depended on the charity of Scott's family until they were able to make their way back to the mainland.[24]

King Island continued to acquire a reputation as a notorious graveyard for ships. In the quarter century that followed the *Neva*'s end, a further six major shipwrecks occurred in the same waters. The worst of these was the loss of the *Cataraqui*, which in 1845 took some 400 British emigrants to the bottom. It remains Australia's worst peacetime shipping disaster. The authorities eventually responded to the continuing carnage by establishing the Cape Wickham lighthouse in 1861.

With the women delivered to Van Diemen's Land, the fate of the *Neva* began to make headlines in Australian newspapers. Eventually those headlines made their way back to Britain and Ireland. With the *George III* already wrecked in April 1835, and the *Amphitrite* having broken up in August 1833, the *Neva* was the third convict shipwreck inside two years. The safety of convict transportation was in question. The authorities were under considerable pressure to provide answers. The circumstances surrounding the loss of the *Neva* had to be explained.

10

Enquiry

The *Sarah Ann* arrived in the mouth of the River Tamar at George Town on the afternoon of Friday 26 June. It brought with it the news of the *Neva*'s demise.[1] The ship was overdue in New South Wales, but the authorities there surely hoped that less tragic circumstances could account for its tardiness. The authorities in Van Diemen's Land may or may not have been aware of the concern in New South Wales. However, the arrival of the *Sarah Ann* put them in the eye of an unwelcome storm.

The first person who had to discharge official responsibility was the port officer at Launceston (upriver from George Town), Matthew Curling Friend. Friend was a brother of the government emigration agent in Cork and had captained the *Norval* on a journey from that city to Hobart, arriving with assisted migrants in July 1832.[2] He was appointed port officer at Launceston around the beginning of 1833. Later that year some controversy arose when it was alleged that part of his remuneration included an excessively generous annual allowance for accommodation.[3]

On Monday 29 June 1835 Friend wrote twice to the Colonial Secretary, John Montagu. Montagu was a veteran of Waterloo and was married to the niece of Van Diemen's Land's most powerful civil servant, Lieutenant Governor Sir George Arthur.[4] In his initial correspondence with Montagu, Friend outlined the basic circumstances of the wreck as 'it appears from the narrative of the Master'. He also noted the names of the survivors and of those left on King Island. Friend proposed sending the cutter '*Shamrock* to bring them off and secure any Government stores that may have washed on shore'. However, during the day he decided that he should write to Montagu a second time and, acknowledging the haste of his first letter, he dispatched a second. This time he notified the governor's office of the presence of '10 Bales of clothing and 30 Puncheons of Rum – stores for the Government at Sydney but which will no doubt be totally lost'. Friend also informed Montagu that:

> … the Master is now writing his narrative of this distressing occurrence which shall be forwarded as soon as possible – and has requested me to move His Excellency the Lieut Governor to institute a Court of Enquiry into his conduct in order to satisfy the Public that no blame was attributable to him, his officers or crew.[5]

In the midst of this correspondence, Matthew Friend specifically praised the actions of Charles Friend, 'who with the greatest personal exertion & risk succeeded in getting the survivors off the Island'.[6] It was little wonder that he did; Charles was his nephew. With his uncle informing the governor's secretary of such bravery, Charles chose the very same day to write to the governor's office. He claimed that he had lost all he possessed when the *Tartar* was wrecked and did not hesitate to state that if the governor felt inclined 'to remunerate me in any way I should feel truly grateful'.[7]

George Deare, the major commandant of the 21st Fusiliers at Launceston, also wrote to the governor's secretary on Monday 29 June. He reported the condition of the surviving convicts and also noted that the *Neva* had 'a mail on board about thirty cask of Rum and some stores of clothing the property of the Government'.[8] It was Deare who had instructed Matthew Friend to send the *Shamrock* to the island and who asked for instructions regarding the initiation of an enquiry. Montagu replied to Deare the next day instructing him to form a committee of enquiry and to report as soon as possible. The committee was to comprise Deare, Matthew Friend 'and any other person you may think proper to appoint'.[9] Montagu's guidelines for the committee were not overly detailed. However, he did outline some facts that he wanted established:

> The time the Vessel Struck, the precise State of the weather, was the Vessel furnished with the necessary Charts, the Australian Directory.
>
> Was the night clear and Starlight [*sic*]?
>
> Had any observation been taken for the latitude, as the Stars came to the Meridian?

Had there been a Meridian Altitude the preceding Noon?

Were there Chronometers on Board? And if so, had sights been taken the preceding afternoon and forenoon, or, if not, when the Longitude by Chronometer had been last ascertained?

When the Longitude had been last calculated from Lunar observation? Had soundings been tried for?

Was the Master on deck the whole of the night?

Montagu also requested that the committee examine the surviving prisoners and establish the quality of their treatment during the voyage and since the wreck. This request may have come as a result of Deare noting that the women had been inclined to complain about such things.[10]

Given the urgency of the communications, Deare most likely received Montagu's letter on Wednesday 1 July. He lost little time in inviting Police Magistrate Lyttleton to join him and Matthew Friend on the committee. They began their deliberations on 3 July. Among the first to give evidence was Benjamin Hutchins Peck. However, a letter from Peck to the *Neva*'s agent in London, revealed annoyance that the enquiry (which it had been claimed he had requested of the governor) would delay his departure:

I thought it my duty to write to you on this melancholy occasion. I should have proceeded hence in this ship, but was detained for the Court of Enquiry to be held which is now about to take place; I have noted and extended my protest and to the best of my knowledge have done all things needful for your benefit; however I shall return home as soon as possible and by the next conveyance to London; the number of persons lost was 224; the ship is to be sold for the benefit of all concerned but I do not expect she will fetch more than £5 … all we saved was 3 casks of flour and about 30 pieces of pork, on which we subsisted about 14 days …[11]

The enquiry was held in Launceston and sat until 6 July. Over the course of those days the survivors were interviewed, with the obvious exception of those still on King Island. Along with Peck, the other principal witnesses were Charles Friend and Joseph Bennett. Less detailed statements were given by Robert Bullard, Thomas Sharp and William Hine. Two other seamen, Charles Willson and Henry Calthorpe, corroborated Hine's statement saying that they had 'heard the statement made by William Hine, and that the circumstances therein related are correct'.[12] Rose Ann Dunn, Ellen Galvin, Mary Slattery, Ann Cullen and Rose Hyland also gave statements to the enquiry.

The enquiry established the basic circumstances of the wreck, as outlined in the previous chapters. On 6 July the members of the committee wrote to Montagu stating that they had complied with instructions and claiming that they had examined the survivors 'separately and apart from each other' and had 'patiently and minutely investigated all the circumstances attending the melancholy loss' of the ship.[13] They concluded that the *Neva* had steered the course outlined by Peck and Bennett, and had run onto a reef where no reef was known to exist. Since no reef was charted in that location, the committee concluded that the Harbinger Reef was incorrectly charted, that the tide had been stronger than usual, or that both of those factors had combined to cause the wreck. As such, only minute error should be attributed to Peck:

In closing this report the Committee ... feel it is their duty to the memory of the late Surgeon Superintendent and to the Master of the vessel to state that it is their opinion that no blame whatsoever can be attributed to them – the officers or the crew – that their reckoning appears to be as correct as possible which must be inferred from their making the land at the very time they expected and the course steered was such as they conceived every judicious seamen would have adopted – and which would under the usual circumstances have carried him at least fourteen miles [twenty-three kilometres] to the Northward of the extreme point of the reef as laid down in the chart.

The Committee can only attribute the ship getting in the reef to the extraordinary strength of the tide in the first instance. The reef being either improperly laid down or an erroneous opinion formed by the Master and crew of their distance from the land when the ship hauled to the wind or more probable the concurrent influence of several minute errors which would united have caused the dreadful catastrophe upon which we are called to report.[14]

The Wreck of the *Neva*

Although the committee acknowledged that Peck and his crew may have formed an erroneous opinion of their distance from land on the night in question, they were keen to forgive the men any error and instead blame the incident on the quirks of Mother Nature. Whether or not Governor Arthur would accept these rather vague conclusions remained to be seen, but he would consider the report under the spotlight of a very interested media. Newspapers had been running reports of the tragedy since the survivors had arrived from King Island and some were raising awkward questions.

Long articles appeared in the *Launceston Advertiser* on 2 July and in the *Hobart Town Courier* on 3 July. Both reported the *Neva* wreck in the context of the loss of the *George III* near Hobart on 12 April. The *Launceston Advertiser* also mentioned the loss of the *Amphitrite*. The third convict shipwreck in two years was certainly shocking, especially when it was considered that in the forty-four years of convict transportation before 1833 not one convict ship was wrecked.

Although the *Launceston Advertiser* erroneously stated that the *Neva* was wrecked south of King Island, it noted the ship's position the day before the wreck and chronicled events on board after she struck the reef. The article stated that 'the survivors were carried on shore at King Island, a distance of about 9 miles [14 kilometres] from where the vessel struck, after being 8 hours in the water'.[15] Charles Friend was credited with the burial of the *Neva*'s dead and Scott the sealer was commended for his considerable assistance to the shipwrecked party. Peck was offended at the suggestion that he had awaited

Friend's arrival before burying the dead and wrote to the newspaper:

> Sir, An error or two have been inserted in your report of the loss of the barque *Neva*, late under my command, which I beg you will correct in your next number.
>
> The first is that the reef which the vessel struck was at the 'South' end of King Island instead of the 'North' end. The second is that 100 bodies were interred by the crew, under the sanction of Mr C. Friend, before he left the Island; whereas, the fact is the bodies were interred by myself, and the men saved from the wreck, immediately upon recovering ourselves from the fatigue to which we had been exposed on reaching the shore.[16]

Yet, at the enquiry Peck explicitly stated that his group had occupied themselves 'for some days' attempting to secure subsistence from the wreckage, before they went in search of others.[17] The *Neva*'s master had contradicted himself.

Where the *Launceston Advertiser* was reluctant to speculate on the cause of the wreck, the *Hobart Town Courier* was less restrained. Describing the wreck 'as a most melancholy and afflictive event, from the horrors of which the mind as it were turns away in vain', the *Courier* then questioned the quality of vessels contracted for convict transportation:

> What can be the reason of these successive and awful shipwrecks now, which since the first settlement of these

distant colonies had never before occurred? The investigation that took place with the circumstances attending the loss of the *George the Third*, showed that the ship was almost too old and frail to have been chartered for so long a voyage with so many souls on board, and if the inquiry which, we learn, the government is now instituting into the circumstances of the present distressing wreck, should come to a similar conclusion, which from the so abruptly falling to pieces of the vessel, we almost anticipate, it will appear that some more care in these points is necessary at head quarters than appears to have been used. Neither can we shut our eyes to the fact of the recent arrangements adopted almost single eyed with a view to economy and saving by which vessels of inferior size and quality have been engaged for the important duty. Compare the fine vessels commanded by able and experienced naval officers, which in former years were employed as transports, with the ships of the present day, and to say nothing of the present catastrophes, the successful voyages of those periods will at least be in some degree accounted for.[18]

The *Courier*'s charge was not entirely without foundation. From the mid 1830s emigration became a lucrative business for ship owners. They therefore tended to employ their best ships and crews in that service.[19] There is no question that convict ships were still rigorously inspected and certified as seaworthy, but it is likely that their quality was beginning to diminish by the time of the *Neva*'s sailing. However, in response, the *Cornwall Chronicle* felt compelled to present a counter-argument:

We regret exceedingly that we have not space to offer a few words in contradiction to the *Courier*'s remarks upon the cause of the losses on the Convict ships. The editor pays but a poor compliment – to the Surveying officers at Lloyds – and to the Surveying Officers of the Navy Board – we will endeavour next week to undeceive him.[20]

When the *Chronicle* defended the quality of convict ships, it did so because it wished to attribute the disaster to another cause. It argued that the coasts of the colony were not correctly surveyed and that the merchant marine would be best employed in the fulfilment of such a survey. The paper made an economic case for the survey by asking:

What will strangers make of these repeated losses? The consequences are evident. Merchants and ship owners will not send their vessels and goods without insuring them, the underwriters will exact premiums in proportion to the risk, which is of course, laid upon the imports, and the consumers, that is, the Colonists have to pay it.[21]

It was against this background of competing critiques of government policy that Montagu considered the committee of enquiry's report before passing it to Governor Arthur. On 7 July Arthur wrote to the Secretary of State for War and the Colonies in London (he assumed this was still T. Spring Rice):

One or two points touched upon in the report appear to me

to require further explanation, which I should have wished to have obtained for your information, but the 'Bolina', by which this communication is transmitted, has cleared out, and is on the point of sailing from Launceston.[22]

The letter made its way to London on the same ship as Peck's letter to the *Neva*'s agent, but they did not arrive until December. Meanwhile Montagu was directed to obtain the 'further explanation' that the governor sought, and on 10 July he wrote to the committee of enquiry as follows:

The Lieutenant Governor having perused the whole of the examination and your report respecting the loss of the ship *Neva*, I am directed to remark that his Excellency is of opinion from the position of the vessel at noon on the 12th May that the course stated to have been steered should have taken her clear of every danger, but it is remarkable that it is not stated in your report nor can His Excellency discover by the evidence where the vessel struck or how far from King Island – his Excellency presumes it must have been the South end of Harbingers Reef, but then he is at a loss to conceive how the vessel came there.

I am to add, that to have run down upon a lee shore at night was the extreme of imprudence as the vessel should have been hove to at 8 o'clock at night and I am further to state that it will be advisable to ascertain whether the vessel had usually over-run her reckoning you will therefore be pleased to make a further report on the point referred to in this letter.[23]

Peck was being criticised for running his ship on a 'lee shore' – that is the shoreline towards which the sea wind is blowing. If further clarification was needed from Peck it may have been difficult to obtain. On 11 July the *Chronicle* reported that he had called at their office to express his thanks to Lieutenant Friend before departing for Sydney.[24] Peck was anxious to leave, but his plans were probably delayed when he was forced to report to the committee a second time. Eventually he left Van Diemen's Land on 12 August and arrived in Sydney aboard the *Nimrod* one week later.[25]

Some of the *Neva*'s crew had beaten him there, arriving aboard the *Currency Lass* in early August.[26] In Launceston, they had benefitted from the charity of Matthew Friend, who was the first to subscribe to a collection for the destitute crew.[27] However, two of their number were forced to rely upon charity a second time, and just over three weeks after they arrived in Sydney a newspaper carried a letter soliciting charitable funds on their behalf.[28] Peck had no need for charity. He was in receipt of 'notarial expenses' shortly before his departure from Launceston.[29] The *Neva*'s master eventually left Sydney on 13 September 1835, bound for London aboard the *Andromeda*.[30] Peck returned to his wife, Ann, in Bergh Apton, Norfolk, but by October 1836 he was back at sea. He died in July 1837, just two years after his rescue from King Island.[31] There is no definitive record of what happened to the remainder of his crew.[32]

Back in Van Diemen's Land, the committee of enquiry responded to Montagu's request for further explanation. On

The Wreck of the *Neva*

17 July 1835 it replied to the colonial secretary and included the map shown below.

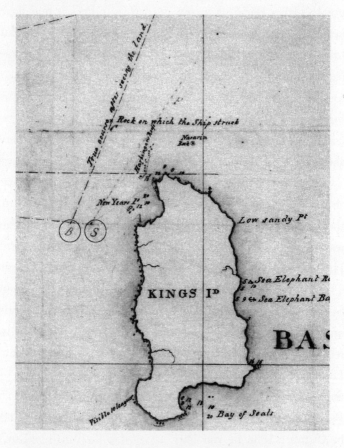

Detail from the map produced as part of the *Neva* enquiry. Captain Peck's stated position on first seeing the island is marked B, and Hobart port officer William Moriarty's estimate for his position of the ship is marked S (both in circles). *Courtesy of State Records NSW: NRS 905, Colonial Secretary; Main series of Letters received, Letters 39/9405 and 39/8104, [4/2441] now [Map 6222]*

The committee reconfirmed its conclusion that the wreck had been an accident, saying that the statement of the first mate and the crew confirmed that of the captain, and that the ship may have struck 'either the N.W. point of the Harbinger Reef or probably a detached portion of the reef where no danger was known to exist, the assumed distance from the land being about three or four leagues'.[33] A league is around 4.83 kilometres, so the captain, the crew and the committee were positioning the reef on which the *Neva* was wrecked between fourteen and nineteen kilometres from Cape Wickham, with the conclusion that it was 'improperly laid down on the Chart'.[34]

However, there was still an element of doubt and the committee was forced to admit that the captain and crew were 'fully sensible of the great difficulty they have to contend with in accounting for an accident, which (was not the melancholy fact before them) they should have considered, could not under the circumstances have taken place'.[35] This time, copies of all witness statements were included with the report.

Governor Arthur still had his doubts; he instructed William Moriarty, the port officer at Hobart in Van Diemen's Land, to examine the papers connected with the wreck. Moriarty had previously been port officer in Launceston and had had first-hand experience of a shipwreck. He was on board the *Letitia* with his wife and two children when she sailed from Cork bound for Van Diemen's Land in 1828. The ship was wrecked at St Jago in August of that year. Moriarty and his family were picked up by an American ship and arrived in Hobart, via

The Wreck of the *Neva*

Rio de Janeiro, in June 1829. Moriarty was a native of Dingle, County Kerry, and a son of Vice-Admiral Sylverius Moriarty. He had entered the Royal Naval Academy at fifteen and took part in the siege of Copenhagen. Moriarty was married to Aphra Crump, the daughter of a doctor in Mary Slattery's home town of Tralee.[36] Crump's failing health was the primary reason that Moriarty was due to move to his property at Westbury, some thirty kilometres west of Launceston, where he would serve as the local police magistrate. Matthew Friend was due to replace Moriarty in Hobart.[37]

Moriarty reported to Montagu on 12 August. He accepted the reported position of the ship at noon the day before the wreck and added that 'the course shaped ought to have taken her clear of every danger'.[38] However, he questioned the ship's position when land had been sighted and the location of the wreck, which he concluded had occurred closer to the island, on the Harbinger Reef. Moriarty dismissed Peck's suggestion that the reef was incorrectly positioned on Matthew Flinders' charts. Flinders had circumnavigated and mapped much of Australia, and had proved that Van Diemen's Land was an island by sailing through Bass Strait. Moriarty suggested that Peck's challenging the cartography of such a famed navigator was little more than wishful thinking:

> From anything that has been elicited in this enquiry I see no reason to suppose that the Harbingers are so far removed from the position assigned them by Flinders, as the spot on which the Committee have placed the wreck of the *Neva*

would seem to indicate, it is a natural infirmity of the human mind to seek to attribute to any cause rather than the real one, misfortunes which may have resulted either from our imprudence or want of correct judgment. I cannot wonder therefore at the Master wishing to believe that the Harbingers are laid down too far to the Eastwards.[39]

Moriarty is even more scathing in his dismissal of Charles Friend's corroboration of Peck's evidence:

Mr Charles Friend concurs in the same view, he is mistaken however in supposing that Flinders considered the Harbingers a solid reef and as he gives no observations by which an opinion can be formed as to whether their position is erroneous or not, I do not consider that statements grounded on such authority should be placed in competition with the remarks of an universally admitted accurate navigator.[40]

Seeking to reconcile the enquiry's positioning of the wreck with the actual location of the Harbinger Reef and the reported position of the ship at noon on 12 May, Moriarty turned to Bennett's positioning of the ship when land had first been sighted:

[Bennett] gives the exact bearing … seeming to have a greater air of authority by being defined. I have adopted it in laying off the ship's place … making her about two and a half miles [four kilometres] nearer to the land than her estimated position.[41]

The Wreck of the *Neva*

There may be an implied criticism of Captain Peck in Moriarty's favouring of Bennett's statement. However, his criticism of the captain for running north and parallel to the coast after land had been sighted is unambiguous:

> On the discovery of the land at two a.m. I consider that the ship should have been brought to the wind on the Starboard Tack ... after making the land it might not have been a question of getting into any particular passage, but how the dangers of a lee shore might be best avoided ... she could not have made good, less than a S.S.W. course, by which she would have drawn considerably off the land and at daylight advantage might have been taken of her situation to pursue such steps as might then appear advisable.[42]

Moriarty was 'sensible of the caution with which one seaman ought to speak of the conduct of another ... were it not drawn from me as an act of duty'. Nonetheless, he considered that the captain had made serious errors of judgement in the three hours after sighting land:

> Had the vessel been hove to at a proper distance from the land, I do conceive the wreck would not have occurred, or had she been brought to the wind, after making the land, on the opposite tack, I do think it would have been equally avoided, a lee shore to a sailor should be an object of the holiest dread; its dangers are seldom to be overcome, its horrors are not to be imagined; it is not from the disastrous waste of human life

attendant on the loss of the *Neva* that these opinions have been formed, it is unfortunately the common routine of such occurrences and should never unnecessarily be encountered, the making a passage a few hours sooner should never be placed in competition with the remotest risk, and I can never agree with that paragraph in the amended Report of the Committee in which they state that they considered the ship was subject to far less danger by running than by laying to.[43]

Unlike the committee of enquiry, Moriarty was quite plain in his remarks. In his opinion, the wreck was caused primarily by Peck's navigational and operational errors, and not by any failure to correctly map the obstacles of Bass Strait.

Having considered the committee's second report, and Moriarty's critique, Governor Arthur wrote to London on 18 September. The recipient of his letter was Charles Grant, 1st Baron Glenelg, who had taken office as the Secretary of State for War and the Colonies in April 1835. Arthur enclosed the second report from the committee, along with the statements of evidence and Moriarty's report.[44] The governor stated that the causes of the disaster were 'fully developed by Captain Moriarty' and he therefore accepted the assertion that the wreck was caused by navigational error and failure to observe proper seafaring protocol.[45]

Governor Arthur did not recommend any further action. Instead his attention turned to the exertions of Charles Friend in rescuing the survivors. London's approval was sought for the payment of £70 to Friend.[46] The committee of enquiry had already written to the colonial secretary on 20 July, enclosing a memorial from Friend and recommending the payment of £75. Interestingly, the *Launceston Advertiser* reported that Charles Friend had been appointed Chief District Constable at Launceston from 15 July.[47] Although he had lost the *Tartar* on King Island, the glowing reports of his behaviour from his uncle Matthew and Captain Peck saw Charles Friend profit from his rescue of the *Neva* survivors. He would go on to spend thirty-one years in the service of the crown in both Van Diemen's Land and Victoria. Known for throwing 'large parties every night', Friend would encounter financial difficulties by October 1838. Ultimately his career would end in ignominy, when, in 1866, as a sub-collector of customs, he was convicted of embezzlement and sentenced to three years' imprisonment.[48]

By October 1835 the authorities in the colony had laid the *Neva* affair to rest. Peck was deemed the villain and there was no need for further action. Yet there were still parts of the story that simply did not make sense. Almost two centuries later, they still don't.

11

Unsolved Mysteries

From London's viewpoint the facts of the *Neva* wreck had been established, even if the sinking had wider ramifications in terms of the organisation and politics of transportation. Later correspondence in England was more concerned with the condition of the ship than reasons for the wreck. To that end, the Admiralty 'directed the Comptroller of Victualling and Transport Services to institute a minute enquiry into every circumstance relating to the *Neva* that could be ascertained in this Country, and also into the character of the Master'.[1] The report concluded that the ship had been expertly inspected and in excellent condition, and the master of good character. The Admiralty would not accept any responsibility for the wreck and wrote to the Home Office, as follows:

I am commanded by their Lordships to acquaint you, satisfactory for the information of Lord John Russell, that the most perfectly safe, roomy and efficient Ships are engaged for the Convict Service, and no Complaint has been made of want of care on this head.[2]

They were not about to have their ship selection questioned. Lloyd's certification also indicated that the craft was perfectly safe. Although the *Belfast Commercial Chronicle* claimed that Lloyd's books were 'good for nothing but deception', it failed to substantiate this charge and still accepted that the *Neva* had been seaworthy.[3] The vessel functioned perfectly until it was run upon a reef, and it is worth noting the assessment of the parliamentarian who observed that 'the loss of the vessel in question had not so much to do with the character of the vessel as with the temerity of the commander in putting it through this difficult strait at night'.[4] But had Peck hit the reef entirely as a result of his temerity and bad navigation? And which reef had he hit?

Given that the reefs closest to Peck's reported wreck site were the Navarine and Harbinger, the ship had almost certainly been wrecked on one of them. Moriarty had concluded that navigational and operational errors had driven the ship onto the Harbinger Reef. However, there are a number of reasons why one may consider the Navarine Reef as the probable location of the wreck. First, its proximity to land meant that the survivors would not have had to drift too far before finding the island. Second, a map thought to date from 1861 marks the position of an unidentified wreck on the Navarine Reef.[5] Reference to the *Encyclopedia of Australian Shipwrecks* indicates that this unidentified wreck may be that of one of several smaller vessels (the *Bertie*, the *Isabella* or the *John*) lost around King Island before 1861.[6] It is also possible that the map marks the location of another unidentified wreck. However, given that the *Neva* was much larger than these three vessels, there is a possibility that the 1861 map identified the location of the *Neva* shipwreck.

The third, and perhaps most compelling, case for the Navarine Reef is the location of the wreckage and bodies washed ashore. The Cape Wickham Lighthouse log for 18 March 1868 recorded that skeletons were found in the vicinity of the lighthouse:

> Superintendent has no doubt that the skeletons found were washed on shore from the 'Neva' wrecked some 35 years ago (with 300 passengers on board) on the Navarine rocks 1½ miles [2.4 kilometres] N.N.W. from where they lay, having heard in 1862 that after a bushfire in 1861 many skeletons were found (and buried by the masons employed building the Tower) between the Lighthouse and Disappointment Bay, the coast being very rocky with small sandy beaches and dense scrub down to high water mark some of which the late bushfires have burned.[7]

Although the log does not specify the number of skeletons found in 1861, it is likely that they were the seven currently buried near the lighthouse. Two years after the wreck John Scott recorded his sleeping in Peck's tents at 'Nord beach' on 23 January 1837.[8] Given that modern-day Disappointment

The Wreck of the *Neva*

Bay is the beach that could be most accurately described as 'Nord', and that two separate bushfires revealed bodies in that vicinity, it seems certain that bodies and survivors from the *Neva* were washed ashore along the north coast of King Island, east of Cape Wickham and close to the Navarine Reef. But could those bodies have come from the Harbinger Reef?

Graves near the lighthouse at Cape Wickham. The plaque in the centre marks the grave containing the seven skeletons thought to be from the *Neva*. *Photo: Kevin Todd*

In the hours immediately after the wreck, many bodies probably came ashore with the *Neva*'s wreckage. Charles Friend reported that he found much of that wreckage, but it is difficult to establish precisely where he located it. Having landed on Yellow Rock Beach, Friend recorded his subsequent passage as follows:

I anchored under the New Years Isles, and landing on the N.W. end of King Island traversed the beach and rocks about thirty five miles [fifty-six kilometres] until I reached Mr B.H. Peck with the men and women survivors from the wreck of the 'Neva' as also the crew of the 'Tartar' cutter belonging to myself which had been wrecked on the same island. In proceeding along twenty miles [thirty-two kilometres] of beach and rocks I could discern nothing more than detached pieces of wreck and staves of casks.[9]

There are some difficulties with Friend's story, as if he walked from the landing point on Yellow Rock Beach north along the shoreline to Disappointment Bay, he could not have covered the 'thirty-five miles' to which he referred. He clearly stated that the fires he sighted were on the northern end of the island, where Scott later located 'Peck's tents'. However, if Friend proceeded beyond these tents and down the east coast to Sea Elephant Bay, he would have covered close to thirty-five miles. This begs the question: did a second encampment exist near Sea Elephant Bay?

The case for such an encampment is quite strong. We know that the *Tartar* was wrecked near the south-east of the island.[10] Friend subsequently stated that the *Tartar* was lost 'about thirty-two miles [fifty-one kilometres] from the spot where the "Neva" wreck came on shore'.[11] The crew of the *Tartar* did not meet the *Neva* survivors until they went in search of them and, for a period, they had an encampment somewhere near the south-east of the island. The most abundant fresh water source in that quadrant is the Sea Elephant River, whilst another substantial source is found at Blow Hole Creek.

Given that Scott was wrecked with them, he may have brought the *Tartar*'s crew to his hut at Yellow Rock. However, if they were at the hut, they did not remain there. Peck's statement described how the *Tartar* crew came to the *Neva* crew and directed them to Scott as he was not with them then. Friend later claimed that the eventual rescue occurred when he anchored 'off the tents of the crew'.[12] His choice of words is interesting; it may be a reference to the crew of the *Tartar* and their initial encampment, rather than the group led by Peck and consisting of crew and convicts. He also claimed that the three he failed to rescue were 'on the other side of the island'.[13] The coast opposite Sea Elephant Bay was the site of Scott's hut at Yellow Rock. This was where the three in question would have gone for the food deposited from the *Sarah Ann*. Had Friend been anchored off Disappointment Bay, 'the other side of the island' was the south coast. It is highly unlikely that any of the survivors had a reason to stray so far.

Friend repeatedly claimed that there were approximately 'thirty-five miles' between his landing point at Yellow Rock, and the encampment where he found Peck. Therefore, it seems reasonable to assume that he walked past the first encampment and signal fires (probably still attended by some survivors) at Disappointment Bay and continued down the east coast to Sea Elephant Bay, where the *Neva*'s survivors had joined those of the *Tartar*.

Friend claimed that during this journey he encountered

a substantial quantity of wreckage over twenty of the thirty-five miles. Unfortunately, he does not tell us whether that was during the first, or the latter, twenty miles. We have already seen that the crew of the *Tartar* spotted wreckage whilst out looking for food; such foraging was more than likely conducted near their encampment on the east coast.[14] Therefore, it seems likely that the wreckage Friend referred to was located east of Cape Wickham, and encountered during the final twenty miles of his journey to Sea Elephant Bay. An analysis of prevailing currents on the night the *Neva* was wrecked also supports this hypothesis.

The *Cornwall Chronicle* of 13 May noted that high tide in Launceston would occur at 11.15 a.m. Using modern tidal charts we can estimate that low tide at Cape Wickham was at 3.15 a.m. High tide was at 10.20 a.m.[15] Thus, when the *Neva* struck the reef at approximately 5 a.m., there was a flood, or inbound, tide at Cape Wickham. By again referring to modern tidal charts we can establish an idea of the currents prevailing when the Cape Wickham tide has been rising for approximately two hours. Those currents first move slowly westwards, away from the Navarine and the Harbingers. However, soon after the ship struck, the currents changed direction and began moving north-eastwards and east, and they gathered pace, moving very rapidly for some three hours after the collision, before slowing again some two hours later, and finally changing direction approximately seven hours after the *Neva* was wrecked. Crucially, during those seven hours one would expect quite an amount of floating wreckage from the

The Wreck of the *Neva*

Navarine Reef to make landfall along the coast east of Cape Wickham. Wreckage from the Harbinger Reef would have moved further east into Bass Strait and comparatively little of it would have reached King Island. The north-westerly wind that prevailed after the collision would also have propelled floating wreckage from the Navarine Reef directly towards Disappointment Bay.

It is probable that most of the wreckage Friend found was east of Cape Wickham, and it is absolutely certain that all of the bodies found in 1861 were found east of Cape Wickham. The bodies of people who drowned at the wreck site may have been subject to currents other than those that prevailed on the surface and could have washed up at various points along the coast. However, those that floated were propelled by winds and currents, and anything that came ashore on Disappointment Bay as a result of those winds and currents was likely to have come from the Navarine Reef. Given that seven survivors died within twenty-four hours of making land, it seems likely that they are the seven bodies re-interred at Cape Wickham and initially found between that point and Disappointment Bay. Therefore, the more likely location of the *Neva* wreck was the Navarine Reef – the same reef upon which an unknown shipwreck was mapped in 1861. But how could the *Neva* have found the Navarine Reef?

In 1835 everybody thought that the exact location of the Navarine Reef had been marked by Flinders in 1802, and the *Neva* enquiry's map was based on his cartography. However, when that map is overlaid with the current Australian

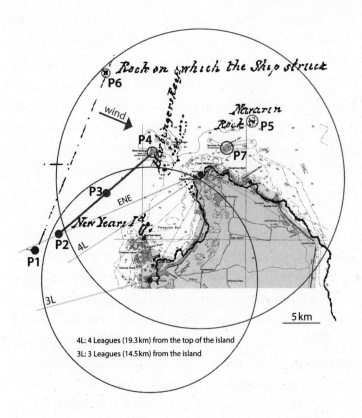

P1: Peck's reported position at 2:00 a.m. on 13 May.
P2: The ship's position as described to the enquiry in relation to the contemporary chart.
P3: Estimated position of the ship when the sails were trimmed at 3:30 a.m.
P4: West Harbinger Reef – correct position.
P5: Navarine Reef as positioned on the enquiry map.
P6: Peck's position for where the ship struck.
P7: Navarine Reef – correct position.

Neva enquiry map overlaid with a contemporary hydrographic chart. Extract of chart AUS 789 is reproduced under licence by permission of the Australian Hydrographic Service.

The Wreck of the *Neva*

Hydrographic Service map for King Island, one can immediately see that Flinders had placed the Navarine Reef much further out to sea (P5) than its actual location (P7). By looking at the statements of Peck, Bennett and Sharp, we can provide further information for our diagram.

Both Peck and Sharp stated the land was three leagues distant when it was first sighted (circle 3L). Bennett stated that the northern extremity of the island was bearing ENE (line ENE). Peck claimed that they then changed course to NNE, and that the northern extremity of the island appeared to be distant about three or four leagues (circle 4L).[16] The intersection of these three bearings occurs at P2, remarkably close to where Peck positioned the ship (P1). If, like Moriarty, we assume that the ship struck the Harbinger Reef (P4), then she had to travel approximately fifteen kilometres from P2 to P4 between 2.00 a.m. and 5.00 a.m. Bullard stated that the sails were trimmed at 3.30 a.m. Thus, we can position the ship at P3 halfway through the three-hour period between P2 and P4. Hine stated that he had come on deck shortly after this, at 4.00 a.m. He did not state precisely when the breakers were sighted, but it would seem to have occurred shortly after he had come on deck.[17] Thus, it seems that at 4.00 a.m. the *Neva* was approximately thirteen kilometres from King Island. As it was a clear night, it must have been obvious that the ship was moving closer to land. By the standards of 1835 the Harbingers were quite accurately charted, so Peck should have known that he was moving towards them. Yet there is no indication that the course was altered after 2 a.m.

Whilst Hine stated that the breakers were sighted after he came on deck at 4 a.m., Sharp claimed that the sighting had come about one hour after he had reefed the topsails at 2 a.m. It is quite possible that Sharp's estimation of 'about an hour' was incorrect. However, it is also possible that *two* sets of breakers were seen – the first caused by the Harbinger Reef, which Peck avoided by moving the *Neva* eastwards, between the reef and the island, and the second, an hour later, when Peck encountered the Navarine Reef where he did not expect it. Alternatively, and less spectacularly, one could posit that Peck hit the Navarine Reef after he attempted a shortcut between the Harbinger Reef and King Island. Such a route would have saved him many kilometres and hours. It would also have taken the *Neva* directly onto the actual location of the Navarine Reef. One contemporary newspaper mentioned what they still considered the 'safe passage' between the Harbinger Reef and the island, but conceded that it was by 'no means a desirable one to attempt'.[18]

Although the crew's evidence can be used to construct cases for both the Harbinger and Navarine reefs, there remains a distinct possibility that this evidence is unreliable. Whilst the evidence is consistent, such uniformity is hardly remarkable. The crew had nearly six weeks on the island, in each other's company, attempting to explain or excuse what had happened. Both the captain and Bennett stated the position of the ship at noon on 12 May with nine-figure accuracy (141°57' E/39°37' S and 141°57' E/39°36' S).[19] It is unlikely that such routine figures would be remembered by both men seven weeks after they were recorded. Such a recollection is even more unlikely when one considers that the later significance of the position could not have been apparent when it was initially taken. The figures they recalled were suspiciously similar, without being incredulously identical. It seems likely that they were recalled, or invented, on King Island after consultations among the crew.

If the *Neva*'s position at noon is questioned, then all other aspects of the crew's statements must be treated with suspicion. In that context attempts to establish which reef the *Neva* struck depend predominantly on the location of the wreckage and the bodies. Efforts to ascertain exactly why she was wrecked must remain speculative. However, we know that she certainly struck either the Navarine Reef (approximately three kilometres from Cape Wickham) or the Harbinger Reef (approximately six-and-a-half kilometres and seven-and-a-half kilometres from Cape Farewell).[20] We know that the ship was much closer to the island than prudence would allow and this might be the reason Peck attempted to locate the wreck approximately nineteen kilometres from land at a location where no reef has ever been charted (P6). Peck's invention of a fictitious rock would seem to be an attempt to disguise foolishness, recklessness, or both. But why would he display such characteristics in notoriously dangerous seas?

Whilst we cannot answer that question definitively, some of the evidence given to the enquiry lends itself to speculation. First, there is the matter of Rose Hyland's testimony. Hyland claimed that when she made her way to the upper deck after the ship had struck, some of the women 'who had been in the main prison' were already in the cuddy, and were hopelessly drunk. Rose Ann Dunn bore witness to similar scenes. But why would a group of women released from the prison upon the ship's striking a reef concern themselves with the excessive consumption of alcohol? Surely remaining sober would be the common sense approach to survival?

The accounts of how the women got on deck also seem contradictory. Peck said that the *Neva* 'raised a midships, and the stanchions of the prison fell down, on which the prisoners all came on deck'. Bullard and Bennett agreed with Peck.[21] However, Ellen Galvin stated that when the ship struck, 'the Captain immediately came down, unlocked the door and released all the women prisoners, as well as those in the black hole and desired us all to come on deck'.[22] Rose Hyland contradicted Galvin when she claimed that Peck had withdrawn the ladder to keep the black-hole prisoners below. Thus, whilst everybody acknowledged that the women were on the upper deck when the ship broke up, they could not agree on how they had escaped the prison. Five of the eleven witness statements made specific reference to the convicts being securely locked in the hold every evening – but were they?

Were some convict women already drinking with the crew before the ship struck the reef? Was this the reason for Hyland seeing so many of them drunk in the cuddy where Peck and Bennett's quarters were located? With good weather, free rum, a ship full of female convicts, and only days to go to Sydney, perhaps the crew were paying more attention to merriment than to navigation. We have already seen that such forbidden intercourse between female convicts and crew frequently occurred on other ships. On the *Neva*, it was even more likely, given that Stephenson was confined to his sickbed. And, if the crew's behaviour was deficient in that regard, it may well have had shortcomings in other areas.

Each of the convicts told the enquiry that she had been treated properly by Peck and his crew. Ellen Galvin was particularly keen to emphasise the point, with four affirmations of good treatment in a 386-word statement:

> During the voyage and up to the time of the wreck of the vessel the Doctor, Captain and Mates behaved to us like fathers ... No intercourse was permitted during the voyage between the prisoners and any of the crew ... I have heard of no causes of complaint during the voyage ... We were all treated with the greatest kindness by the Captain throughout the voyage and since the wreck.[23]

Yet, we have seen that there were tensions on King Island. Bennett had emphasised Hyland's bad behaviour and the indifferent behaviour of two others.[24] Those tensions seemed to reach breaking point when Hyland initially refused to leave the island. Major Commandant Deare, writing to the colonial secretary, claimed that by the time the convicts reached Launceston, some of them were inclined to complain of their treatment at the hands of Peck and Bennett.[25] There was one primary reason why the women might have been aggrieved. Nine of the *Neva*'s twenty-six-man crew survived the sinking, yet only six of her 213 women and children left King Island alive. That is a survival rate of 35 per cent for the crew, and less than 3 per cent for the women and children.[26] Although the *Neva* shipwreck occurred almost twenty years before the policy of 'women and children first' began to evolve, it is difficult to avoid the conclusion that Peck, Bennett and the rest of the crew were not particularly concerned with the women's safety. We know that, of the six surviving convicts, Margaret Drury was romantically linked with a surviving seaman. After her gushing praise of the master and crew, Ellen Galvin specifically told the enquiry that Bennett had saved her life, so it is possible that she had formed a relationship with him. When Bennett claimed that three of the surviving women were well behaved, he almost certainly included Galvin and Drury among that number. Hyland was not part of that club, so she may have felt aggrieved at her treatment and that of some of her friends. On the morning she departed King Island, anger and fear may have mingled with the rum she admitted to having in her blood. Her consumption of rum on the morning of her departure raises further questions. How much rum was on King Island? And where did it all go?

Peck and Charles Friend each stated that few of the thirty puncheons of rum aboard the *Neva* had washed ashore and none were salvageable. Yet William Hine told the enquiry that 'three puncheons of rum half full were washed on shore and whilst we were on the island we had as much as we liked by going to fetch it'.[27] Peck admitted that he had distributed rum to the survivors from 'part of a puncheon' that had washed ashore.[28] When the cutter *Shamrock* returned from King Island in August with the three survivors who were initially left behind, Matthew Friend wrote to Montagu stating that no government stores were washed ashore or saved. Yet on 2 September 1835 G. H. Barnes from Customs in Launceston also wrote to Montagu asking about a quantity 'of spirits saved from the wreck of the *Neva*'.[29] Furthermore, in January 1836 the commissariat in Hobart was in receipt of correspondence enquiring of the salvage price for 'rum belonging to Government and saved by Mr Joseph Penny from the wreck of the barque *Neva*'.[30] The letter went on to schedule 485 gallons (2,204 litres) in puncheons and kegs and to state that the last shipment from England had been valued at 1s 10d per gallon. At that rate, the total value of the salvaged rum was more than £44. Such a quantity of rum would have weighed in excess of 2,500 kilograms and required considerable effort to move from King Island to Launceston. Penny may well have used a sloop that he owned to remove some, or all, of that rum. That sloop was called *Sarah Ann*, the same ship Charles Friend had sailed from the island![31]

In February 1836 the government in New South Wales received a letter from Leonard Roberts of Launceston. Roberts enclosed a petition from a John Peter Armstrong regarding 'the salvage of goods saved by him and others from the barque *Neva*'. This communication implied that Armstrong sought remuneration for goods (not just rum) bound for New

South Wales, from the governor of that territory. In case the governor required a corroboration of Armstrong's petition, he was provided with an affidavit, as sworn by one Charles Friend![32]

Interestingly, although Charles Friend had managed the trip with the survivors from King Island to George Town in around two days, the *Shamrock* took more than four weeks to get to the island and back. Therefore it would appear that the vessel spent two or three weeks in Bass Strait. The survivors from the *Tartar* wreck were also conspicuously absent from reports of both the first and second rescues. They were never mentioned by name, and there is no record of any official interview with them. In fact Friend stated that he took twelve people off the island, leaving behind Margaret Drury and two of the *Neva*'s crew.[33] The *Neva* wreck had fifteen survivors. Thus, it would appear that Friend left the *Tartar*'s crew on the island, along with Kidney, Robinson and Drury. The survivors indicated that food was running low when Friend eventually took them from the island. Why then would he have left the crew of the *Tartar* behind? And if the *Tartar*'s crew did indeed have a separate encampment on the east coast, why would they have stayed there alone instead of joining Scott at Yellow Rock? Is it possible that they were guarding something?

It could be that the *Tartar* was smuggling rum and used the opportunity provided by the *Neva*'s wreck to legitimise the contraband. Whilst Charles Friend claimed that he was on his way to Port Fairy when he stumbled upon the wreck of his own ship, it seems much more likely that he had procured the *Sarah Ann* to search for the *Tartar*.[34] If that was the case, his failure to admit that he sought out the *Tartar* is another reason to suspect that vessel's involvement in illegal trade.

So, what happened to the *Neva*'s rum? Was there rum on the *Tartar*? Did the rum that turned up in Launceston in September really originate on the *Neva* wreck? How did the *Sarah Ann*'s owner come into possession of rum that was allegedly salvaged from the *Neva*? Why did the *Shamrock* spend some three weeks rescuing survivors from the island? Why were those survivors left behind, when food was supposed to be in short supply? Who were the *Tartar* crewmen and why did the authorities never seek to speak to them? Did Peck and Friend really attempt to sail from King Island to Port Fairy? And if they did, what might they have carried with them?

Unfortunately we can provide only speculative answers to these questions. There were certainly some highly suspicious anomalies surrounding the *Neva*'s rum. However, the smuggling of significant quantities of rum from King Island would have required the collusion of convicts, crew, ship owners and government agents. Yet such collusion is certainly possible in an environment where everybody had something to hide. Peck may not have wanted the authorities to know that the *Neva* had turned into a party ship as soon as Stephenson had taken ill. The convicts may not have wanted anybody to know of their participation in those parties. Charles Friend and his crew would certainly have wanted to keep secret the presence of any rum aboard the *Tartar*, or their possible removal of any rum from King Island aboard the *Sarah Ann*. Matthew Friend may have sought to disguise his nephew's part in the plot by dispatching the *Shamrock* so quickly. And the government agents aboard the *Shamrock* may have sought to profit by their removal of the remaining rum. Just twenty-seven years after the infamous rum rebellion, it was not entirely inconceivable that government officials would place personal profit ahead of duty to the colony. Charles Friend's subsequent conviction for embezzlement is evidence that he was certainly motivated by personal profit some thirty years after these events.

However, in July 1835 there was not enough evidence to suspect that rum was removed from King Island. As far as the authorities were aware, the only removals from the island were the *Neva*'s survivors. Now, the six surviving women were about to enter the colonial convict system.

12

Colonial Australia

When they stepped off the *Sarah Ann* in George Town, the survivors of the *Neva* had finally arrived in colonial Australia. It was a society that was simultaneously different and similar to that they had left behind. Colonial Australia was a country of two distinct classes: the colonists who formed, governed and sustained the colony, and the convicts who served them. This class system was not entirely different to that which prevailed in Ireland. The *Neva*'s survivors were always cast in the role of servants and there were certain positions they could never hope to fill. Nonetheless, this emerging nation also presented them with certain opportunities: convicts could improve their situation in life and achieve a status that Ireland could never have given them. However, they worked towards that improvement within a society that was still dominated by England and traditional English values. The Australian colony was the brainchild of the English aristocracy and it was governed according to their whims.

The first convicts arrived with the first fleet just forty-seven years before the *Neva* was wrecked. They were immediately put to work establishing and maintaining a system of agriculture to preserve the colony. Few of them had the skills necessary for this task and food grew increasingly scarce. The arrival of the second fleet in 1790 did little to alleviate the situation. Its ill, dead and dying convicts placed an even greater drain on the colonists' limited resources. The appalling scenes that greeted the arrival of the second fleet's neglected convicts were partially replicated when the third fleet arrived in 1791, pressuring the administration into regulating the transportation of convicts. However, the arrival of dead and dying convicts from the second and third fleets ensured that opposition to transportation was ever present among the colonists.

In 1791 the *Queen* brought the first Irish convicts transported directly from their homeland. The Irish presented a dilemma because they brought a culture of disobedience with them. Among their number were Whiteboys, other groups of agrarian agitators and, after 1798, separatist republicans. All of these lived by their own rules and not those that an English government imposed. Thus, the potential for disruption of English law and order was ever present, and eventually, in 1804, it boiled over.

The Castle Hill rebellion began on 4 March 1804, when a group of convicts, led by former United Irishman Phillip Cunningham, seized firearms and ammunition in the Castle Hill area of Sydney. The rebellion met with some initial success until substantial portions of the convict army descended into disorganisation. Eventually, by employing a number of tricks to delay the rebel advance, the professional soldiers of the British Army caught up with the convicts near Rouse Hill. Chaos followed, with the untrained rebels fleeing after sustaining only twenty minutes of fire. In honour of the United Irishmen's last stand in Wexford six years previously, the engagement was called the 'Battle of Vinegar Hill'. For the Irish, it had similar results. The leaders were rounded up and hanged, whilst the rank-and-file rebels were publicly flogged. English colonists grew increasingly suspicious of Irish disloyalty. Although up to half of the rebels were actually English convicts, some in colonial Australia would not allow such facts to detract from their simplistic stereotype of the disloyal Irish rebel.

Disloyalty was not the only stereotypical behaviour associated with the Irish. The colony inherited much of its intellectual value system from its British masters, and its Irish stereotypes were similar to those of nineteenth-century Britain. Just two years before the *Neva* came to grief, Edward Ford Bromley, the surgeon superintendent of the *Surrey II*, revealed an anti-Irish prejudice that was entirely acceptable to the British establishment:

The great difficulty I experienced among the Irish prisoners was a rooted dislike to every kind of cleanliness, which it was difficult to eradicate. Beyond this their general conduct was as good as could be expected from such a class of people.[1]

Bromley was not the only surgeon who made general assumptions about prisoners based on nationality or class. Similar sentiments were expressed by William C. Watt of the *Edward* when he mused that the 'lower class of Irish are fond of swallowing drugs'.[2] While many surgeons made no such assumptions, and there were others who were specifically complimentary of the Irish, the idea that Irish prisoners were different was prevalent and prejudices against the Irish went unchallenged.[3]

In the colony, as in Ireland, the ordinary Irish people still had one trait that made them very different to the governing classes: their Roman Catholicism. On both sides of the British Empire, some Anglican gentlemen were intensely suspicious of all Roman Catholics. The Castle Hill rebellion led to a severe backlash against Catholicism. The prominent Anglican clergyman, Rev. Samuel Marsden, attended many of the floggings of the Vinegar Hill rebels and was most impressed with the brutality displayed. The few priests who had the right to celebrate Mass had that right withdrawn. When the Vatican attempted to appoint a prefect apostolic to the colony, the authorities sent him back to London. However, the British reacted to this highly visible suppression of religious freedom and colonists were consequently forced to soften their attitude to Catholicism – by 1820 they had accepted a Catholic mission. In 1821 the authorities allowed, and even supported, the building of a Roman Catholic cathedral in Sydney.

Whilst the colonial government slowly relaxed its attitude to Catholicism, the same could not be said for all of colonial society. Old anti-Catholic prejudices were still present. Indeed the Anglican church was not formally disestablished until the year after the *Neva*'s survivors arrived. Of the *Neva*'s six female survivors, five were Roman Catholics.[4] The prejudices they encountered were not substantially different to those they left behind in Ireland. Roman Catholics found the Australian colonists as tolerant of their faith as the Irish ascendancy was.

If their criminal convictions, nationality and religion were not enough to place the *Neva*'s survivors at the very bottom of the social ladder, their gender certainly was. In the early days of Australian society most white women were convict women. Although that situation was changing, old anti-female prejudices certainly survived. Indeed such prejudices were enforced by governmental administration at all levels. Historian Robert Hughes has noted that:

> … there was rarely a comment on colonial society, scarcely a passage of evidence to the various Select Committees on Transportation, hardly a tract or a diary or a letter home, that missed the chance to describe the degeneracy, incorrigibility and worthlessness of women convicts in Australia. Military officers believed this, and so did doctors, judges, parsons, governors and, of course, their respectable wives. Convict men might in the end redeem themselves through work and penance, but women almost never. It was as though women had passed the ordinary bounds of class and become a fiction, not far from pornography: crude raucous Eve, sucking rum and mothering bastards in the exterior darkness, inviting contempt rather than pity from her social superiors, rape rather than help from men.[5]

This prejudice had its origins in the colony's earliest days. British and Irish women's primary function upon arrival was to provide breeding partners for the colony's men. As such, they were perceived as little more than sexual objects. Upon arrival, some of the earliest female convicts were simply lined up on the deck of the ship which had conveyed them, so that local colonists, soldiers and ex-convicts could chose their partners from among the new arrivals. Some of these women were subsequently cast aside by colonists who grew weary of them. This left them entirely dependent on their wits, and sometimes on the sale of sexual favours.[6]

The perception of colonial Australia's founding mothers as roving vagabond whores was always prevalent. The authorities allowed the behaviour of some women to colour their perception of an entire gender. In doing so they developed a willingness to accept, without question, any evidence that seemed to bolster their prejudices. The most notable example of such corrupted evidence came in the form of a 'Female Register' created by Rev. Samuel Marsden in 1806. Marsden surveyed each woman in the colony and assigned her the simplistic status of 'married' or 'concubine'. He found that for every married woman the colony homed, it homed two-and-a-half concubines. Of course, there were some significant flaws in his method of classification. All of his 'married' women were married in the Anglican church, so the most significant grouping that Marsden had failed to categorise as married was the many Irish women married by the Roman Catholic church. Considering that more Irish than British women were already married upon their arrival in the colony, this was a substantial omission.

If Marsden's definition of marriage was fundamentally flawed, so was his definition of 'concubine'. He employed this word to describe all women who cohabited with their partners. Many of the women he described so glibly were in long-term, established relationships and shared their lives with a partner in exactly the same way that any wife would. Many of them had several children, all of whom were fathered by one partner. A substantial number of Marsden's concubines remained with the father of their children until death finally parted them.[7]

Whilst cohabitation without marriage certainly was not the norm in Britain and Ireland, there were reasons why it was common in Australia. First, colonial society indoctrinated its citizens with a different set of values. Those who struggled for survival in the harsh and alien environment, without the support network or prying eyes of an extended family, did not conform to the moral standards of the British Isles as a priority. Second, those who did prioritise such contemporary moral values may still have found conformity somewhat difficult. If a convict woman wanted to marry the man she had chosen to cohabit with, where would she find a priest? As Portia Robinson has noted, 'for many ... there was no alternative to an unblessed union, and they simply declared themselves man and wife in the sight of God and waited for the arrival of a priest of their faith to legalise their union'.[8]

Female convicts faced one final charge from their detractors: their portrayal as a drain on the limited resources of the emerging colony. Men were put to work in the fields, built the houses and created the infrastructure that the colony needed to sustain itself. However, it was more difficult to find a use for women. The values of the time dictated that only specific forms of labour were appropriate for women, mainly in the domestic sphere. However, the number of maids could never match the number of men. If the proportion of women in the colony was ever to rise to that of a normal society, additional employment would have to be found for increasing numbers of women; female convicts would have to pull their weight and add to productivity. If they did not, they would present further ammunition to those who wished to paint simplified pictures of lecherous whores. The solution was the 'Female Factory' and that was where the *Neva*'s survivors were bound.

In George Town the *Neva*'s women were probably placed aboard a smaller vessel and moved up the River Tamar towards Launceston. It is likely that they made that trip aboard a steamer similar to the one that had taken them down Cork's River Lee six months previously. The Tamar had seen the arrival of its first steamer, also named *Tamar*, in the previous year. She was used to ply the river between George Town and Launceston, and it is likely that the *Neva* survivors joined her on one of her upstream journeys.[9] The place names on the north coast of Van Diemen's Land reflected its settlement by English colonists. The river separated Devon and Cornwall, whilst Launceston shared its name with a village in the latter county. Launceston had a population of around 6,000, and the administrative centre at Hobart was populated by approximately 14,000.[10] The total population of the colony in 1835 was estimated at 40,283, and they lived in an area almost exactly the size of the present-day Republic of Ireland.[11] Thus, whilst George Town, with its 400 people, may have felt busy after the isolation of King Island, it was considerably quieter than the city of Cork.

Sketch of the town of Launceston in 1830, Lieut William Thomas Lyttleton. Lyttleton was the police magistrate at Launceston and sat on the committee of enquiry into the *Neva. Image: William Thomas Lyttleton. Mitchell Library, State Library of NSW. SV6B/ Laun/3*

As the survivors parted from the *Sarah Ann*, they probably reserved a special place in their affections for their rescue ship. However, she too was touched by the *Neva*'s curse when, twelve months later, she was wrecked at Port Fairy.[12]

Steaming away from George Town and into a quieter landscape, the women probably noted the differences between this and their previous river journey. The high, wooded hills with their gum trees were in stark contrast to the cleared green fields that rose from the banks of the Lee. Clearances on the hills above the Tamar were only partial, having occurred wherever landholders could take advantage of free convict labour. As they neared Launceston, the women passed Matthew Friend's 250-acre estate, overlooking the river at Newnham. At that time the owner was in the process of seeking a tenant for his riverside residence, although its third floor was still incomplete.[13]

The women's journey down the Lee had taken place in winter, and now they were experiencing their second winter in seven months. Although Launceston is ten degrees closer to the equator than Cork, the winter temperatures are similar. As they moved upstream they probably noted the increased shipping traffic. Launceston was a vibrant trade centre; fifteen of Van Diemen's Land's seventy-one ships were based there. In addition, ships on their way to Hobart, Sydney and Europe made regular visits.[14] The *Neva*'s survivors saw the *Lochiel* waiting to sail for Leith in Scotland. The *Dublin Packet* may have reminded Rose Ann Dunn of her time in Kilmainham. That ship was bound for Sydney, having stopped off on her way from King George Sound (later Albany, Western Australia). Matthew Friend's old ship, the *Norval*, was also Sydney bound, whilst the *Vibilia* had recently arrived from London on its way to Hobart. The *Lavinia* had just unloaded cargo and was outbound for Sydney. A local newspaper advertised the newly arrived cargo as follows: 'Taylor's Brown Stout, Dunbar's bottled ale and porter, West India Rum in puncheons, English soap, men's waterproof hats, oven doors, coffee mills, potato and dung forks and Chubb's patent 7 and 8, 3 bolt, 2 keyed locks.'[15]

These goods were sold in the shops and markets of a rapidly expanding town. However, Launceston was only two decades old and some of its infrastructure was not as advanced as that of British and Irish cities. A visitor to the colonial town in 1830 described it:

> Built on a flat, the remainder rises gradually to the summit of a moderate elevation. It is of some extent, contains in all about 2,500 inhabitants and is not badly laid out; but I cannot say much in favour of some of the streets, as in wet weather the sloughs are deeper than is convenient for those who get into them, the bullocks not unfrequently perishing while attempting to extricate themselves and the dray from such a disagreeable situation. At least that was the case in 1830; and I was informed when in the colony in November 1832, that very little improvement had been made.[16]

We know that the population of Launceston had more than doubled as part of a boom experienced throughout the colony. The population of Van Diemen's Land rose from 24,504 to 45,846 between 1830 and 1838. By 1838 the total convict population was 16,968, of whom only 2,054 were women. Given that there were only 780 births and 525 deaths (a net natural increase of 255) in 1835, it is clear that both convict arrivals and immigration were having a significant impact on the colony.[17]

The 'Female Factory' was a short walk from the wharves of the North Esk river, a tributary of the Tamar. The walk took the convicts past the government reserve, military barracks, hospital, treadmill and gaol on their way to the imposing sandstone building.[18] The factory was run by the superintendent, Mr Paterson; his wife was the matron. It was a relatively new building when the survivors arrived. Completed in July 1834, and furnished in September of the same year, it was opened in November, when prisoners from George Town were moved in. The building was of octagonal design, whereby the superintendent could watch each and every part of the institution from the windows of his octagonal quarters right at the factory's heart. At the time it was considered a marked improvement on the decrepit and overcrowded facility at George Town.[19]

In theory, these factories served a dual function. First, they separated a group categorised as morally depraved from the rest of society. Second, they provided labour for women who could not be placed in domestic service. In order to achieve these goals the administration enforced a strict regime, an essential part of which was the class structure of the factory: all inmates were divided into three distinct classes in accordance with their behaviour:

The 1st. Class shall consist of those Women who may be placed in the Establishment on their arrival from England, without any complaint from the Surgeon Superintendent, of those who are returned from service with good characters, and of those who have undergone at least three months' probation in the second, after their sentence in the third class has expired. The Women of this class alone shall be considered assignable, and shall be sent to service when proper situations can be obtained.

The 2d. Class shall consist of Females who have been guilty of minor offences, and of those who, by their improved conduct, merit removal from the Crime Class.

The 3d., or Crime Class, shall consist of those Females who shall have been transported a second time, or who shall have been guilty of misconduct on their passage to the colony, of those who shall have been convicted of offences before the Supreme Court, who shall have been sent in under the sentence of a Magistrate, or who shall have been guilty of offences within the walls, – they shall never be removed from the 3d. to the 1st. Class.[20]

The work a convict was given depended on the category in which she was placed. Third-class prisoners were employed mainly in washing for the various prisons, or in spinning or carding wool. Second-class women were employed in the manufacture of convict clothing. Those from the first class still awaiting assignment were employed as cooks, hospital attendants or task women. The task women were the equivalent of the shipboard matrons in that they exercised authority over their fellow prisoners, operating as supervisors in various capacities.

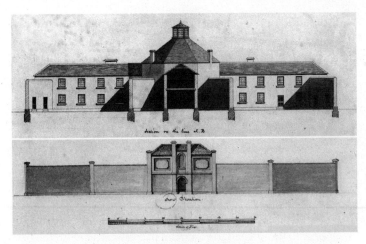

The Female Factory at Launceston where the surviving women were sent. *Images (details from): Tasmanian Archive and Heritage Office, PWD266-1-898 and PWD266-1-900 (drawings of the Female Factory, Launceston)*

Each class was issued prison clothing consisting of a dress, an apron, a jacket, a straw bonnet and a petticoat, all made from 'cheap and coarse materials'. Third-class prisoners were distinguished by a yellow letter 'c', which adorned the back of their petticoat and the right-hand sleeve and rear of their jacket. Second-class prisoners wore a similar 'c' on their left-hand sleeve, whilst first-class prisoners bore no marks that distinguished their station.[21]

The significance of the *Neva* women's arrival is attested by the fact that they were examined on a Sunday by the colonial surgeon, who reported that they had 'no severe wounds or injuries but are in good health'.[22] Nonetheless, their clothing and personal hygiene doubtlessly required attention. The factory had strict rules, and the women were certainly washed and clothed before admittance. However, these women did not immediately join the general population. Major Commandant Deare had formed an opinion of them, based on information Peck had relayed to him. On 27 June he wrote to Colonial Secretary Montagu:

> The women saved are reported by the Master to be of not very good character on Board, I have therefore had them separated in the Factory and desired that they should be kept so. They appear to be inclined to complain of mistreatment on the part of the Master and Superintendent.[23]

Whilst this separation may have attached greater credibility to their statements to the forthcoming enquiry, it also had consequences for the women. Within the factory they were categorised as third-class prisoners. They would remain at Launceston attempting to work their way up to the first class for a period. Considering that those who made their way from third to second class should then serve three months' probation, one would expect that a period longer than ninety days would need to have passed before the *Neva*'s women were assigned to labour outside the factory. Yet it was only approximately ninety days when one of them definitely gained an external assignment.[24] In September 1834 newspapers had reported a serious shortage of domestic servants in Van Diemen's Land; perhaps the labour shortage led to a more liberal interpretation of the rules.

Although the survivors were assigned in Van Diemen's Land, their ultimate destination was the subject of some debate, as the *Neva* was originally bound for New South Wales. Consequently her convicts became the objects of a curious legal conundrum involving the changing status of territories on both sides of the British Empire. Although Van Diemen's Land had been part of New South Wales, it became a separate colony in 1825. The *Neva's* human cargo had originally been bound for the care of the governor of New South Wales, not for that of his counterpart in Van Diemen's Land. On 7 August 1835 Montagu asked the governor whether the survivors should be forwarded to New South Wales.[25] The governor felt that the women should be retained in Van Diemen's Land and this wish was communicated to London. Glenelg, the Secretary of State for War and the Colonies agreed, and in January 1836 he wrote to the governor of New South Wales to inform him of that decision.[26] However, nobody thought to inform the authorities in Dublin, and on 12 February 1836 the lord lieutenant's office wrote to the governor of New South Wales to 'transfer the services' of the *Neva's* survivors to his colony.[27] The governor of New South Wales simply forwarded the documents to the governor of Van Diemen's Land. Legal advice was then sought by the authorities in Van Diemen's Land. It was given as follows:

In reply to Your Excellency's question respecting the female convicts landed in Van Diemen's Land from the wreck of the transport *Neva*, originally directed for New South Wales, I have the honour to report that, by the Act ... where a ship conveying convicts from the United Kingdom to a particular Colony, shall by stress of weather or other circumstances convey them to another Colony, the Governor of such last mentioned Colony may retain such convicts, & they shall be subject to the same laws, as if contracted originally to be delivered to him.

It seems remarkable, that the rest of the Act applies in terms to convicts transported only from Great Britain, and the laws of Ireland authorise transportation only to New South Wales – of which (if this colony were known at all in Ireland, in those days) V.D. Land was generally considered to be a part. But the section referred to has the words 'United Kingdom of Great Britain and Ireland'.

I am of the opinion, that the landing of the *Neva* convicts in one of the islands of this government, tho from the wreck only of that vessel, is within the provision of the Act, – & consequently that they may be lawfully detained as convicts in this Colony.[28]

The 'laws of Ireland' referred to were those made by the separate parliament that sat in Ireland until the Acts of Union dissolved it in 1800. Ireland had never legislated for her convicts to be transported to the separate colony of Van Diemen's Land. However, the more recently established 'United Kingdom of Great Britain and Ireland' had provided that any of its convicts stranded in any colony (thereby including Van Diemen's Land) other than the one for which they were originally destined could remain in that colony if the governor wished to retain them. Fortunately for the *Neva*'s survivors, Governor Arthur wished to keep them in Van Diemen's land.

The original five were joined by Margaret Drury when she returned from King Island aboard the *Shamrock* on 11 August.[29] They had just survived the worst convict shipwreck in Australian history. What was next for the *Neva*'s survivors?

13

Life after the *Neva*

News travelled slowly in 1835. It was almost Christmas before reports of the *Neva* tragedy began to trickle through to the Irish newspapers. On 8 December *The Freeman's Journal* broke the story with the following statement: 'By an arrival from Sydney on Saturday morning, with dates to the 4th of July, we learn the loss of the *Neva* convict ship, from Cork to New South Wales, with 241 souls on board, consisting of 150 female convicts, nine free women, and 55 children.'

In the next few days local newspapers picked up on the story and soon it was news across Ireland. Those who could not read English no doubt heard the news from neighbours and friends. But the details of May's events in Bass Strait were of little consequence to most who happened upon them. Many Irish people were far too engaged with their own daily existence to ponder the particulars of a faraway tragedy involving a group of criminals completely unknown to them. Yet there were some 200 families that watched the news carefully. Those were the families who knew that their loved one may have perished on the ship. Louisa Mellefont's son probably remembered the tearful farewell he had bade his mother in a Cork courthouse. Now *The Constitution or Cork Advertiser* left him in no doubt of the finality of this separation, reporting: 'Mrs Mellefont was on board this ship.'[1] In the days that followed various newspapers published the names of the six survivors.

Convict Mary Slattery's father, Jeremiah, owned a butcher shop in Tralee. His wife, Ellen, lived with him, and the couple had eight children. Whilst Mary claimed that her father had sought her transportation in frustration at her habitual thieving, his real motivation remains unclear. He may have sought to banish his daughter, or he might have wished to provide her with the means to emigrate. Either way, Mary was still his flesh and blood and he and his other children doubtlessly wondered what had become of her. On 10 December *The Constitution* printed the names of the *Neva*'s survivors. The Slattery family then knew that Mary was saved.

One of Mary's first assignments in Van Diemen's Land was with a Mr W. A. McCannon in 1835. By 1838 she was assigned to labour in Longford town, some twenty kilometres south of Launceston. When she walked its streets, she would have seen a clustered settlement which had recently sprung up around the Longford Hotel. The surrounding area had just been settled by farmers from Norfolk Island. As Slattery was categorised a house servant, she was engaged in domestic labour for one of these early settlers.

She was a model servant. The conduct register for convicts

in Van Diemen's Land at that time contains not one single entry against Slattery's name. She was one of only a handful to avoid punishment of any kind. However, it may be that she spent a considerable part of her time in Longford on a sickbed. When she had first arrived in Launceston, she was the only one of the survivors whose complexion was described as 'pale'. There were no detected signs of illness, but her paleness might have been the outward manifestation of a constitution weakened by her ordeal. Perhaps that weakness was part of the reason why Mary Slattery died just shy of three years after her arrival in the colony. She was buried in Longford, Van Diemen's Land, on 20 April 1838. Although her burial was recorded, her name never appeared among the lists of convict deaths routinely dispatched to the Colonial Office in London. Thus, it was never reported to the Home Office or to Dublin Castle. The Slattery family knew that Mary had survived the *Neva* wreck, but they could not have known that she died less than three years later. And, if nobody thought to inform Dublin Castle that the survivors were to remain in Van Diemen's Land, the Slatterys could not have known where Mary ended her days.[2]

Curiously, on the day that Slattery was buried, the *Neva* crossed the mind of the new governor of New South Wales, Major Sir George Gipps. On that day he wrote to the Colonial Office in London seeking a copy of the ship's assignment list. He claimed: 'Such information is necessary to enable the local Government to answer satisfactorily the inquiries which are now so frequently made respecting the fate of convicts in this country, as the local authorities for the want of it, incur the suspicion of gross negligence or inaccuracy.'[3]

We cannot say whether queries regarding the *Neva* survivors had been directed to New South Wales. Indeed Gipps appeared to be labouring under the misapprehension that the ship had originated in England. Nonetheless it is plain that the tragedy was quickly forgotten down under. In the three years that followed the loss of the *Neva*, nobody had thought to look for the list of those who died. By the time the new governor put pen to paper, Mary Slattery was already dead. But what became of the other five?

Rose Hyland's first recorded assignment was to Mr Munce in October 1835. Whilst in his employ she recorded her first offence as a colonial convict. On 23 October 1835 Hyland was found absent without leave and sentenced to seven days' solitary confinement on bread and water. As soon as she was released from the factory and returned to service, she re-offended. This time her offence was drunkenness and she was sentenced to a further fourteen days' confinement. Having returned to service in November, Hyland was re-interned for insolence on 19 December and spent Christmas of 1835 alone in a solitary cell.

Although her behaviour improved somewhat, Hyland had clocked up three more offences before the beginning of October 1836. All related to unauthorised absences from service or drunkenness. Having obtained the permission of the authorities, she married Thomas Dorkin of Campbelltown on 24 October 1836. She was then assigned to her new husband

and it seems that they settled at Kangaroo Point. Married life did not curtail Hyland's rebelliousness; on 20 November she was heard 'making use of bad language on the streets' and was found in a drunken condition the next day.

Hyland and Dorkin were still together when Hyland received her ticket of leave between August 1839 and March 1840. Hyland was making progress towards her freedom, but she continued to commit occasional petty offences. However, from April 1840 her husband's name was absent from the few reports of her petty misdemeanours. In February 1841 she was punished for 'keeping a disorderly house'. This offence did not prevent her from obtaining a certificate of freedom and by the end of 1841 Rose Hyland was a free woman.[4] At this point the *Neva*'s tearaway dissenter should have disappeared from the annals of the convict system. However, in March 1842 Hyland was arrested again. This time she was 'remanded on a charge of robbery at Kangaroo Point'. Her accomplice was not her husband, but a man by the name of James Simpson. It appears that they were guilty of the theft of £1 from their victim.[5]

Hyland's poor behaviour is hardly surprising. Before she had left Ireland she had already become a thief. The entire penal system, into which she was then inserted, was hardly conducive to rehabilitation. Any convict arriving in Australia had already spent months in the closest of confinement with the worst of British and Irish society. Female convicts were then placed in a societal structure that positioned them at the very bottom of the social ladder. Their colonial masters were fed a staple diet of appalling anecdotes centred on the notion of the convict whore and her corrupting influence. They treated convict women with the disdain that their contemporaries demanded. Many convict women were bound to react to such negativity. The more they were treated like reprobates, the more that some of them would behave like reprobates. They would not value a society that did not value them. There was nothing unusual about Hyland's behaviour. She was not even the most badly behaved of the *Neva*'s contingent. That dubious distinction fell to Rose Ann Dunn.

While Hyland committed thirteen recorded offences, mostly of a minor nature, Dunn committed sixteen, some of them quite serious. On 23 September 1835 Dunn became the first of the *Neva* survivors who sought to marry. She agreed to become the wife of William Mears just three months after her arrival in the colony. The haste of this union would suggest that Mears was one of the many men who sought out a match at the female factory. Such marriages were usually arranged over a period of hours. If both parties agreed that the arrangement was of mutual benefit, the ceremony was conducted as soon as the convict had received permission to marry. In Dunn's case, that permission was granted and she married Mears in Longford parish on 26 October 1835.[6] It appears that the couple then resided in the district of Longford/Norfolk Plains, under the watchful eye of local magistrate A. W. Horne. It was whilst in this situation that Dunn's first act of drunkenness occurred and she was returned to the factory at Launceston for two months' hard labour. By

July 1836 Dunn had committed a further four offences, two related to drunkenness and two to unauthorised absences. The recording of the latter two offences affords us an insightful glimpse into Dunn's nocturnal activities and the character traits she had carried to her new home.

On 30 May 1836 Dunn was found 'absent without her husband's leave all night'. She was returned to gaol and it was further stipulated that 'if appearing that her husband has encouraged her in prostitution it is recommended that she may not be allowed to live with him again'. However, Dunn was returned to Mears, and on 18 July she was deemed guilty of another unauthorised absence. This time she was sentenced to four days' solitary confinement on a diet of bread and water. In addition, she was 'removed from her service and not to be again assigned in this district'. This time the sentence was carried out and she was not returned to her husband. It seems possible that he had not been in search of a wife as much as a supplemental income when he had arrived at the factory the previous year. On 15 October 1836 Dunn was found drunk whilst assigned to service elsewhere.

Dunn absconded from service in November 1836 and had six months added to her term of transportation. This did not deter her from further misbehaving; just three days later she was found in a disorderly house after hours. This may hint at her continued practice of prostitution. The offence resulted in her relegation to crime class (third class) and her consequential return to the factory. However, her stay behind the factory walls did not last as long as it should have, and she was found guilty of further drunkenness whilst on assignment in March 1837.

The downward trajectory of Dunn's behavioural pattern continued when she was again found in a drunken condition on 25 April 1837. This time she was described as 'a most abandoned character' and was sentenced to confinement for twelve months. However, she refused to be returned to the house of correction. Having been dragged there under protest, she began her two-week stay in a solitary cell. Upon release from solitary, Dunn served a further three months peaceably. Then on 7 August she was returned to solitary confinement when found fighting in the crime-class dining-room. The remainder of Dunn's twelve-month sentence passed without incident. However, it appears that, upon her release, she had had her fill of the convict system. At some point after 25 April 1838 Dunn again absconded from the supervision of the convict department. This time she began to pass herself off as a free woman. Her deception did not last long, however, for on 17 July she was apprehended and returned to the infamously turbulent Cascades Factory in Hobart for four months' hard labour.

Upon her release she committed three more minor offences. Then on 1 July 1839 she was again found drunk in service. This time she was returned to the factory to await the next vessel bound for Bruni Island. Having served some time on the island, she was guilty of a further offence on 5 August. She was returned to the factory to await assignment in the country. It appears that prison authorities were actively seeking to remove Dunn from the urban surroundings of

The Wreck of the *Neva*

Hobart and the company that she kept. It is likely that she was still operating as a prostitute. It is also possible that she had become a part of a particularly notorious group of female convicts known as the 'Flash Mob'. The Flash Mob shocked some colonial journalists to their core, and one of them described it as follows:

We have appended to the title of this article, the term 'Flash Mob;' that this term is technical, is sufficiently obvious; but few of our readers, – few indeed, of any who possess the ordinary attributes of human nature, can even conjecture the frightful abominations which are practised by the women who compose this mob. Of course, we cannot pollute our columns with the disgusting details, which have been conveyed to us; but we may, with propriety, call the notice of the proper Functionaries to a system of vice, immorality, and iniquity, which has tended, mainly, to render the majority of female assigned servants, the annoying and untractable animals that they are. The Flash Mob at the Factory consists, as it would seem, of a certain number of women, who, by a simple process of initiation, are admitted into a series of unhallowed mysteries, similar, in many respects, to those which are described by Goethe, in his unrivalled Drama of Faust, as occurring, on particular occasions, amongst the supposed supernatural inhabitants of the Harz Mountains. Like those abominable Saturnalia, they are performed in the dark and silent hour of night, but, unlike those, they are performed in solitude and secrecy, amongst only the duly initiated. With the fiendish fondness for sin, every effort, both in the Factory, and out of it, is made by these wretches, to acquire proselytes to their infamous practices; and, it has come to our knowledge, within these few days, that a simple-minded girl, who had been in one and the same service since she left the ship, – a period of nearly six months, – very narrowly escaped seduction (we can use no stronger term) by a well known, and most accomplished member of this unholy sisterhood. This practice constitutes one of the rules of the 'order;' and we need not waste many words to show how perniciously it must act upon the 'new hands,' exposed to its influence. Another rule is, that, should any member be assigned, she must return to the Factory, so soon as she has obtained (we need not say by what means) a sufficient sum of money to enable herself and her companion to procure such indulgences as the Factory can supply, – or, rather, as can be supplied by certain individuals connected with the Factory. This sufficiently accounts for the contempt, which the majority of female prisoners entertain for the Factory, while it shows, also, why the solitary cell is considered the worst punishment.[7]

Dunn's degenerate behaviour provides evidence of a real possibility that she belonged to this group. She was a convicted prostitute and had practised that trade in the colony. She was much more sexually promiscuous than the average female convict. At a time when lesbianism was strictly taboo, women like Dunn may have been more willing than others to experiment with its physical manifestation. Her confinement on six different occasions throughout 1839 may be indicative of her desire to be reunited with a partner in the factory. The authorities' desire to remove her from the urban area and its influences may have indicated their desire to separate Dunn from the Flash Mob.

In any event, by 24 February 1840 the convict system had decided that it had seen enough of Rose Ann Dunn, and the governor general used his authority to 'remit the extended sentences of this woman' and grant to her her freedom. Dunn walked from the factory in Hobart a free woman. We cannot say what friends or lovers she may have left behind. There is nothing to suggest that she ever returned to the husband who had once 'encouraged her in prostitution'.[8] Dunn was unlucky in her choice of partner. In that regard, she had something in common with Ellen Galvin.

Like all the other female *Neva* survivors, it is likely that Ellen Galvin was assigned soon after arriving at Launceston. However, it was 1836 before she first broke the rules of her service. Her first offence was an unauthorised absence and she was punished with ten days' solitary confinement on bread and water. By the end of 1836 she had committed that same offence on two further occasions. On the second occasion she had also added the use of obscene language to her repertoire. Between 25 March and 26 September 1837 Galvin clocked up another seven offences. She spent much of this time assigned to a man named Heaney in the vicinity of Norfolk Plains. Repeated drunkenness was a feature of Galvin's life whilst in Heaney's employ. However, her most serious

offences came on 25 March, when she had six months added
to her term of transportation for absconding from service,
and on 18 August, when she was found guilty of larceny and
had a further two months added. This accumulation of bad
behaviour cannot have assisted her greatly when, on 3 January
1838, she applied for permission to marry free man Patrick
Devlin. Nonetheless, the authorities granted their approval
for the marriage. However, somebody changed their mind and
the union never took place. At this point Galvin's behaviour
improved dramatically and she managed to avoid any form of
punishment until 25 June 1838, when she was sentenced to
fifteen days' solitary confinement for 'drunkedness [_sic_] and
insolence to her mistress'.

On 28 September 1838 she applied for permission to
marry William Lawrence, a convict who had arrived on board
the _Juliana_ in 1820. He was convicted in Middlesex, England,
and transported for life for the theft of a horse. Lawrence's
behaviour in English gaols was described as 'bad'. However,
after his transfer to the prison hulk, it improved to 'good'.
In Van Diemen's Land he had committed many of the usual
petty offences whilst in service, and between 1823 and 1833
he received a total of 150 lashes. Lawrence also served twelve
months in the prison on Maria Island, off the east coast of
Van Diemen's Land, for assaulting a military guard and
attempting to liberate the prisoner he guarded. On 19 October
1838 he was granted a conditional pardon, which allowed him
all the rights of a free man except the right to return to his
native land.[9] Ten days after he received his pardon, Lawrence

married Ellen Galvin in the parish of Longford. His new wife was eventually granted her freedom in 1842.[10]

Bridget Hayes, the sister whom Ellen had left at the Cork depot, arrived in New South Wales with her eighteen-month-old son in February 1836. She spent some time in the factory at Parramatta before marrying her second husband, William Brooks, in 1837. Hayes was granted her freedom just before Christmas in 1841.[11] There is no evidence to suggest that the two sisters were ever reunited.

Margaret Drury was assigned by 25 November 1835. On that date she was reprimanded for drunkenness. This comparatively minor offence did not prevent her from seeking the hand of the man with whom she had tarried on King Island. On 1 December 1835 she sought permission to marry Peter Robinson. They wed in the parish of St John, Launceston, on 12 January 1836.

Drury's time under sentence was comparatively uneventful. She was reasonably well behaved and generally seemed to avoid the attention of the authorities. Nonetheless, she seemed to be a character of some daring and a streak of rebelliousness occasionally manifested itself. On 21 March 1836 Drury and Robinson were caught harbouring an absconded convict by the name of Margaret Jones. Jones was a pickpocket who had arrived on the *Sovereign* in 1827. After her visit to the Drury-Robinson household she was returned to prison, where she served one month's solitary confinement on bread and water.[12] Drury occupied a nearby solitary cell for twenty-one days, her sentence for harbouring the fugitive.

Almost one year later, on 25 February 1837, Drury was sentenced to six months in the factory's crime class. This time she had indecently exposed herself whilst in a drunken condition. However, it was more than two years later that the most mysterious chapter of Drury's life was written, when, on 2 July 1839, she was returned to the factory at Launceston. The lieutenant governor directed that she spend six months in the factory 'for having been found residing upon the islands in Bass Straits without permission'. Thus, it seems that Drury had returned to Bass Strait at some point between August 1837 and July 1839. Approximately fifty small islands are dotted around the strait. In Drury's time few of them were inhabited. However, she was particularly well acquainted with King Island as she and her husband had lived with John Scott for some time after the rest of the *Neva*'s survivors had departed. Did Drury and Robinson return to the island where they were shipwrecked some years previously? Alas, the answer must remain the subject of mere speculation.

Whilst serving her six-month sentence in crime class, Drury was deemed guilty of disobedience, banished to her cell and restricted to a diet of bread and water for thirty days. No further incidents involving the Roscommon woman were reported and she was eventually granted her freedom in 1840.[13]

Margaret Drury and Peter Robinson's marriage was not a manufactured match, but rather one of mutual affection. The couple had met each other on a doomed convict ship and lived through its trauma together. On 14 February 1844, more than eight years after their marriage, the Robinsons had a son, Henry. Henry eventually relocated to Seymour, Victoria. Many of Drury's descendants are living in Australia today and some were of enormous assistance in the writing of this book.[14]

The last of the *Neva*'s survivors to break free of the convict system was Ann Cullen. Cullen had received a life sentence and consequently was destined to spend more time in the penal system than her five surviving female shipmates. Upon admission to the factory, she declared herself a 'farm servant'.[15] Consequently any assignment she received may have involved labouring in that capacity. Her first known assignment was to W. G. Elliston in 1835.[16] Her first known offence came in the form of insolence whilst serving with H. Rowecroft in September that year. From that date until January 1838, Cullen was punished for minor offences on six separate occasions. However, the most significant event that occurred during that time was the birth of her child, Mary Ann. Mary Ann's birth was registered in Launceston on 11 February 1837. The child's father was John Devereaux, a convicted thief who had been transported aboard the *Manlius* in 1830. Cullen and Devereaux did not marry, and the child was lodged in an orphanage in Hobart in January 1840.

By the time she finally sought permission to marry, Cullen's behaviour had deteriorated significantly. On 6 June 1838 she was found in a disorderly house after hours. She paid for that offence with ten days in solitary confinement. On 2 July she was guilty of being 'out after hours' and once again returned to the factory. Upon her admission, several articles of jewellery and a substantial sum of money were found concealed on her person. For this offence her initial sentence of twelve days in crime class was extended by one month. During that month Cullen received two weeks' solitary confinement on a diet of bread and water when she disobeyed orders by lighting a cigarette when not permitted to do so. No sooner was she returned to service than she encountered trouble again. This time she represented herself as a free woman to some constables who questioned her. In February and October 1838 she was found in public houses, and on the second occasion returned to the factory at Launceston for a period of one month. Having returned to the assignment class in January 1839, she was involved in a physical altercation with some of her fellow servants. It appears that she struck more than one of them before absenting herself without leave. She was duly punished, but by March 1839 was once again outside the factory's walls and once again found absent without leave. By now, the authorities had had enough of her degenerate behaviour and, as in the case of Rose Ann Dunn, it was recommended that she be reassigned to a rural area. This certainly seemed to have the desired effect; Cullen did not reoffend for some time.

On 25 October 1840 Cullen sought permission to marry William Jones. Jones had been convicted of the theft of two asses at the Chester Assizes in August 1834. He arrived in Van Diemen's Land aboard the *Norfolk* later that year. His English gaol report described him as a 'bad character'. He had previously served three months for the crime of 'bastardy'.

The Wreck of the *Neva*

Cullen and Jones failed to secure permission for their union at the first attempt as she was serving six months' hard labour for her disorderly conduct on 2 October 1840. The couple reapplied in December 1841. Although William Jones had been granted his freedom certificate by that time, Cullen's second application to marry him was turned down when it was considered that she should serve six months' further probation on her life sentence.

At this point Jones and Cullen went their separate ways. For William Jones, a marriage was more of a convenient partnership than an enduring life-long love affair, as he already had a wife and child in England. Cullen's name was recorded among disciplinary reports again in July 1841, when she was sentenced to seven days in solitary for an unauthorised absence. However, this did not prevent her from applying to marry once again; this time her intended was William Howard.

Howard was also a convict. He had been transported for fourteen years upon his fourth conviction for theft and arrived in the colony on the *Lord Lyndoch* in November 1831. Like Jones before him, Howard also sought out a life partner even though he had left a wife and three children in Sheffield. However, Cullen was not an unlucky woman who continued to pledge her hand to adulterous men. At that time there was nothing unusual about Howard's behaviour. In fact married convicts were permitted to remarry when they had been separated from their previous spouse for more than seven years, provided that the spouse remained in Ireland or Britain. Thus, the authorities were aware that Howard was already married when they reviewed his application to marry Cullen in February 1844. The application was granted and the couple were married in Launceston on 13 March.

As Ann Cullen had been sentenced to life she did not qualify for a freedom certificate. However, in 1847 she received a conditional pardon and was then free to do as she wished provided that she remained within the colony.[17] She was the final *Neva* survivor to receive her freedom. The authorities made no mention of her previous ordeal, recommending her pardon on the basis that she had 'held a ticket of leave two years and her conduct during that period, and for a long time previously having given good proof of reformation'.[18]

Little Mary Ann Cullen had been returned to her mother in Launceston around the time of her fifth birthday, in February 1845. Mary Ann would later settle in Mount Misery, Victoria, and have three children by Richard Young, before the couple were eventually married in 1905. Several of Mary Ann's descendants have been traced and assisted greatly in the researching of this book.[19]

Back in Ireland, the relatives of the *Neva*'s dead had little option but to accept the untimely loss of their loved ones. In Longford those who remembered Mary Ryan knew that the free woman and her daughter, Elizabeth, were never reunited with their husband and father Bryan. As is the case with all the male convicts who lost wives and children to the *Neva* tragedy, there is no evidence to suggest that Bryan Ryan ever remarried. Indeed it seems that he returned to his native county at the height of the famine in 1847.[20]

The Wreck of the *Neva*

The family of another Longford Whiteboy, William McCue, still held out some hope of his wife Mary's survival. They were most distressed to hear of the *Neva*'s wreck, and indeed that of the *Hive*, which had departed Cork some eight months after the *Neva* and was wrecked just short of Sydney on 10 December 1835. Only one life was lost when the *Hive* was wrecked, but the McCue family were not immediately aware of that fact. They hoped that Mary McCue had not been aboard either of the wrecked vessels. After a brief exchange of correspondence (none of which survives) between Longford gentleman John Kingston of Mosstown and the authorities in Dublin Castle, Kingston wrote:

Sir,

I have made inquiry and cannot find 'Mary Dininy wife of John McHugh' referred to in your letter of the 5th inst. But a Mary Dineny wife of William McHugh [*sic*] left this neighbourhood on the 27th Dec 1834 for Cork to be forwarded in a Gov transport to New South Wales, to her husband who had been transported about the year 1826. Her family have not heard any tidings of her since she left Cork and now in great distress of mind not knowing whether she has suffered in one of the vessels lost on passage to that colony. They will feel very grateful for any information you can give respecting her. They do not know in what vessel she sailed. They only can say that she sailed sometime after her arrival in Cork in early January 1835.[21]

Age has almost consumed the reply Kingston received. What remains of it is preserved on microfilm by the National Archives of Ireland. Still, its few discernible words stand as an emotive reminder that this terrible tragedy had a human face. The final legible phrase confirms for Kingston that Mary Dineny (McCue) was 'embarked on transport "the *Neva*" '.[22] Now her family knew. Mary and her nine-year-old son were forever lost, somewhere between Ireland and Australia.

Conclusion

Almost two centuries have elapsed since the *Neva* shipwreck erased the lives of 224 people. Of the 209 convict ships that departed Ireland, the *Neva* met with the most tragic end. Yet, in Ireland, her name is not known. Neither are those of her convicts. Indeed, little is known of the criminal classes that settled another continent. Like millions of Irish emigrants, time erased them from memory and wrote them into the history of another nation. One famous folk song tells of a fictional character named Michael, who was transported from County Galway after his conviction for the theft of corn. Written by Pete St John in the 1970s, 'The Fields of Athenry' stands as Ireland's most popular memorial to its exiled convicts. Whilst Michael is doubtlessly representative of the many convicts who were transported for crimes of necessity, his story should not be misunderstood as that of a typical convict. Neither should the stories of the *Neva*'s convicts.

The overwhelming majority of the *Neva*'s convicts never made it to dry land. However, more than 40,000 Irish people concluded their journey and settled in the colonies we now call Australia. These people were partly responsible for the construction of a new nation and their memory is preserved by the descendants who bear their surnames and by an emerging interest in the history of transportation. That interest has seen the preservation of historical convict sites at places such as Cockatoo Island, Port Arthur and the Cascades. Enhanced access to genealogical records has also resulted in increasing numbers of Australian people researching their convict ancestry. However, only two of the *Neva*'s convicts have known descendants and the *Neva* tragedy is not widely remembered in either country.

Uncovering the *Neva*'s story took us to five different cities on two separate continents. In each place we could sense that time was the most prominent barrier between us and the women we researched. Although they have since been trod by some of Ireland's most famous patriots, the dreary corridors of Kilmainham's west wing are not much changed since Margaret Drury first felt their cold stone floors beneath her feet. Although Elizabeth Fort's buildings were burned during the Irish revolution, its outer walls still reach skyward from their lofty perch. On the other side of the world, the surf of Bass Strait still crashes noisily on the sand and rocks of Disappointment Bay. Human hands have since added a lighthouse to the refined landscape, but the sounds of the ocean remain as they were when Ellen Galvin first heard them punctuate her terror. Van Diemen's Land has changed its name to Tasmania, but the River Tamar still winds its way peacefully between Launceston and George Town. The same hills watch that river's journey, although their former wilderness has been partially consumed by human agrarian activities.

Back in Cork, Cove became Queenstown before reverting

The Wreck of the *Neva*

to its old name with a Gaelic spelling – Cobh. From the hills of the town it is easy to look upon a peaceful harbour and think of the *Neva*'s children playing on her decks in the cold January air. Eight-year-old Michael Doyle probably watched Peck and Bennett in innocent admiration. Five months later, amidst the frightening screams of fearful women, he watched those men desert him, before the remains of his life were stolen by the ocean waves.

Now, as Irish naval vessels move through waters once reserved for British warships, they pass the disintegrating pier that saw *Titanic*'s final passengers leave Ireland. Nearby, the *Lusitania* monument overlooks the quaysides that took that liner's dead from the ocean that claimed them. Cork harbour has long been associated with some of the world's most famous, and infamous, ships. This text may restore to consciousness the harbour's forgotten association with the most tragic of all the convict ships: the *Neva*. The names of those who sailed on her are listed in Appendix II. It has taken 178 years for those names to appear in print.

The tide steals time, from those who watch,
The water changed, the river's not,
These silent hills, the very same,
Their time is gone, their place remains.

Cal McCarthy

244

Appendix I

Convict Voyages from Ireland to Australia

Date of departure	Name	From	To	Male convicts	Female convicts	Male deaths	Female deaths	Master	Days at sea	Notes
16/04/1791	*Queen*	Cork	NSW	133	22	7	0	Richard Owen	173	Date of departure per *Hibernian Chronicle*, 18 April 1791
15/02/1793	*Boddingtons*	Cork	NSW	125	20	1	0	Robert Chalmers	173	
12/04/1793	*Sugar Cane*	Cork	NSW	110	50	1	0	Thomas Musgrave	157	Man who died was executed for mutinous intent
09/08/1795	*Marquis Cornwallis*	Cork	NSW	163	70	11	0	Michael Hogan	186	Seven men executed after mutiny was squashed
10/12/1796	*Brittania I*	Cork	NSW	144	44	10	1	Thomas Dennot	169	
24/08/1799	*Minerva*	Cork	NSW	165	26	3	0	Joseph Salkeld	140	
24/08/1799	*Friendship*	Cork	NSW	133	0	19	0	Hugh Reed	176	
26/06/1800	*Anne I*	Cork	NSW	130	24	3	0	Jas Stewart	240	
20/11/1801	*Hercules I*	Cork	NSW	140	25	44	0	Luckyn Betts	209	Port of departure per *Cork Mercantile Chronicle*, 30 November 1801; three escaped

29/11/1801	Atlas I	Cork	NSW	151	28	63	2	Richard Brooks	220	Port of departure per Cork Mercantile Chronicle, 30 November 1801
30/05/1802	Atlas II	Cork	NSW	193	0	4	0	Thomas Musgrave	153	
04/11/1802	Rolla	Cork	NSW	122	37	3	0	Robert Cumming	189	
31/08/1805	Tellicherry	Cork	NSW	130	36	5	1	Thomas Cuzens	168	
31/08/1805	William Pitt	Cork	NSW	1	119	0	2	Jn Boyce	223	
21/01/1809	Experiment II	Cork	NSW	0	60	0	0	Joseph Dodds	155	
10/03/1809	Boyd	Cork	NSW	139	0	5	0	Jn Thompson	157	
15/05/1812	Archduke Charles	Cork	NSW	147	54	2	0	J.P.Jeffries	227	
05/12/1814	Canada (3)	Cork	NSW	156	0	0	0	Jn Grigg	243	
05/12/1814	Francis & Eliza	Cork	NSW	54	69	2	4	Wm Harrison	246	
04/11/1815	Alexander II	Ireland	NSW	0	84	0	3	Wm Hamilton	152	
1815	Guildford (2)	Ireland	NSW	221	0	1	0	Magnus Johnson	Unknown	
14/07/1816	Surrey I (2)	Cork	NSW	150	0	0	0	Thomas Raine	159	
09/03/1817	Pilot	Cork	NSW	117	0	0	0	Wm Pexton	142	

Date	Ship	Port	Destination					Master		Notes
14/03/1817	Chapman (1)	Cork	NSW	198	0	12	0	Jn Drake	134	Crew panicked on mutiny rumour. Shots fired on two occasions
21/03/1817	Canada (4)	Cork	NSW	0	89	0	0	Jn Grigg	138	
14/11/1817	Guildford (3)	Cork	NSW	199	0	1	0	Magnus Johnson	138	
01/01/1818	Minerva I (1)	Ireland	NSW	160	0	3	0	Jn Bell	119	
26/07/1818	Elizabeth I (2)	Cork	NSW	0	101	0	0	Wm Ostler	116	
07/08/1818	Earl St Vincent (1)	Cork	NSW	160	0	3	0	Sam Simpson	131	
10/08/1818	Tyne	Cork	NSW	180	0	1	0	Casey Bell	Unknown	Port and date of departure established by reference to Southern Reporter, 11 August 1818
18/08/1818	Martha	Cork	NSW	170	0	0	0	Jn Apsey	128	
25/04/1819	Bencoolen	Cork	NSW	150	0	0	0	Jos. B. Anstice	123	
25/05/1819	Mary I	Cork	NSW	160	0	1	0	Jn Lusk	123	
28/05/1819	Daphne	Cork	NSW	180	0	2	0	Hugh Mattison	116	
26/08/1819	Minerva I (2)	Cork	NSW	172	0	1	0	Jn Bell	113	
01/09/1819	Lord Wellington	Cork	NSW	0	121	0	0	Lew Hill	Unknown	
03/10/1819	Castle Forbes (1)	Cork	VDL	140	0	0	0	Thomas Reid	116	Four males landed Sydney

05/12/1819	Janus		Cork	NSW	0	104	0	0	Thomas J. Mowat	150	Allegations of prostitution on the Janus were investigated in Australia. Englishwomen also sailed on the Janus
02/04/1820	Hadlow (2)		Cork	NSW	150	0	2	0	Jn Craigie	125	
05/05/1820	Dorothy		Cork	NSW	190	0	0	0	Jn Hargraves	137	
22/08/1820	Almorah (2)		Waterford	NSW	160	0	1	0	Thomas Winter	122	
19/09/1820	Prince Regent II (1)		Cork	NSW	144	0	1	0	Fran Clifford	112	
04/11/1820	Lord Sidmouth (2)		Cork	NSW	160	0	0	0	James Muddle	107	
16/06/1821	John Barry (2)		Cork	NSW	180	0	0	0	Roger Dobson	144	
25/07/1821	John Bull		Cork	NSW	0	80	0	0	Wm Corlett	146	
04/11/1821	Isabella I (2)		Cork	NSW	200	0	0	0	Jn Wallis	125	
18/11/1821	Southworth (1)		Cork	NSW	101	0	0	0	David Sampson	111	
21/06/1822	Mangles (2)		Cork	NSW	190	0	0	0	Jn Cogill	140	
03/09/1822	Countess of Harcourt (2)		Cork	NSW	172	0	1	0	Geo. Bunn	109	
08/11/1822	Brampton		Cork	NSW	172	0	0	0	Sam Moore	165	
25/01/1823	Woodman (1)		Cork	NSW	0	97	0	3	Hy. Ford	151	
05/04/1823	Recovery (2)		Cork	NSW	180	0	0	0	Wm Fotherly	116	

Date	Ship	Origin	Destination					Master	
29/04/1823	Earl St Vincent (3)	Cork	NSW	157	0	1	0	Peter Jn Reeves	133
05/09/1823	Medina (1)	Cork	NSW	177	0	1	0	Robert Brown	115
28/09/1823	Castle Forbes (2)	Cork	NSW	140	0	1	0	Jn W. Ord	109
1823	Isabella I (3)	Ireland	NSW	200	0	5	0	Jn Wallis	Unknown
13/02/1824	Prince Regent I (2)	Cork	NSW	180	0	3	0	Alex Wales	153
06/04/1824	Almorah (3)	Cork	NSW	0	109	0	1	Geo. Hay Boyd	136
08/09/1824	Ann & Amelia	Cork	NSW	200	0	0	0	Wm Ascough	116
29/10/1824	Asia I (3)	Cork	NSW	190	0	0	0	Thos F. Stead	116
05/01/1825	Hooghly (1)	Cork	NSW	195	0	2	0	Peter Jn Reeves	107
12/03/1825	Mariner (2)	Cork	NSW	0	113	0	1	Wm Fotherly	120
16/05/1825	Lonach	Cork	NSW	144	0	1	0	Wm H. Driscoll	111
11/07/1825	Sir Godfrey Webster (2)	Cork	NSW	194	0	3	0	Jn Reynoldson	176
05/08/1825	Henry Porcher (1)	Dublin	NSW	176	0	1	0	Jn Thompson	120
23/10/1825	Mangles (4)	Cork	NSW	190	0	0	0	Jn Cogill	118
19/01/1826	Lady Rowena	Cork	NSW	0	100	0	0	Boum Russell	118
16/03/1826	Regalia	Dublin	NSW	129	0	0	0	Robert Burt	142
29/06/1826	Boyne	Cork	NSW	199	0	0	0	Wm L. Pope	121
27/08/1826	Phoenix III	Dublin	NSW	190	0	1	0	Alex Anderson	120
03/10/1826	Brothers (2)	Cork	NSW	0	161	0	3	Charles Motley	122

14/01/1827	*Mariner* (3)	Cork	NSW	160	0	2	0	Robert Nosworthy	129	
14/02/1827	*Countess of Harcourt* (4)	Dublin	NSW	194	0	2	0	Wm Harrison	134	
02/06/1827	*Cambridge*	Dublin	NSW	200	0	2	0	Richard Pearce	107	
19/07/1827	*Eliza II* (1)	Cork	NSW	192	0	0	0	Dan Leary	112	
27/08/1827	*Elizabeth II*	Cork	NSW	0	194	0	2	Walt Cock	138	
27/09/1827	*Marquis of Huntley* (2)	Cork	NSW	160	0	0	0	Wm Ascough	125	
03/11/1827	*Morley* (5)	Dublin	NSW	195	0	3	0	Harry Williams	121	
11/02/1828	*Borodino*	Cork	NSW	200	0	0	0	Richard Mentrup	152	
23/02/1828	*Mangles* (5)	Dublin	NSW	200	0	3	0	Wm Carr	100	
23/06/1828	*City of Edinburgh* (1)	Cork	NSW	0	80	0	0	James R. Clendon	142	
15/09/1828	*Sophia*	Dublin	NSW	192	0	2	0	Thos A. Elley	124	
21/09/1828	*Governor Ready* (2)	Cork	NSW	200	0	0	0	Jn Young	117	
16/11/1828	*Fergusson*	Dublin	NSW	216	0	2	0	Jn S. Groves	130	
01/01/1829	*Edward* (1)	Cork	NSW	0	177	0	3	James Gilbert	115	
02/03/1829	*Eliza II* (2)	Cork	NSW	170	0	3	0	Wm Nicholas	110	
12/07/1829	*Guildford* (8)	Dublin	NSW	200	0	4	0	Robert Harrison	115	
16/08/1829	*Larkins* (2)	Cork	NSW	199	0	3	0	Wm Campbell	128	
10/09/1829	*Asia I* (5)	Cork	NSW	0	199	0	3	Thos F. Stead	125	
02/10/1829	*James Pattison* (1)	Dublin	NSW	200	0	1	0	Joseph Grote	110	

Date	Ship	Origin	Dest					Surgeon	No.	Notes
01/01/1830	Forth I	Cork	NSW	118	0	3	0	Dav. Proodfoot	115	
03/06/1830	Forth II	Cork	NSW	0	120	0	0	James Robertson	131	
03/07/1830	Hercules II (2)	Dublin	NSW	200	0	1	0	Wm Vaughan	121	
16/08/1830	Florentia (2)	Ireland	NSW	200	0	4	0	Jn Jeffrey Drake	121	
28/08/1830	Andromeda II (1)	Cork	NSW	180	0	8	0	Robert Parkin	112	
17/10/1830	Edward (2)	Cork	NSW	158	0	5	0	James Gilbert	128	
18/12/1830	Waterloo (2)	Dublin	NSW	200	0	1	0	Stephen Addison	133	
23/03/1831	Palambam	Cork	NSW	0	116	0	2	Geo. Willis	130	
29/04/1831	Jane I	Cork	NSW	130	0	2	0	James Baigrie	190	
24/06/1831	Hooghly (3)	Cork	NSW	0	184	0	0	Peter Jn Reeves	95	
06/08/1831	Asia V (2)	Cork	NSW	217	0	11	0	Harry Ager	118	
16/08/1831	Bussorah Merchant (3)	Dublin	NSW	198	0	0	0	Jn Moncreif	120	
15/10/1831	Norfolk (3)	Cork	NSW	199	0	4	0	Wm Henniker	117	
05/11/1831	Captain Cook (1)	Dublin	NSW	200	0	2	0	Wm Steward	154	
10/11/1831	Pyramus (1)	Cork	NSW	0	149	0	2	Alex Wilson	116	Originated in England
06/02/1832	Southworth (3)	Cork	NSW	0	134	0	1	Jn J. Coombes	129	
18/03/1832	City of Edinburgh (2)	Cork	NSW	139	0	0	0	Giles Wade	101	
10/05/1832	Eliza II (4)	Cork	NSW	198	0	2	0	Jn S. Groves	119	

Date	Ship	Port	Colony					Surgeon	
01/07/1832	Dunvegan Castle (2)	Dublin	NSW	200	0	0	0	Jn Duff	107
08/10/1832	Roslin Castle (3)	Cork	NSW	195	0	1	0	Wm Richards	120
05/11/1832	Surrey II	Cork	NSW	0	139	0	0	Wm Veale	124
21/02/1833	Portland (2)	Cork	NSW	192	0	8	0	Wm Ascough	125
15/04/1833	Caroline	Cork	NSW	0	120	0	0	Alex McDonald	113
04/06/1833	Royal Admiral (2)	Dublin	NSW	220	0	5	0	Dav. Fotheringham	144
24/07/1833	Java	Cork	NSW	206	0	5	0	Jn Todd	117
06/09/1833	Royal Sovereign (1)	Dublin	NSW	170	0	2	0	Jn Henderson	135
29/10/1833	Parmelia (2)	Cork	NSW	220	0	2	0	James Gilbert	124
16/02/1834	James Laing	Dublin	NSW	200	0	3	0	Geoff Tomlin	133
25/05/1834	Andromeda II (3)	Cork	NSW	0	175	0	2	Ben Gales	115
27/07/1834	Blenheim I (1)	Cork	NSW	200	0	2	0	James Temple Brown	110
27/09/1834	Royal Admiral (3)	Dublin	NSW	203	0	2	0	Dav. Fotheringham	117
21/10/1834	Forth	Cork	NSW	196	0	1	0	Hy. Hutton	105
27/10/1834	Lady Kennaway	Cork	VDL	293	0	19	0	Thos Bolton	109

08/01/1835	Neva (2)	Cork	NSW	0	150	0	144	Benjamin H. Peck	Wrecked	Numbers reflect the 150 named convicts embarked (per Appendix II) and mentioned in Peck's statement to the enquiry. Whilst Bateson claimed that 151 convicts embarked, he may have been in error, or one convict may have been re-landed
15/03/1835	Hero	Dublin	NSW	199	0	2	0	Harry C. Dowson	169	
12/06/1835	Blackwell	Cork	NSW	150	0	0	0	Dalrymple Dowson	109	
23/06/1835	Lady McNaghten	Dublin	NSW	300	0	2	0	Geoff Hustwick	125	
24/08/1835	Hive (2)	Cork	NSW	250	0	2	0	Jn Nutting	108	Wrecked off NSW
28/10/1835	Roslin Castle (5)	Cork	NSW	0	165	0	3	Wm Richards	120	
09/01/1836	Surrey I (9)	Cork	NSW	227	0	5	0	Geo. Sinclair	129	

19/02/1836	Thomas Harrison	Cork	NSW	0	112	0	0	Thos O. Harrison	111
21/05/1836	Waterloo (5)	Cork	NSW	224	0	2	0	Jn Cow	108
05/07/1836	Captain Cook (3)	Cork	NSW	229	0	1	0	Geo. W. Brown	131
20/08/1836	Pyramus (2)	Cork	NSW	0	120	0	0	Geo. N. Livesay	116
27/08/1836	Earl Grey (1)	Cork	NSW	291	0	3	0	James Talbert	126
13/09/1836	St Vincent (1)	Cork	NSW	191	0	1	0	James Muddle	114
24/01/1837	Margaret (1)	Cork	NSW	0	153	0	2	Ed. Canney	126
16/03/1837	Heber	Dublin	NSW	218	0	1	0	Jn Campbell	118
19/04/1837	Calcutta II	Dublin	NSW	340	0	10	0	Joseph Brown	108
11/08/1837	Sir Charles Forbes (4)	Dublin	NSW	0	148	0	1	James Leslie	136
27/08/1837	Neptune II	Dublin	NSW	200	0	3	0	Joseph Nagle	128
28/11/1837	William Jardine (1)	Dublin	NSW	212	0	2	0	Jn Crosbie	139
29/11/1837	Diamond	Cork	NSW	0	162	0	1	James F. Bisset	114
27/04/1838	Westmoreland (3)	Dublin	NSW	217	0	4	0	Jn Brigstock	117
11/05/1838	Clyde I (3)	Dublin	NSW	190	0	0	0	Jn Matches	122
01/09/1838	Margaret (2)	Dublin	NSW	0	167	0	1	Ed. Canney	126
08/09/1838	Elphinstone (3)	Dublin	NSW	232	0	0	0	Thos Fremlin	112
18/02/1839	Whitby	Dublin	NSW	0	133	0	1	Thos Wellbank	125
22/02/1839	Waverley (1)	Dublin	NSW	176	0	0	0	James Morgan	115
19/05/1839	Blenheim I (3)	Dublin	NSW	200	0	4	0	Jn Grey	131

06/07/1839	Middlesex	Dublin	NSW	200	0	8	0	Charles Munro	203	
18/08/1839	Minerva II (2)	Dublin	NSW	0	118	0	2	Geoff Brown	130	
17/09/1839	Nautilus (2)	Dublin	NI	200	0	1	0	H. F. Alloway	145	
11/11/1839	Augusta Jessie (3)	Dublin	NI	161	0	1	0	J. S. Sparke	136	
05/03/1840	Isabella II	Dublin	NSW	0	119	0	0	Alex McAusland	141	
28/04/1840	King William	Dublin	NSW	180	0	0	0	Geoff Thomas	111	
30/04/1840	Margaret (3)	Dublin	NSW	0	131	0	1	Ed. Canney	109	
10/07/1840	Pekoe	Dublin	NSW	180	0	3	0	Sampson Keen	119	
19/08/1840	Egyptian (2)	Dublin	VDL	170	0	0	0	Jn Skelton	115	
27/11/1840	Mary Ann III (2)	Dublin	VDL	0	125	0	1	Adolphus Holton	112	
16/12/1840	British Sovereign	Dublin	VDL	180	0	0	0	Jn Cow	92	
25/04/1841	Waverley (2)	Dublin	VDL	176	0	2	0	James Morgan	140	
07/08/1841	Prince Regent II (2)	Dublin	VDL	181	0	3	0	Jn T. Barclay	149	
12/08/1841	Mexborough	Dublin	VDL	0	145	0	2	Jn H. Bridgeman	136	
15/11/1841	Richard Webb	Dublin	VDL	193	0	4	0	Robert McLachlan	109	
10/04/1842	Hope	Dublin	VDL	0	139	0	2	Jn Goss	129	
01/05/1842	Isabella Watson	Dublin	VDL	197	0	2	0	Jn A. McDonald	94	
10/07/1842	Kinnear (1)	Dublin	VDL	174	0	2	0	Wm Liddesdale	105	
04/09/1842	Waverley (3)	Dublin	VDL	0	149	0	0	James Morgan	102	
22/09/1842	Navarino (2)	Dublin	VDL	180	0	2	0	Chris A. Warning	110	

20/12/1842	North Briton	Dublin	VDL	179	0	1	0	Thos Fyall	105
09/05/1843	Constant	Dublin	VDL	204	0	3	0	Jn Hemery	112
10/05/1843	East London	Dublin	VDL	0	133	0	17	James Parley	133
12/08/1843	Orator	Dublin	VDL	170	0	1	0	Wm Tayt	101
21/09/1843	Duke of Richmond	Dublin	VDL	111	0	0	0	Dav. Clarke	103
05/03/1844	Greenlaw	Dublin	VDL	0	120	0	5	Jn Edgar	119
09/04/1844	Cadet (1)	Dublin	VDL	164	0	0	0	Jn C. Hillman	137
14/07/1844	Emily II	Dublin	VDL	205	0	0	0	Harry H. Greaves	108
25/09/1844	Phoebe	Dublin	VDL	0	129	0	1	Wm Dale	99
15/02/1845	Elizabeth & Henry	Dublin	VDL	200	0	1	0	Clarke	114
19/05/1845	Ratcliffe (1)	Dublin	VDL	215	0	0	0	James Gilbert	103
02/09/1845	Tasmania (2)	Dublin	VDL	0	140	0	1	Wm Black	93
23/09/1845	Samuel Boddington	Dublin	VDL	143	0	0	0	Harry Tamott	117
19/04/1846	Lord Auckland (2)	Dublin	VDL	180	0	4	0	Robert Brown	120
11/11/1846	Tory (2)	Dublin	NI	200	0	5	0	Jn Young	127
22/11/1846	Arabian	Dublin	VDL	0	150	0	1	Jn Robertson	95
18/07/1847	Waverley (4)	Dublin	VDL	0	134	0	5	James Morgan	99
24/01/1848	John Calvin (2)	Dublin	VDL	0	171	0	1	Jn Davison	115
16/06/1848	Kinnear (2)	Dublin	VDL	0	144	0	5	Robert Heard	113
20/09/1848	Pestonjee Bomanjee (3)	Dublin	VDL	300	0	2	0	Jn Baker	104

Date	Ship	Port	Dest.					Captain	
11/10/1848	Lord Auckland (3)	Dublin	VDL	0	200	0	1	Thos Bacon	101
1848	Blenheim II (1)	Dublin	VDL	300	0	1	0	A. S. Watson	Unknown
05/04/1849	Maria II	Dublin	VDL	0	166	0	1	F. W. Plank	109
23/05/1849	Hyderabad (2)	Dublin	VDL	300	0	3	0	T. A. Castle	95
26/06/1849	Australasia	Dublin	VDL	0	200	0	3	James Connell	95
17/12/1849	Earl Grey (4)	Dublin	VDL	0	240	0	4	H. E. Landesdowne	143
13/09/1850	Hyderabad (3)	Q'town	VDL	287	0	0	0	T. A. Castle	91
20/12/1850	London (2)	Dublin	VDL	288	0	3	0	J. Sceales	89
1850	Duke of Cornwall	Dublin	VDL	0	200	0	2	Jn Whitehead	Unknown
24/01/1851	Blackfriar	Dublin	VDL	0	261	0	1	T. Greeves	125
29/07/1851	Blenheim II (3)	Cork	VDL	310	0	2	0	Alex S. Molison	94
24/09/1851	Rodney (2)	Q'town	VDL	300	0	0	0	Alex MacLean	87
28/12/1851	John William Dare	Dublin	VDL	0	172	0	3	Thos Walters	146
30/04/1852	Lord Dalhousie (1)	Cork	VDL	324	0	2	0	W. T. Ferris	106
08/06/1852	Martin Luther	Dublin	VDL	0	212	0	0	Ken Ross	85
29/09/1852	Lord Auckland (4)	Cork	VDL	248	0	2	0	Geo. Thompson	122
17/11/1852	Midlothian	Dublin	VDL	0	168	0	1	J. Gibson	99
24/11/1852	Rodney (3)	Cork	VDL	342	0	3	0	Alex MacLean	80
02/06/1853	Phoebe Dunbar	K'town	WA	295	0	10	0	T. Michie	89
Total				28,746	8,806	465	249		

Appendix I

Notes:

This table is constructed primarily from the work of Charles Bateson as published in his book *The Convict Ships, 1787–1868*. Where Bateson's work is expanded on, the source material for such expansion is noted in the 'Notes' column of this table. Where Roman numerals appear next to the name of a ship, they formed a part of that vessel's name. Where Arabic numerals appear within brackets next to the name of a ship, they represent the number of the convict voyage being undertaken by that vessel, per Bateson's method. For example, '*Asia I* (3)' refers to the third convict voyage of the *Asia I*. It should be remembered that most convict voyages departed from Britain. Thus, the first two convict voyages undertaken by the *Asia I* do not appear on this table.

K'town denotes Kingstown (now Dun Laoghaire) – an artificial harbour just south of Dublin Bay.

Q'town denotes Queenstown (now Cobh) – part of Cork's lower harbour.

NSW denotes New South Wales.

VDL denotes Van Diemen's Land.

WA denotes Western Australia.

NI denotes Norfolk Island.

Appendix II

THE *NEVA*'S CONVICTS

	Name	Age	Place of conviction	Date of conviction	Crime	Term of transportation	Sources
1	Jane McIlvenna	33	Antrim	28 January 1834	Theft of a hat	7 yrs	*Belfast Commercial Chronicle*, 1 February 1834
2	Mary Jordan	39	Antrim	April 1834	Larceny	7 yrs	*Belfast Commercial Chronicle*, 23 April 1834
3	Mary Anne Develin	23	Antrim	April 1834	Receiving stolen goods		*Belfast Commercial Chronicle*, 23 April 1834
4	Rose Ann Hyland	24	Antrim	June 1834	Stealing money	7 yrs	NAI/MFGS51/042, Kilmainham HRA/1/18, pp. 147–8; TAHO, CON13/1/8, CON16/1/1 & CON40/1/5
5	Esther Raw	14	Antrim	2 July 1834	Theft of a cloak	7 yrs	*Belfast Commercial Chronicle*, 7 July 1834
6	Mary McQuillan	27	Antrim	24 July 1834	Stealing a substantial sum of money	7 yrs	*The Belfast Commercial Chronicle*, 27 July 1834
7	Mary Smith	30	Armagh				
8	Martha McClure	46	Armagh	October 1833	Breaking and entering	7 yrs	*Newry Commercial Telegraph*, 22 October 1833
9	Sarah Gallagher	50	Armagh				
10	Mary Ann Hughes	18	Armagh				

	Name	Age	County	Date	Offence	Sentence	Source
11	Mary McCarthy	30	Clare	March 1834	Stealing wearing apparel	7 yrs	*Limerick Chronicle*, 1 March 1834
11a	Patrick	3 y 6 m	Clare	N/A	N/A	N/A	
12	Bridget Kennedy	23	Carlow				
13	Mary Headon	30	Carlow	22 October 1834	Larceny	7 yrs	*Carlow Morning Post*, 25 October 1834
13a	Elizabeth	1 y 1 m	Carlow	N/A	N/A	N/A	
14	Catherine Dolan	25	Cavan				
15	Rose Ann Dunn	20	Cavan	Summer 1832	Vagrancy	7 yrs	TAHO, CON13/1/8, CON16/1/1 & CON40/1/3
16	Catherine Murray	28	Cavan				
17	Margaret Drury	23	Cavan	2 March 1833	Theft of a watch and seal	7 yrs	*Impartial Reporter*, 3 March 1833. TAHO, CON13/1/8, CON16/1/1 & CON40/1/3
18	Mary Gaffney	28	Cavan	March 1834	Larceny	14 yrs	*Enniskillen Chronicle*, 13 March 1834
19	Catherine Molloy	40	Cavan				
20	Catherine Rahill	36	Cavan				

No.	Name	Age	County	Date	Crime	Sentence	Source
21	Jane Cruise	25	Cavan				
22	Louisa Mellefont	47	Cork	March 1833	Forgery	Life	*The Constitution or Cork Advertiser*, 26 March 1833
23	Mary Russell	32	Cork	September 1833	Theft of cloth	7 yrs	NAI/MFGS/51/008-9, Cork County Prison Register
23a	John	5 y	Cork	N/A	N/A	N/A	
24	Margaret Kelliher	20	Cork	Spring 1834	Theft of evening apparel	7 yrs	NAI/MFGS/51/023, Cork City Gaol Register
25	Mary Sullivan	20	Cork				
26	Honora Buckley	21	Cork				
26a	William	5 m	Cork	N/A	N/A	N/A	
27	Mary Donovan	20	Cork	Spring 1834	Stealing money	7 yrs	NAI/MFGS/51/023, Cork City Gaol Register
28	Mary McNamara	21	Cork				
29	Margaret McShee	19	Donegal	March 1834	Stealing wearing apparel	7 yrs	*Enniskillen Chronicle*, 27 March 1834
30	Rachael Robinson	19	Down				
31	Mary Campbell	19	Down				
32	Mary Johnston	28	Down	March 1834	Vagrancy	7 yrs	*Belfast Commercial Chronicle*, 2 April 1834

33	Anne Smith	19	Down	March 1834	Vagrancy	7 yrs	*Belfast Commercial Chronicle*, 2 April 1834
34	Jane Gordon	19	Down	21 March 1834	Theft of scissors	Unknown	*Belfast Commercial Chronicle*, 24 March 1834
35	Margaret Fulton	60	Down	21 March 1834	Two separate thefts of shirts and shifts	7 yrs	*Belfast Commercial Chronicle*, 24 March 1834 & 2 April 1834
36	Catherine Kennedy	19	Down	8 April 1834	Theft of a cloak and separate theft of silver coin	7 yrs	*Newry Examiner*, 9 April 1834
37	Eleanor McMullan	18	Down	April 1834	Theft of three yards of muslin	7 yrs	*Newry Commercial Telegraph*, 15 April 1834
38	Mary Anne Stewart	20	Down	April 1834	Theft of three yards of muslin	7 yrs	*The Newry Commercial Telegraph*, 15 April 1834
39	Anne Rogers	17	Down				
40	Cath O'Neil or Crawford	43	Down				
41	Ellen Magennis	23	Down	30 July 1834	Theft of shoes and other articles	7 yrs	*Newry Examiner*, 8 August 1834
42	Mary Redmond	24	Dublin	1 August 1833	Theft of cloak and silver spoons	7 yrs	NAI/MFGS/51/042, Kilmainham Prison Register
43	Jane Williams	24	Dublin	16 June 1834	Theft of ten barrels of oats	7 yrs	*Evening Freeman*, 17 June 1834 & NAI/MFGS/51/042, Kilmainham Prison Register

43a	Mary	5 m	Dublin	N/A	N/A	N/A	NAI/MFGS/51/042, Kilmainham Prison Register
44	Bridget McDonnell	27	Dublin	15 October 1834	Theft of banknotes	7 yrs	
45	Mary or Cath Fitzgerald	37	Dublin				
46	Martha Rochford	53	Dublin				
47	Judith Connor	30	Dublin				
48	Anne Kelly	21	Dublin				
49	Cath Kavanagh or Kenny	24	Dublin				
50	Jane Fox	17	Dublin				
51	Anne Dunne	20	Dublin	26 February 1834	Theft of money	7 yrs	Evening Freeman, 27 February 1834
52	Julia Delany	33	Dublin				
52a	Mary	3 y 6 m	Dublin	N/A	N/A	N/A	
52b	Julia	10 m	Dublin	N/A	N/A	N/A	
53	Sarah White or Nicholson	29	Dublin				
54	Mary Doyle	36	Dublin				
54a	Bess	9 y	Dublin	N/A	N/A	N/A	

55	Eliza Cotter	21	Dublin	March 1834	Stealing several articles of plate	7 yrs	*Evening Freeman*, 27 February 1834
56	Eliza Brien	31	Dublin				
57	Mary Strahan or Boardman	18	Dublin	March 1834	Petty larcenies (old offender)	7 yrs	*Evening Freeman*, 3 April 1834
58	Margaret Halloran	23	Dublin		Petty larcenies (old offender)	7 yrs	*Evening Freeman*, 3 April 1834
59	Bridget Fegan or Boranna	25	Dublin				
60	Margaret Harford or Murphy	25	Dublin				
61	Eleanor Hughes or Cardiff	35	Dublin				
61a	Margaret	6 y	Dublin	N/A	N/A	N/A	
62	Mary Fox or Scott or Higgins	36	Dublin				
62a	Catherine	11 y	Dublin	N/A	N/A	N/A	
62b	Mary	8 y	Dublin	N/A	N/A	N/A	
63	Eliza Farrell or Halpin	30	Dublin				

63a	Michael	3 y 6 m	Dublin	N/A	N/A	N/A	
64	Eleanor Heysberry	35	Dublin				
64a	Thomas	5 y 6 m	Dublin	N/A	N/A	N/A	
65	Mary A. McDonnel or Curry	17	Dublin				
66	Rose Connolly or Davis	19	Dublin				
67	Margaret Ryan or Lunt	29	Dublin			N/A	
67a	Mary Anne	7 y	Dublin	N/A	N/A	N/A	
68	Elizabeth Murphy	44	Dublin				
69	Catherine Heath	20	Dublin				
70	Catherine Brady	18	Dublin	August 1834	Theft of money, jewellery and wearing apparel	7 yrs	*Clonmel Advertiser*, 6 August 1834; *Dublin Evening Mail*, 1 and 3 September 1834; *Evening Freeman*, 30 August 1834

71	Mary Cassidy	19	Dublin	6 September 1834	Theft of a pocket handkerchief	7 yrs	*Clonmel Advertiser*, 6 September 1834
72	Mary Reynolds	18	Dublin	7 September 1834	Theft of valuable property from the house in which she served	7 yrs	*Morning Register*, 8 September 1834
73	Esther Brady	42	Dublin	1 September 1834	Theft of a stone weight of starch	7 yrs	*Dublin Evening Mail*, 3 September 1834
74	Mary Hynis	18	Dublin				
75	Mary A. Charles	16	Dublin				
76	Mary McDermott	40	Fermanagh	July 1834	Stealing or having in their possession knowing to be stolen, a silver watch, and seal keys	7 yrs	*Enniskillen Chronicle and Erne Packet*, 27 July 1834
77	Marg Kennedy	22	Galway				
78	Bridget Houlaghan	19	Galway	4 January 1834	Larceny	7 yrs	*Connaught Journal*, 9 January 1834
79	Margaret Doyle	26	Galway	22 March 1834	Larceny	Unknown	*Galway Advertiser*, 29 March 1834

80	Mary Sullivan	22	Galway					
81	Bridget Concannon	28	Galway					
82	Anne Carter	33	Galway	18 July 1834	Theft of bedding and wearing apparel	7 yrs		*Connaught Journal*, 21 July 1834
83	Mary Kerrigan	30	Galway	18 July 1834	Theft of a table cloth	7 yrs		*Connaught Journal*, 21 July 1834
84	Mary Slattery	22	Kerry	14 January 1834	Theft of silver spoons worth £10	7 yrs		*Tralee Mercury*, 18 January 1834 & TAHO, CON40/1/3, CON13/1/8 & CON16/1/1
85	Ellen Mullane	35	Kerry	11 March 1834	Larceny	7 yrs		*Tralee Mercury*, 15 March 1834
86	Ellen White	29	Kerry	11 March 1834	Larceny	7 yrs		*Tralee Mercury*, 15 March 1834
87	Honora O'Brien	20	Kerry	11 March 1834	Theft of wearing apparel	7 yrs		*Kerry Evening Post*, 12 March 1834 & *Tralee Mercury*, 15 March 1834
88	Catherine Reilly	35	Kerry	June 1834	Larceny	7 yrs		*Western Herald*, 30 June 1834
88a	Honora	7 y	Kerry	N/A	N/A	N/A		
88b	Catherine	6 m	Kerry	N/A	N/A	N/A		
89	Margaret Hassett	21	Kerry	June 1834	Larceny	7 yrs		*Western Herald*, 30 June 1834

	Name	Age	County	Date	Crime	Sentence	Source
89a	Mary	3 y		N/A	N/A	N/A	
90	Catherine Connor	24	Kerry		Theft of a sheet	7 yrs	*Kerry Evening Post*, 9 July 1834
91	Jane Tims	30	Kildare				
92	Mary Cody	18	Kilkenny	Summer 1834	Larceny from a shop	7 yrs	NAI/CSOOP/1834/106, Calendar of Prisoners for Trial at Kilkenny County Gaol
93	Catherine Cleary	22	Kilkenny	Summer 1834	Stealing banknotes	7 yrs	NAI/CSOOP/1834/106
94	Anne Cullen	21	Kilkenny	Summer 1834	Possessing a stolen cow	Life	NAI/CSOOP/1834/106; TAHO, CON13/1/8, CON16/1/1 & CON40/1/5
95	Mary Sullivan	34	Kilkenny				
95a	James	1 y	Kilkenny	N/A	N/A	N/A	
96	Catherine Donohoe	24	Kilkenny				
97	Bridget Dunn	17	Kings				
98	Catherine Plunkett	29	Kings				
99	Judith Dooley	33	Kings				
100	Eliza Colreany	35	Leitrim	July 1833	Larceny	7 yrs	*Enniskillen Chronicle*, 25 July 1833; *Roscommon & Leitrim Gazette*, 20 July 1833
101	Mary Cullen	26	Leitrim	14 July 1834	Vagrancy	7 yrs	*Roscommon & Leitrim Gazette*, 14 July 1834

No.	Name	Age	Place	Date	Crime	Sentence	Source
102	Mary Rochford	24	Limerick				
103	Mary Clue	24	Limerick				
104	Eliza Smith	26	Limerick				
105	Judith Whealan	20	Limerick				
106	Cath Shanny or Danagher	30	Limerick	January 1834	Larceny	7 yrs	NAI/MFGS51/084-85, Limerick Prison Register
107	Johanna Sweeney	28	Limerick	March 1834	Stealing money and apparel	7 yrs	*Limerick Chronicle*, 8 and 12 March 1834; the Limerick Prison register recorded Johanna Sweeney's age as 30 – however, the assignment list made her 28
108	Johanna Galvin	64	Limerick	March 1834	Stealing money and apparel	7 yrs	*Limerick Chronicle*, 8 and 12 March 1834; the Limerick Prison register recorded Johanna Galvin's age as 60 – however, the assignment list made her 64
109	Catherine Ryan	30	Limerick	March 1834	Larceny of silk	7 yrs	NAI/MFGS51/084-85, Limerick Prison Register
109a	Michael	1 y 1 m	Limerick	N/A	N/A	N/A	

110	Ellen Galvin	19	Limerick	April 1834	Larceny	7 yrs	NAI/MFGS51/084-85, Limerick Prison Register; TAHO, CON40/1/3, CON13/1/8 & CON16/1/1
111	Lucy Minehan	20	Limerick	April 1834	Larceny	7 yrs	NAI/MFGS51/084-85, Limerick Prison Register
112	Elizabeth Greany	35	Limerick	April 1834	Larceny	7 yrs	NAI/MFGS51/084-85, Limerick Prison Register
113	Mary Hickey	26	Limerick	April 1834	Larceny	7 yrs	NAI/MFGS51/084-85, Limerick Prison Register
114	Anne Frawley	30	Limerick	April 1834	Receipt of stolen goods	7 yrs	NAI/MFGS51/084-85, Limerick Prison Register
114a	Michael	1 y 1 m	Limerick	N/A	N/A	N/A	
115	Honora Sheedy	24	Limerick	April 1834	Larceny	7 yrs	NAI/MFGS51/084-85, Limerick Prison Register
116	Mary Malone	24	Limerick	July 1834	Possession of stolen goods	7 yrs	NAI/MFGS51/084-85, Limerick Prison Register
116a	Catherine	1 y 6 m	Limerick	N/A	N/A	N/A	
117	Jane Hamilton or Connor	28	Londonderry				
117a	Charles	4 y	Londonderry	N/A	N/A	N/A	

118	Mary Williams	21	Longford				
119	Margaret Crane	23	Meath				NAI/MFGS51/042, Kilmainham Register
120	Jane Farrell	31	Meath				NAI/MFGS51/042, Kilmainham Register
121	Catherine Byrne	28	Meath				NAI/MFGS51/042, Kilmainham Register
122	Judith King	23	Meath				NAI/MFGS51/042, Kilmainham Register
123	Anne Stenson	37	Monaghan	March 1833	Highway robbery	Life	*Newry Commercial Telegraph*, 8 March 1833
124	Anne McCardle	24	Monaghan				
125	Mary Smith	26	Queens	13 March 1833	Larceny	7 yrs	NAI/MFGS/51/145, Queens County Prison Register
126	Anne Delaney	35	Queens	23 October 1833	Larceny	7 yrs	NAI/MFGS/51/145, Maryborough Register; *Leinster Express*, 2 November 1833
127	Margaret Brooks	39	Queens	23 October 1833	Larceny	7 yrs	NAI/MFGS/51/145, Maryborough Register; *Leinster Express*, 2 November 1833
127a	Catherine	6 y	Queens	N/A	N/A	N/A	

128	Mary Ryan	33	Queens	8 April 1834	Stealing geese	7 yrs	NAI/MFGS/51/145, Maryborough Register
128a	Patrick	1 y	Queens	N/A	N/A	N/A	
129	Anne Regan	40	Sligo				
129a	Bridget	10 m	Sligo	N/A	N/A	N/A	
130	Bridget Strang	45	Tipperary	March 1834	Sheep stealing	Life	*Clonmel Advertiser*, 29 March 1834
130a	Mary	8 y	Tipperary	N/A	N/A	N/A	
130b	Margaret	3 y	Tipperary	N/A	N/A	N/A	
131	Margaret Condon	23	Tipperary				
132	Cath. McDermott	26	Tipperary				
132a	Ellen	3 y	Tipperary	N/A	N/A	N/A	
132b	John	9 m	Tipperary	N/A	N/A	N/A	
133	Anne McCormick	33	Tyrone				
134	Catherine Gormley	38	Tyrone				
134a	Jane	10 m	Tyrone	N/A	N/A	N/A	
135	Mary Johnston or Gormley	60	Tyrone				
136	Johanna Power	25	Waterford	June 1833	Vagrancy	Unknown	*Waterford Mail*, 17 June 1833

137	Margaret Harrington	30	Waterford				
138	Anne Hixon	22	Waterford	April 1834	Theft of a cloak and a quilt	7 yrs	*Waterford Mail*, 5 March and 12 April 1834
139	Bridget King	21	Wexford	March 1833	Manslaughter	Life	*Impartial Reporter*, 7 March 1833; *Waterford Mail*, 13 March 1833
139a	Patrick	2 y	Wexford	N/A	N/A	N/A	
140	Anne Everington	24	Wexford	March 1834	Theft of money	7 yrs	*Waterford Mail*, 5 March 1834
140a	Mary Anne	2 y	Wexford	N/A	N/A	N/A	
141	Judith Henning	22	Wexford				
142	Mary Martin	24	Wexford	14 July 1834	Theft of wearing apparel	Unknown	*Kilkenny Journal*, 19 July 1834
143	Bridget Lynn	31	Westmeath				
144	Jane Doyle	20	Westmeath	1 March 1834	Stealing 16 shillings	7 yrs	*Athlone Independent*, 12 March 1834
145	Margaret Hamilton	17	Westmeath	1 March 1834	Larceny	Unknown	*Athlone Independent*, 5 March 1834
146	Anne Lynch	28	Westmeath	October 1834	Theft of Oxford grey cloth and a piece of cotton	7 yrs	*Athlone Independent*, 22 October 1834

147	Catherine Lynch	24	Westmeath				
148	Margaret Shaw	50	Westmeath	October 1834	Theft of Oxford grey cloth and a piece of cotton	7 yrs	*Athlone Independent*, 22 October 1834
149	Jane Gaffney	26	Wicklow				
149a	Mary	4 y 6 m	Wicklow	N/A	N/A	N/A	
149b	James	1 y 6 m	Wicklow	N/A	N/A	N/A	
150	Anne Thomas	24	Wicklow				

Appendix II

Notes:

Names and places of conviction established by reference to: SRNSW, Col. Sec. Letters Received (NRS905), Letter No. 39/9405 [4/2441], *Neva* Assignment List. Details of crimes and sentencing established primarily by reference to local newspapers from 1833 and 1834.

Blank boxes imply that appropriate information was unavailable. As digitisation of newspaper sources begins and progresses, further information may become available.

The ages of some convicts vary slightly between different records. Where records are directly referenced in the main text, the convict's age is given as per the record in question. In this appendix the convict's age is given as per the surviving assignment list (SRNSW, Col. Sec. Letters Received (NRS905), Letter No. 39/9405 [4/2441], *Neva* Assignment List). The difference is usually accounted for by the period of time between arrest and the *Neva*'s sinking, a period of up to 24 months. In a few cases that two-year period cannot account for the discrepancy. It is thought that reasons such as transcription error by office clerks, ignorance of date of birth by some convicts, lies about age, or other miscellaneous errors account for these few discrepancies.

Every effort was made to ensure that the women on the assignment list were matched correctly with women in various Irish records. Wherever Irish records generated two possible matches for a woman on the assignment list, those Irish records were ignored. Thus, every woman for whom Irish records are referenced was the only possible match for an identical name on the assignment list.

Appendix III

THE *NEVA*'S FREE WOMEN AND THEIR CHILDREN

County	Woman's name	Children's names	Children's ages
Cork city	Johanna Sullivan		
Wexford	Mary Browne or Bulgers	Miles Moses Ellen	14 11 9
Louth	Catherine Langan or Quinn	Thomas Christopher	19 13
Longford	Mary Dininy or McCue	John	9
Tipperary	Mary Street or Hickey	Mary	9
Westmeath	Rose Doyle	Michael	8
Longford	Mary Ruien (Ryan)	Elizabeth	9
Tipperary	Mary Brophy or Hunt	Catherine Margaret Winifred Johana James Catherine (daughter of Catherine above)	20 15 12 9 7 1½
Mayo	Jane O'Hara or McLoughlin	Mary Bridget Jane Elizabeth Edward James	20 19 17 15 14 12

Appendix IV

The *Neva*'s Crew[1]

John Stephenson	Surgeon
B. H. Peck	Master
Joseph Bennett	First Mate
W. H. Laws	Second Mate
Charles Hagman	Third Mate
John May	Fourth Mate
Henry Hollis	Steward
Edwin Forbes	Carpenter
Anthony Edwards	Cook
William Wright	Seaman
Mr Miller	do
William Kidney	do
Peter Robinson	do
Charles Willson	do
Thomas Sharp	do
Thomas Haines[2]	do
Edward Calthorpe[3]	do
George Brown	do
Henry Pearson	do
Robert Bullard	do

Frederick Pengally	do
William Bridger	do
John Faisey	do
John Foley	do
John Murray	do
Joseph Firrell	boy
Thomas Quinn	boy

Endnotes

Abbreviations and Acronyms

ADM	Admiralty
CON	Convict Papers
CSOOP	Chief Secretary's Office Official Papers
CSORP	Chief Secretary's Office Registered Papers
FS	Free Settlers Papers
HMSO	Her Majesty's Stationery Office
HRA	Historical Records of Australia, Series 1, Volume 18 (1/18)
NAI	National Archives of Ireland
NSWSL	New South Wales State Library
PRO	Public Record Office
SRNSW	State Records Authority of New South Wales
TAHO	Tasmanian Archive and Heritage Office, Convict Department (CON)

1 Ireland and Transportation

1 Shaw, *Convicts and the Colonies*, p. 36.
2 *Ibid.*, p. 143.
3 *Ibid.*, p. 166.
4 *Ibid.*
5 When the *Neva* is excluded, the female mortality rate is 1.2 per cent.
6 Robson, 'The Convict Settlers of Australia', pp. 74–5, in Daniels, *Convict Women*, p. 52; Oxley, *Convict Maids*, p. 135.

7   Soon after the emptying of the hulks in 1837, Cork's female depot at Elizabeth Fort was converted to a constabulary barracks (OS Map 1842). The gaol at North Gate Bridge was removed in 1826, whilst the gaol at the South Gate stood only until 1818 (Middle Parish Chronicle). The city had a gaol at Sunday's Well, and the county housed its criminals near Western Road. The Sixteenth Report of the Inspectors General on the General State of the Prisons of Ireland 1838 (House of Commons, Parliamentary Papers) did not report on the Cork depot, where its predecessors had, so it seems that Elizabeth Fort depot ceased to function in November 1837. The inspectors' fifteenth report indicated that plans to create a convict depot at Newgate in Dublin were proceeding. However, these plans were continually frustrated by overcrowding in various Dublin prisons, and Kilmainham continued to provide temporary accommodation for male convicts (National Archives of Ireland (NAI), Chief Secretary's Office Registered Papers (CSORP) 1838/2333). By 1838 Grangegorman provided a similar function for females (NAI/MFGS/51/027, Grangegorman Prison Register & House of Commons Parliamentary Papers, Sixteenth Report of the Inspectors General on the General State of the Prisons of Ireland 1838). By 1839 the expectation was that all convicts would be transferred to Dublin for transportation (NAI/CSORP/1839/123, 132).

8   Shaw, *Convicts and the Colonies*, estimates that 20 per cent of convicts transported from Ireland were convicted in Dublin.

2 Kilmainham

1   NAI/MFGS51/042, Kilmainham Prison Register.

2   *Impartial Reporter*, 14 March 1833; Tasmanian Archive and Heritage Office (TAHO), Convict Papers (CON) 40/1/3, CON13/1/8, CON16/1/1.

3   Kelly, *A History of Kilmainham Gaol*, p. 29.

4   Historical Records of Australia (HRA), Series 1, Volume 18 (1/18), p. 148; TAHO, CON40/1/3, CON13/1/8 & CON16/1/1.

5   HRA/1/18, p. 73. Whilst there is no known record that pinpoints Drury's location in the prison, it is likely that she was held at the rear of the west wing nearest the female exercise yards as marked in the Park Neville diagrams from the 1830s (Kilmainham Archive). In addition to its proximity to the female exercise yards, the west wing also housed the matron, who was charged with the supervision of all female prisoners. It is considered likely that all female prisoners were held near the matron and close to their exercise yards. The west wing, as Drury probably saw it, was slightly altered shortly after she left it, and later detained the 1916 rebels before their execution.

6   O'Sullivan, *Every Dark Hour*, p. 21.

7   NAI/MFGS51/042, Kilmainham Register.

8   *Ibid.*

9   *Newry Commercial Telegraph*, 8 March 1833.

10   NAI/MFGS51/042, Kilmainham Register.

11   *Impartial Reporter*, 7 March 1833; *Waterford Mail*, 13 March 1833.

12   State Records Authority of New South Wales (SRNSW), Col. Sec. Letters Received (NRS905), Letter No. 39/9405 (4/2441), *Neva* Assignment List.

13   NAI/MFGS51/145, Queens County Register.

14   NAI/MFGS51/042, Kilmainham Register.

15   The *Cork Evening Herald* of 15 January 1834 recorded that eighty-one prisoners had originated in Dublin and arrived in Cork aboard the *Erin*. As only fifty-four came from Kilmainham (NAI/MFGS51/042), twenty-seven prisoners came from elsewhere. At that time Newgate was the only other Dublin prison that housed female convicts under sentence of transportation (House of Commons, Parliamentary Papers, The Eleventh & Twelfth Reports of the Inspectors General on the General State of the Prisons of Ireland 1833 & 1834).

16   *Cork Evening Herald*, 8 January 1834.

17   *Ibid.*, 20 January 1834.

18   *Cork Mercantile Chronicle*, 10 January 1834.

19   *Cork Evening Herald*, 10 January 1834.

20   *Cork Mercantile Chronicle*, 24 January 1834.

21   Public Record Office (PRO), Admiralty (ADM)/101/62/4, Surgeon's Journal *Pyramus*.

22   Cadogan (ed.), *Lewis' Cork*, pp. 203–4. Initially published in 1837, Samuel Lewis' publication *A Topographical Dictionary of Ireland* is the primary source for contemporary accounts of Irish places throughout this book.

23   NAI/CSORP/1835/2430; CSORP/1829/10296; CSORP/1825/11274; CSORP/1822/72; CSORP/1822/2544; CSORP/1822/3193; *Cork Historical and Archaeological Society Journal*, Vol. 93, 1988. The exact location of Cork's convict hulk, as approved by the chief secretary's office, was attained by reference to CSORP/1822/2550.

24   Rynne, 'An Archaeological Survey of Elizabeth Fort'. In addition, Thomas Holt's map of Cork city in 1832 identifies Elizabeth Fort as a 'Convict Depot'. The Inspectors General Reports on the General State of the Prisons of Ireland 1823–1837 indicate that there had been a convict depot for both genders in an old barracks in Cork since before 1823.

25   House of Commons, Parliamentary Papers, Twelfth Report of the Inspectors General on the General State of the Prisons of Ireland 1834.

26   *Cork Mercantile Chronicle*, 2 May & 16 May 1834. Thirty-three women identical in name and place of conviction, whilst similar in age (ages often vary as many people in nineteenth-century Ireland did not know their date of birth) were, according to the Kilmainham Register, shipped on board the *Erin* to Cork, and then appeared on the *Andromeda II* assignment list.

27   House of Commons, Parliamentary Papers, Twelfth and Thirteenth Reports of the Inspectors General on the General State of the Prisons of Ireland 1834 & 1835.

28   *Cork Mercantile Chronicle*, 11 August 1834. The convict was named as Dillon from Clonmel, his accomplice simply as McDonnell.

3   The Second Shipment

1   NAI/MFGS51/042, Kilmainham Register.

2   The *Neva*'s assignment list described Mary Williams as a five-month-old infant. This implies that the child was born in August 1834. The *Evening Freeman* of 17 June 1834 described Williams and her co-accused as 'rather decent looking people'.

3   *Dublin Evening Mail*, 18 June 1834.

4   *Evening Freeman*, 17 June 1834.

5   Mayberry, *Irish Convicts to New South Wales*, Internet-based database: http://members.pcug.org.au/~ppmay (Mayberry website).

6   House of Commons, Parliamentary Papers, Eleventh, Twelfth & Thirteenth Reports of the Inspectors General on the General State of the Prisons of Ireland 1833, 1834 & 1835.

7   NAI/MFGS51/042, Kilmainham Register. The *Enniskillen Chronicle and Erne Packet* of 13 March 1834 details Gaffney's conviction for larceny.

8   *Enniskillen Chronicle and Erne Packet*, 27 July 1834.

9   Mayberry website, http://members.pcug.org.au/~ppmay.

10   NAI/MFGS51/042, Kilmainham Register; *Athlone Independent*, 5 March 1834.

11   *Newry Commercial Telegraph*, 22 October 1833.

12   NAI/MFGS51/042, Kilmainham Register.

13   *Enniskillen Chronicle and Erne Packet*, 27 March 1834.

14   *Galway Advertiser*, 2 August 1834.

15   *Newry Commercial Telegraph*, 15 April 1834.

16   *Ibid.*, 28 March 1834.

17   *Belfast Commercial Chronicle*, 2 April 1834.

18   *Newry Commercial Telegraph*, 11 April 1834; *Newry Examiner*, 6 August 1834.

19   *Belfast Commercial Chronicle*, 24 March 1834.

20   *Ibid.*, 7 July 1834; NAI/MFGS51/042, Kilmainham Register; HRA/1/18, pp. 147–8.

21   *Belfast Commercial Chronicle*, 1 February 1834, 23 April 1834 & 7 July 1834.

22 *Ibid.*, 27 July 1834.

23 NAI/MFGS51/042, Kilmainham Register; *Waterford Mail*, 5 March 1834.

24 NAI/MFGS51/042, Kilmainham Register.

25 *Carlow Morning Post*, 25 October 1834.

26 *Athlone Independent*, 22 October 1834. The newspaper's 'Linch' is a less-frequent variant of the spelling of 'Lynch'.

27 Crowley, *A Drift of 'Derwent Ducks'*, p. 98.

28 The shipping columns of the *Cork Evening Herald*, *Cork Mercantile Chronicle* and *Southern Reporter* did not record the arrival of any other female convict transport (other than the *Andromeda*) in the time between the *Erin*'s first arrival and the departure of the *Neva*. Thus, the women held in Newgate and convicted after *Erin*'s first sailing can have arrived in Cork only as part of the second shipment. The situation at Newgate had not changed since the inspectors' reports of 1833 and 1834, and it was still the only other Dublin prison that held female convicts under sentence of transportation (House of Commons, Parliamentary Papers, Thirteenth Report of the Inspectors General on the General State of the Prisons of Ireland 1835; NAI/CSORP/1834/625, NAI/MFGS51/140, Richmond Register).

29 *Dublin Evening Mail*, 3 September 1834.

30 *Ibid.*, 1 September 1834.

31 *Evening Freeman*, 30 August 1834.

32 *Clonmel Advertiser*, 6 August 1834.

33 *Evening Freeman*, 30 August 1834.

34 *Ibid.*, 27 February 1834.

35 *Ibid.*, 3 April 1834.

36 *Ibid.*, 4 March 1834.

37 *Cork Mercantile Chronicle*, 17 November 1834, and *Southern Reporter*, 18 November 1834, reported that the *Erin* arrived on 16 November. However, the *Cork Evening Herald* and *The Constitution or Cork Advertiser* stated that the ship arrived on 15 November. At this distance in time, the only reasonable

The Wreck of the *Neva*

conclusion is that the *Erin* arrived during the early hours of 16 November, generally considered the night of 15 November.

38 NAI/CSORP/1834/4213, CSORP/1835/2430 & CSORP/1834/4186.

39 *Cork Evening Herald*, 14 November 1834.

4   Logistics and Operation

1 Mawer, *Most Perfectly Safe*, pp. 56–77. The *George III* that was wrecked off Bruny Island was certainly the same ship that had tendered for the *Neva* assignment, as only one ship of that name appeared on Lloyd's Registers for 1834 and 1835. By further coincidence, a ship called *Enchantress* was also wrecked off Van Diemen's Land in 1835. However, the tonnage and master of the wreck do not match the tonnage of the vessel that tendered for the *Neva's* convicts, so this wreck appears to have been one of the other four ships named *Enchantress* registered by Lloyd's.

2 HRA/1/18 Report by Comptroller of Victualling and Transport Services, p. 276.

3 *Ibid.*

4 *Ibid.*, p. 277; Select Committee on Causes of Shipwrecks, Paper 567, Vol. XVII, p. 373; Parliamentary Papers 1836, Series 3, Vol. 32, Commons Sitting 15 April 1836.

5 Bateson, *The Convict Ships*, p. 89.

6 NAI/CSORP/1834/2778.

7 *Ibid.*

8 NAI, Chief Secretary's Office Official Papers (CSOOP), 1837/392.

9 Shaw, *Convicts and the Colonies*, p. 116.

10 NAI/CSOOP/1837/392.

11 NAI/CSOOP/1839/123 & CSORP/1834/2939.

12 NAI/CSORP/1818/102A.

13 Hughes, *The Fatal Shore*, p. 148.

14 Bateson, *The Convict Ships*, p. 233.

15 *Sydney Monitor*, 29 June 1831.

16   Bateson, *The Convict Ships*, p. 274.
17   For details of Stephenson's service, see his surviving diaries, PRO, ADM101/23/1, ADM101/31/5, ADM101/40/3 & ADM101/73/3; Mawer, *Most Perfectly Safe*, pp. 9–18. For his obituary, see *The Freeman's Journal*, 17 December 1835. For details of his personal life see *The Times*, 14 December 1835.
18   NAI/CSORP/1835/389.
19   PRO, ADM101/31/5 & ADM101/73/3, Surgeons' Journals *Guildford* and *Waterloo*.
20   NAI/CSORP/1835/389.
21   House of Commons, Parliamentary Papers, Twelfth Report of the Inspectors General on the General State of the Prisons of Ireland 1834.
22   Lohan, 'Sources in the National Archives for Research into the Transportation of Irish Convicts to Australia (1791–1853)', pp. 13–28; O'Donnell, *Robert Emmet*, pp. 153, 162, 185, 205, 260, 270–3; NAI/CSORP/1818/C88.
23   NAI/CSORP/1835/389.

5   Cork

1   *The Constitution or Cork Advertiser*, 26 March 1833.
2   NAI/MFGS51/008-9, Cork County Prison Register.
3   NAI/CSORP/1831/3317.
4   Mayberry website, http://members.pcug.org.au/~ppmay.
5   Lohan, 'Sources in the National Archives for Research into the Transportation of Irish Convicts to Australia (1791–1853)', pp. 13–28.
6   Daniels, *Convict Women*, pp. 53–4.
7   *Cork Evening Herald*, 2 May 1834.
8   NAI/MFGS51/084–85, Limerick Prison Register.
9   *The Limerick Chronicle*, 12 March 1834. 'Berrin' was a colloquialism probably derived from the Gaelic word 'beir', referring to a taking, in this case connected to the mythical 'fairies'. 'Philter' is probably a misspelling of 'philtre'. 'Mames' appears to be a colloquialism derived from 'maim'. Although

Bridget Hynes is here referred to by that name, it is more likely
that her name was Bridget Hayes, as entered on the Limerick
Prison Register beneath that of Johanna Galvin. The newspaper
used a slightly different spelling for Johanna Sweeney's
surname. Such variations were common in nineteenth-century
Ireland.

10 *Limerick Chronicle*, 12 March 1834.

11 NAI/MFGS51/084–85, Limerick Prison Register & TAHO,
CON40/1/3, CON13/1/8 & CON16/1/1.

12 Mayberry website, http://members.pcug.org.au/~ppmay.

13 *Clonmel Advertiser*, 29 March 1834.

14 *Galway Advertiser*, 29 March 1834.

15 *Western Herald or Kerry Advertiser*, 30 June 1834.

16 *Tralee Mercury*, 2 July 1834; *Kerry Evening Post*, 2 July 1834.
The latter newspaper reported that Reilly was not to be
transported, but was sentenced to twelve months' hard labour.
However, given that no other Catherine Reilly was convicted
around this time, that Catherine Reilly's name is above that of
Margaret Hassett on the *Neva* assignment list (it was common
for accomplices to appear together), and that the former
newspaper reported that Reilly had received the same sentence
as all her accomplices, it is reasonable to assume that the report
of the *Kerry Evening Post* was incorrect.

17 *Kerry Evening Post*, 9 July 1834. Note that it is mistaken in the
statement that Connor was removed to the hulk. No women
were held aboard the hulk.

18 *Waterford Mail*, 5 March 1834.

19 *Ibid.*, 17 June 1833.

20 TAHO, CON16/1/1.

21 HRA/1/18, Mary Slattery's statement specifically mentioned
her boarding the vessel on 4 January. It is likely that the
Waterford convicts did likewise.

22 *Cork Mercantile Chronicle*, 31 December 1834.

23 These convicts were initially matched with their wives by
reference to the *Neva* free settlers list, and the assignment lists

reproduced on the Mayberry website, http://members.pcug.
org.au/~ppmay.

24 NAI/CSORP/1828/715; SRNSW 4/4013/87, SRNSW 4/2032
(29/4276) & SRNSW 4/2188.

25 SRNSW 4/4012 & 4/2188.

26 NAI, Prisoners Petition Cases (PPC), 3331. Bryan Ryan had
several names and aliases. Various transcriptions of various
handwritten records have resulted in four derivations of his
surname: Ryan, Ruien, Royan and Rovcen.

27 *Westmeath Journal*, 9 March 1826; NAI, Free Settlers Papers
(FS) 1836, B13.

28 Mayberry website, http://members.pcug.org.au/~ppmay.

29 Shaw, *Convicts and the Colonies*, pp. 173–83.

30 Jane was known by two surnames (one being her maiden name):
McLoughlin and O'Hara. A search of the Mayberry website
(http://members.pcug.org.au/~ppmay) for male convicts from
Mayo bearing either of those names unearths only one real
possibility: Edward McLoughlin.

31 NAI/FS/1834/1.

32 Although the task was daunting, and certainly gruelling for
twelve-year-old James McLoughlin, the McLoughlin family
probably arrived in Cork before 5 January. The *Neva*'s assignment
list (or a copy of same) recorded that the family were embarked
with the convicts on 5 January.

33 NAI/CSORP/1825/12423.

6   Farewell to Ireland

1 For references to surgeons visiting the Cork depot days before
departure, see PRO, ADM101/22/6 & ADM101/70/3, Surgeons'
Journals *Edward* and *Surrey II*.

2 *Cork Evening Herald*, 5 January 1835. The journalist in question
was misinformed regarding the numbers departing the depot.
The *Neva* carried 150 female convicts, 13 free settlers and 51
children. At least seven Kerry convicts and their three children
boarded the ship in Cove on 4 January (HRA/1/18, Statement

of Mary Slattery). Thus 13 free settlers, up to 143 convicts and as many as 48 children left Elizabeth Fort. For the purposes of this analysis, those aged over 18 are considered adults. It is worth noting that two of the *Neva*'s 150 convicts were less than 18 years old (see Appendix II).

3   Cadogan (ed.), *Lewis' Cork*, pp. 168–70.

4   *Cork Mercantile Chronicle*, 9 January 1835; *Southern Reporter*, 6, 8 & 10 January 1835.

5   PRO, ADM3805, Report of Comptroller for Victualling and Transport Services.

6   *Cork Mercantile Chronicle*, 10 & 11 December 1816.

7   PRO, ADM3805, Report of Comptroller for Victualling and Transport Services; Mawer, *Most Perfectly Safe*, pp. 9–18.

8   PRO, ADM101/56/6, Surgeon's Journal *Neva* (1833).

9   Mayberry website, http://members.pcug.org.au/~ppmay.

10   PRO, ADM101/56/6, Surgeon's Journal *Neva* (1833).

11   PRO, ADM101/56/7, Surgeon's Journal *New Grove*. The *New Grove*'s surgeon, David Thomson, stated: 'The hospital in the *New Grove* was situated in the after part of the lower deck, a situation in every respect preferable to the bows of the ship where it was formerly placed.' As the *New Grove* made only one convict voyage, he was referring to all convict ships and not specifically the *New Grove*.

12   This location also kept the distance between the crew and the hospital.

13   Dana, *Two Years Before the Mast*, pp. 16–17.

14   HRA/1/18, Statement of Rose Ann Hyland. Hyland indicated that the door from her punishment cell led directly to the prison deck. The layout of the *Neva*, as described, is drawn from multiple sources. These include diagrams by Eric McGraffin reproduced by G. W. Mawer, State Library of Tasmania; plans of *Anson* – as fitted out for a female convict ship; and multiple photographs and drawings of convict ships and models as reproduced on various Internet sites. This information was adapted for the *Neva* by reference to the various surgeon's

journals and the *Neva* witness statements. Whilst we cannot say that this was the exact layout of the ship, it is considered likely that any differences between our representation and the actual layout are minimal.

15   PRO, CO280/59, Peck to Board of Enquiry.

16   Bateson, *The Convict Ships*, in Hughes, *The Fatal Shore*, p. 156.

17   PRO, ADM3805, Report of the Comptroller of Victualling and Transport Services; PRO, Prob 11/1882, Last Will and Testament of Benjamin Hutchins Peck.

18   HRA/1/18, Statements of Bennett, Bullard, Hine and Sharp.

19   Bateson, *The Convict Ships*, pp. 86–7.

20   PRO, ADM101/73/3, Surgeon's Journal *Waterloo*.

21   PRO, ADM101/22/6, Surgeon's Journal *Edward*.

22   PRO, ADM101/38/7, Surgeon's Journal *John Bull*. Refers to relatives boarding *John Bull* at Cork, and those who did not board rowing around the ship.

23   *Southern Reporter*, 8 January 1835.

24   *Cork Evening Herald*, 7 January 1835.

25   McIntyre, *Free Passage*, p. 138.

26   *The Constitution or Cork Advertiser*, 6 January 1835; *Cork Evening Herald*, 7 January 1835.

27   HRA/1/18, Statement of Mary Slattery.

7   The Voyage

1   Her Majesty's Stationery Office (HMSO), Parliamentary Papers 1834, Volume 5, Instructions to Surgeons Superintendent on board convict ships proceeding to New South Wales or Van Diemen's Land.

2   PRO, ADM101/22/6, Surgeon's Journal *Edward*.

3   PRO, ADM101/31/5, Surgeon's Journal *Guildford*.

4   PRO, ADM101/22/6, Surgeon's Journal *Edward*.

5   Dana, *Two Years Before the Mast*, p. 4.

6   PRO, ADM101/38/7, Surgeon's Journal *John Bull*.

7   PRO, ADM101/17/3, Surgeon's Journal *City of Edinburgh*.

8   Cunningham, *Two Years in New South Wales*; Mawer, *Most*

Perfectly Safe, p. 12.

9   NAI, CSORP/1839/95/2–95/10730.

10 HMSO, Parliamentary Papers 1834, Volume 5, Instructions to the Masters of Convict Ships.

11 HMSO, Parliamentary Papers 1834, Volume 5, Instructions to Surgeons Superintendent on board convict ships.

12 HRA/1/18, Statement of Rose Ann Hyland.

13 PRO, ADM101/22/6, Surgeon's Journal *Edward*. William Watt's diary from the *Edward*'s voyage in 1828 is of particular relevance. Like most of the diaries used to construct this narrative, it referred to a female convict ship that left Ireland during the same period as the *Neva*. The specific routine enforced by Watt aboard the *Edward* received a note of approval from General Superintendent of Convicts Edward Trevor.

14 PRO, ADM101/56/7, Surgeon's Journal *New Grove*.

15 PRO, ADM101/31/5, Surgeon's Journal *Guildford*.

16 HMSO, Parliamentary Papers 1834, Volume 5, Instructions to Surgeons Superintendent on board convict ships.

17 PRO, ADM101/31/5, Surgeon's Journal *Guildford*.

18 PRO, ADM101/31/5 & ADM101/40/3, Surgeons' Journals *Guildford* and *Katherine Stewart Forbes*.

19 PRO, ADM101/38/7 & ADM101/70/3, Surgeons' Journals *John Bull* and *Surrey II*.

20 HRA/1/18, Statement of Joseph Bennett.

21 HMSO, Parliamentary Papers 1834, Volume 5, Instructions to Surgeons Superintendent on board convict ships.

22 *Ibid.*

23 PRO, ADM101/62/5, Surgeon's Journal *Pyramus*.

24 PRO, ADM101/38/7, Surgeon's Journal *John Bull*.

25 Five women submitted statements to the enquiry. Only two were capable of signing a name, with three opting for an X. Of the six survivors, three claimed an ability to read; only two of those could write. See TAHO, CON16/1/1.

26 PRO, ADM101/40/3 & ADM101/17/3, Surgeons' Journals *Katherine Stewart Forbes* and *City of Edinburgh*. Both surgeons

(Stephenson on *Katherine Stewart Forbes*) specifically commented on the inability of one single patient to speak English, which implies that this was a rare occurrence.

27   PRO, ADM101/38/7 & ADM101/62/4, Surgeons' Journals *John Bull* and *Pyramus*.

28   HMSO, Parliamentary Papers 1834, Volume 5, Instructions to Surgeons Superintendent on board convict ships.

29   Smith, *A Cargo of Women*, p. 28.

30   Damousi, *Depraved and Disorderly*, p. 9.

31   *Westmeath Journal*, 24 October 1833.

32   PRO, CO201/277, Enquiry *John Renwick*.

33   HRA/1/18, Statement of Benjamin Hutchins Peck.

34   PRO, ADM101/22/6, Surgeon's Journal *Edward*.

35   *Ibid.*

36   PRO, ADM101/31/5 & ADM101/73/3, Surgeons' Journals *Guildford* and *Waterloo*.

37   Damousi, *Depraved and Disorderly*, p. 25.

38   PRO, ADM101/38/7, Surgeon's Journal *John Bull*.

39   HMSO, Parliamentary Papers 1834, Instructions to Surgeons Superintendent on board convict ships.

40   For an account of the various sightings aboard an 1830s voyage from the United Kingdom to Australia, see New South Wales State Library (NSWSL), Croker Millar Journal, ML MSS 6110.

41   For an account of a particularly quarrelsome night in the prison of a female convict ship, see PRO, ADM101/38/7, Surgeon's Journal *John Bull*.

42   *Westmeath Journal*, 24 October 1833.

43   PRO, ADM101/65/3, Surgeon's Journal *Royal Admiral*.

44   PRO, ADM101/38/7, Surgeon's Journal *John Bull*.

45   Mawer, *Most Perfectly Safe*, pp. 13–15; Hughes, *The Fatal Shore*, pp. 143–57.

46   Damousi, *Depraved and Disorderly*, p. 21.

47   HRA/1/18, Statement of Thomas Sharp.

48   HMSO, Parliamentary Papers 1834, Instructions to Surgeons

Superintendent on board convict ships.

49   PRO, ADM101/38/7, Surgeon's Journal *John Bull*.

50   PRO, ADM101/31/5, Surgeon's Journal *Guildford*.

51   PRO, ADM101/40/3, Surgeon's Journal *Katherine Stewart Forbes*.

52   *Ibid*.

53   PRO, ADM101/56/7, Surgeon's Journal *New Grove*.

54   *Ibid*.

55   PRO, ADM101/38/7, Surgeon's Journal *John Bull*.

56   Stone, *Beautiful Bodies*, p. 70.

57   *Ibid*.

58   Browning, *The Convict Ship*, pp. 298–307. Browning's text was a proposed outline for the ideal organisation of a convict voyage as dictated by the author's experience of three of them.

59   HMSO, Parliamentary Papers 1834, Volume 5, Instructions to Surgeons Superintendent on board convict ships.

60   PRO, ADM101/38/7, Surgeon's Journal *John Bull*.

61   TAHO, NS816, Reminiscences of the Voyage of the 'Garland Grove 2' by Abraham Harvey, 2nd Officer, reproduced on femaleconvicts.org.au.

8   The Wreck

1   PRO, ADM101/23/1, Surgeon's Journal *Eleanor*.

2   HRA/1/18, Statement of Benjamin Hutchins Peck.

3   For an explanation of the watch system operated aboard nineteenth-century merchant vessels, see Dana, *Two Years Before the Mast*, p. 6. Robert Bullard's statement to the *Neva* enquiry indicated that four-hour watches were the norm aboard the ship.

4   PRO, ADM101/38/7, Surgeon's Journal *John Bull*. The women subsequently admitted that they had spoken of the *Lady Shore*, but assured the surgeon that they had no mutinous intent. They returned to the usual daily routine as soon as they pledged good behaviour.

5   Dana, *Two Years Before the Mast*, p. 26.

6   *Cornwall Chronicle*, 4 July 1835. None of the survivors specifically reported a stop at St Paul's, so the newspaper report may be incorrect. However, given that it was written immediately after the survivors arrived at Launceston in Van Diemen's Land, it is assumed that the journalist had a reliable source.

7   HRA/1/18, Statement of Benjamin Hutchins Peck.

8   *Ibid.*

9   James Horsburgh, *The India Directory*, 3rd edition, London 1826, p. 101, in Mawer, *Most Perfectly Safe*, p. 80.

10   HRA/1/18, Statement of Joseph Bennett.

11   PRO, ADM101/70/3 & ADM101/62/5, Surgeons' Journals *Surrey II* and *Pyramus*.

9   King Island

1   TAHO, G. W. Barnard, Survey of King Island 1827, Dispatch No. 73/1827. See also: *Hobart Town Gazette*, 21 March 1827.

2   This account of the survivors' time on King Island is constructed from cross-reference to the reports of the Boards of Enquiry contained in HRA/1/18. More specific references are given where required. Questions as to the accuracy of those reports, and the testimony on which they were based, are dealt with in subsequent chapters.

3   The statements of Bennett and Sharp each mentioned the boy specifically. Peck stated that ten crew members made it to King Island alive. Consequently we can conclude that the boy mentioned was one of the crew.

4   For references to these tents, see *Cornwall Chronicle*, 4 July 1835. See also: TAHO, NS1612/1/1, *Journal recording details of life on King Island by John Scott who had children with Mary, an Aboriginal woman.* Copied by Anne Drysdale, who cared for his children after he drowned.

5   *Launceston Advertiser*, 9 July 1835.

6   HRA/1/18, Report by Board of Enquiry.

7   TAHO, AB760/1/6, Cape Wickham Lighthouse Log 1868–

69, p. 563; HRA/1/18, Statements of Peck and Bennett; *The West Australian*, 13 April 1935; *Launceston Advertiser*, 2 July 1835; *North Western Advocate and Emu Bay Times*, 26 September 1910.

8 *Sydney Gazette*, 7 July 1835; HRA/1/18, Report by Board of Enquiry.

9 TAHO, CSO1/809/17293, Charles Friend to Arthur. Although Dunderdale's *The Book of the Bush* claimed that the fires were started with a flint musket that washed ashore, *The Book of the Bush* is not considered the most reliable of sources. It was written several decades after the events in question and directly contradicts the eyewitness accounts on several occasions. It also omits many of the details provided by the survivors. Friend was there and he wrote to Arthur in June 1835, and thus his account is considered much more reliable. It is also considered more likely that fire was transferred to the *Neva* camp from Scott's hut, via the *Tartar* camp.

10 Gough, 'The Ranger: Seeking the Hidden Figure of History'.

11 TAHO, NS1612/1/1, Scott's Journal.

12 TAHO, CSO1/809/17293; *Cornwall Chronicle*, 4 July 1835. Both of these sources refer to Scott's 'passenger' status aboard the *Tartar*. Scott was definitely resident on the island when he began his journal (TAHO, NS1612/1/1) in late 1836. However, that journal's references to his family's ages and the replacement of his 'old' hut in late 1836, along with continuous references to the existence of his hut at Yellow Rock in May 1835 by several of the *Neva*'s survivors and by Charles Friend, indicate that Scott and his family were already resident on the island at the time of the *Neva* tragedy. Numerous newspaper accounts of the wreck, dating from 1835 onwards, refer to Scott's residency on King Island.

13 See Chapter 13 for details of tickets of leave in respect of the *Neva* survivors.

14 TAHO, NS1612/1/1 Scott's Journal; the *Argus*, 24 May 1884.

15 TAHO, CSO1/809/17293, Memorial of Mr Charles Friend.

16   *Sydney Gazette*, 7 July 1835.
17   TAHO, CSO1/809/17293, Memorial of Mr Charles Friend.
18   *Ibid.*
19   *Ibid.*
20   *Ibid.*
21   HRA/1/18, Statement of Rose Ann Hyland. This establishes that the convicts left the island in the morning. TAHO, CSO1/809/17293, Ronald C. Gunn to Superintendent of Convicts. This letter establishes that the date of departure from King Island was 24 June.
22   HRA/1/18, Statement of Joseph Bennett.
23   HRA/1/18, Statement of Rose Ann Hyland.
24   TAHO, NS1612/1/1, Scott's Journal.

10   Enquiry

1   PRO, ADM1/4260, Peck to Soutler.
2   O'Byrne, *A Naval Biographical Dictionary*.
3   *Sydney Gazette and New South Wales Advertiser*, 19 December 1833.
4   Reynolds, John, 'Montagu, John (1797–1853)', in *Australian Dictionary of Biography*.
5   TAHO, CSO809/17293/127/8, Friend to Montagu.
6   *Ibid.*
7   TAHO, CSO809/17293/127/8, Friend to Arthur.
8   TAHO, CSO809/17293/127/8, Deare to Montagu.
9   HRA/1/18, p. 136.
10   TAHO, CSO809/17293/127/8, Deare to Montagu.
11   PRO, ADM1/4260, Peck to Soutler.
12   PRO, CO280/59.
13   SRNSW Col. Sec., Letter No. 39/9405 [4/2441].
14   *Ibid.*
15   *Launceston Advertiser*, 2 July 1835.
16   *Ibid.*, 9 July 1835.
17   HRA/1/18, Peck to Board of Enquiry.
18   *Hobart Town Courier*, 3 July 1835.

The Wreck of the *Neva*

19 Bateson, *The Convict Ships*, pp. 215–16.

20 *Cornwall Chronicle*, 4 July 1835.

21 *Ibid.*

22 PRO, CO280/58/92118, Arthur to Spring Rice.

23 PRO, CO201/247, Montagu to Board of Enquiry.

24 *Cornwall Chronicle*, 11 July 1835.

25 *Sydney Gazette and New South Wales Advertiser*, 22 August 1835.

26 *Ibid.*, 1 August 1835.

27 *Cornwall Chronicle*, 27 June 1835.

28 *The Australian*, 25 August 1835.

29 *Cornwall Chronicle*, 10 June 1874.

30 *The Colonist*, 17 September 1835.

31 PRO, Prob 11/1882, Last Will and Testament of Benjamin Hutchins Peck.

32 Although some records of men with similar names might relate to the *Neva*'s crew, those names (and derivations of them) were too common to declare a reasonable likelihood that the records are relevant to this story. Nonetheless, it is worth noting that Joseph Bennett may have owned a shop in Evandale, Van Diemen's Land (*The Mercury*, 14 June 1866), and may have been involved in a second maritime disaster when the *Penola*, on which a Joseph Bennett was a passenger, collided with the *City of Launceston* in November 1865 (*Cornwall Chronicle*, 25 August 1866). Thomas Sharp might have returned to sea. In 1868 a man of that name was involved in a drunken riot aboard the *Harrowby* during its passage from Britain to Australia (*Launceston Examiner*, 8 February 1868). Robert Bullard may also have returned to sea. A man of that name sailed from London aboard the *Waterwitch* in November 1836 (PRO, BT98/384).

33 PRO, CO280/59/92118, Board of Enquiry to Montagu.

34 *Ibid.*

35 *Ibid.*

36 Hansen, Jill T., 'Moriarty, William (1792–1850)', in *Australian*

Dictionary of Biography.

37   *Cornwall Chronicle*, 18 and 25 April 1835.

38   PRO, CO280/59/92118, Moriarty to Montagu.

39   *Ibid.*

40   *Ibid.*

41   *Ibid.*

42   *Ibid.*

43   *Ibid.*

44   PRO, CO280/59/92118, Arthur to Glenelg.

45   *Ibid.*

46   *Ibid.*

47   *Launceston Advertiser*, 23 July 1835.

48   *Cornwall Chronicle*, 6 October 1866; Archer, *The Scott Letters*, pp. 39 & 63.

11   Unsolved Mysteries

1   HRA/1/18, Wood to Maule.

2   HRA/1/18, Wood to Phillips.

3   *Belfast Commercial Chronicle*, 21 December 1835.

4   House of Commons, Parliamentary Papers 1836, Series 3, Vol. 32, Commons Sitting, 15 April 1836.

5   The map is on file with the heritage officer at Parks Tasmania. There is no precise date on the map; however, it is thought to originate from the construction of the Cape Wickham Lighthouse in 1861.

6   Stone, *Encyclopedia of Australian Shipwrecks*, at http://oceans1. customer.netspace.net.au/easw.html. See also: Broxam and Nash, *Tasmanian Shipwrecks*.

7   TAHO, AB760/1/6 (1868–69, p. 563).

8   TAHO, NS1612/1/1, Scott's Journal.

9   HRA/1/18, Friend to Board of Enquiry.

10   *Cornwall Chronicle*, 4 July 1835.

11   TAHO, CSO809/17293/127/8, Friend to Arthur.

12   *Ibid.*

13   HRA/1/18, Friend to Board of Enquiry.

The Wreck of the *Neva*

14 See map in Chapter 9, p. 153.

15 Tidal charts provided by Tidetech (www.tidetech.org).

16 HRA/1/18, Statements of Peck, Bennett, and Sharp.

17 *Ibid.* Thomas Sharp stated that breakers had been sighted about one hour after he had gone below. He had gone below having reefed the topsails before 2 a.m. (Peck and Bennett statements). This implies that the breakers had actually been sighted at 3 a.m. However, Sharp's impression that the warning of breakers had come 'about an hour' after he had gone below hardly lends itself to the establishment of a precise timeline.

18 *Colonial Times*, 1 September 1835.

19 HRA/1/18, Statements of Peck and Bennett.

20 Given the renowned accuracy of Admiralty charts, and the continuing evolution of hydrography in the two centuries since the *Neva* was wrecked, the possibility of an uncharted rock at Peck's location is discounted.

21 HRA/1/18, Statements of Peck, Bullard, and Bennett.

22 HRA/1/18, Statement of Ellen Galvin.

23 *Ibid.*

24 See Chapter 9, pp. 162–3.

25 TAHO, CSO809/17293/127/8, Deare to Montagu.

26 Figures are adjusted for the three deaths and one birth that occurred between Cork and King Island.

27 HRA/1/18, Statement of William Hine.

28 HRA/1/18, Statement of Benjamin Hutchins Peck.

29 TAHO, CSO809/17293/127/8, Barnes to Montagu.

30 TAHO, CSO809/17293/127/8, Board of Survey to Commissariat, Hobart.

31 Parsons, *Ships of Australia and New Zealand before 1850 – Part Two*, p. 54.

32 SRNSW, Col. Sec., 36/1150 [4/2334–5].

33 TAHO, CSO809/17293/127/8, Memorial of Charles Friend.

34 If Friend had come in search of the *Tartar*, it seems that he and Peck lied about their attempt to provision workers at Port Fairy.

12   Colonial Australia

1   Damousi, *Depraved and Disorderly*, p. 29.

2   PRO, ADM101/22/6, Surgeon's Journal *Edward*.

3   PRO, ADM101/62/5, Surgeon's Journal *Pyramus*.

4   TAHO, CON16/1/1, Convict Indent.

5   Hughes, *The Fatal Shore*, pp. 244–5.

6   *Ibid.*, pp. 252–3.

7   *Ibid.*, pp. 247–8.

8   Robinson, *The Women of Botany Bay*, p. 204.

9   See gravesoftas.dyndns.org – Free Settler: Alexander Wales; see also: *Launceston Advertiser*, 20 November 1834.

10 *Statistical Returns of Van Diemen's Land from 1824 to 1839* – figures from 1838 Census.

11 *Ibid.*

12 Broxam and Nash, *Tasmanian Shipwrecks*.

13 *Cornwall Chronicle*, 27 June 1835.

14 *Statistical Returns of Van Diemen's Land from 1824 to 1839*.

15 Shipping details from the *Cornwall Chronicle*, 27 June 1835.

16 Breton, *Excursions in New South Wales*, p. 307.

17 Statistical Returns of Van Diemen's Land from 1824 to 1839.

18 National Library of Australia: RM 1213. Plan of the Town of Launceston VDL Smythe, H. W. H. 1835. http://nla.gov.au/nla.map-rm1213-sd-cd.

19 See www.femaleconvicts.org.au.

20 *Hobart Town Courier*, 10 October 1829. See also: www.femaleconvicts.org.au.

21 *Ibid.*

22 PRO, ADM1/4260, Deare to Montagu.

23 TAHO, CSO1/809/17293, Deare to Montagu.

24 TAHO, CON40/1/1, Conduct registers for female convicts.

25 TAHO, CSO1/809/17293, Matthew Curling Friend to Montagu (associated correspondence).

26 PRO, CO201/246/92118.

27 TAHO, CON13/1/8.

28 *Ibid.*

29   TAHO, CSO809/17293/127/8, Matthew Curling Friend to John Montagu.

13   Life after the *Neva*

1   *The Constitution or Cork Advertiser*, 10 December 1835.

2   Information on Mary Slattery is drawn from multiple sources. See: TAHO, CON13/1/8, CON16/1/1 & CON40/1/9. See also: PRO, CO280/94, CO280/96, CO280/97 & CO280/104; www.irishgenealogy.ie; KY/RC/BA/477631, KY/RC/BA/453593, KY/RC/BA/462185 & KY/RC/BA/477631. The Convict Indent (TAHO, CON16/1/1) recorded Slattery's place of trial as Galway. However, the same document recorded her birthplace as Tralee and named the Tralee publican from whom she stole £10 worth of silver spoons. No other *Neva* record makes any reference to Mary Slattery being tried in Galway. An exhaustive trawl of Galway newspapers (because no official court records survive) from 1833 and 1834 did not reveal a single Mary Slattery tried in Galway at that time. For those reasons it is considered that the indent recorded the place of trial incorrectly.

3   PRO, CO201/272.

4   Information on Rose Ann Hyland is drawn from multiple sources. See: TAHO, CON13/1/8, CON16/1/1 & CON40/1/5.

5   *Colonial Times*, 29 March & 5 April 1842.

6   TAHO, CON52/1/1, p. 115; Ancestry.com, *Australia Marriage Index, 1788–1950*.

7   *Colonial Times*, 10 March 1840, at femaleconvicts.org.au.

8   Information on Rose Ann Dunn is drawn from multiple sources. See: TAHO, CON13/1/8, CON16/1/1 & CON40/1/3. See also: TAHO, CON52/1/1, p. 115.

9   TAHO, CON31/1/27. See also: TAHO, CSO1/1/403.

10   Information on Ellen Galvin is drawn from multiple sources. See: TAHO, CON13/1/8, CON16/1/1 & CON40/1/3. See also: TAHO, CON52/1/1, p. 115; Ancestry.com, *Australia Marriage Index, 1788–1950*.

11 SRNSW, Series 12212, Item 4/4509 & Series 12210, Item 4/4370.

12 TAHO, CON40/1/5.

13 Information on Margaret Drury is drawn from multiple sources. See: TAHO, CON13/1/8, CON16/1/1 & CON40/1/3.

14 Research on the Drury line was conducted with reference to the papers of Victor Malheim.

15 TAHO, CON16/1/1, Convict Indent.

16 PRO, Microfilm Publication, HO10, Piece 50.

17 Information on Ann Cullen, William Jones and William Howard is drawn from several sources. See: TAHO, CON40/1/1, CON13/1/8, CON16/1/1, CON31/1/26, CON18/1/18, CON23/1/2, CSO/1/1/820, CON52/1/2, pp. 85–6 & 365. See also: Ancestry.com, *Australia Marriage Index, 1788–1950.* Two separate William Joneses sailed on the *Norfolk*. Cullen certainly sought approval to marry the William Jones mentioned (Prisoner No. 857). She then sought permission to marry William Jones again. By that time both of the *Norfolk*'s William Joneses were free men. Consequently neither one would have had their prisoner numbers recorded on the application. This text assumes that Cullen sought to marry the William Jones cited as 857 on a second occasion. Although she may have sought to marry the other William Jones, that possibility is considered unlikely.

18 PRO, CO280/205.

19 Genealogical research on Mary Ann Cullen was drawn from the papers of Lynette McKimm and Dianne Snowden.

20 McIntyre, *Free Passage*, p. 209.

21 NAI/FS1836/B13.

22 *Ibid.*

Appendix IV

1 PRO, CO201/247 92118, p. 367.

2 Variations of Christian name and surnames were common among records of this time. For example, Peter Robinson is

sometimes referred to as Sydney Robinson among different records of the *Neva* tragedy. For that reason, and given the repeated statements from various survivors regarding the numbers of the *Neva*'s crew and complement, it is thought likely that 'Haines' is an alternative spelling of Hine (sometimes Hines), and that Thomas was a name sometimes used by William. It is considered highly unlikely that a man whose name was not on the official crew list gave a statement to the authorities.

3   Like William Hine and Peter Robinson, it seems that Henry Calthorpe used different variations of his name. It is thought that Edward Calthorpe and Henry Calthorpe were the same person.

Select Bibliography

Alexander, A., *Tasmania's Convicts: How Felons Built a Free Society* (Allen & Unwin, Crows Nest, NSW, 2010)

Ancestry.com, *Australia Marriage Index, 1788–1950* [online database] (Provo, UT, USA: Ancestry.com Operations, Inc., 2010)

Archer, D. J. L. (transcriber), *The Scott Letters: VDL & Scotland 1836–55* (Regal Publications, Launceston, Tas., 2009)

Australian Dictionary of Biography [online] (National Centre of Biography, Australian National University, Canberra, 2006), http://adb.anu.edu.au

Barrington, G. and Rickard, S., *George Barrington's Voyage to Botany Bay: Re-telling a Convict's Travel Narrative of the 1790s* (Leicester University Press, London, 2001)

Bateson, C., *The Convict Ships, 1787–1868* (A. H. and A. W. Reed, Sydney and London, 1974)

Boyce, J., *Van Diemen's Land* (Black Inc., Melbourne, 2009)

Breton, Lieut W. H., *Excursions in New South Wales, Western Australia and Van Diemen's Land During the Years 1830, 1831, 1832 and 1833* (Richard Bentley, London, 1834)

Brooke, A. and Brandon, D., *Bound for Botany Bay: British Convict Voyages to Australia* (National Archives, Kew, Surrey, 2005)

Browning, C. A., *The Convict Ship and England's Exiles* (Hamilton, Adams & Co., London, 1847)

Broxam, G. and Nash, M., *Tasmanian Shipwrecks* (Navarine Publishing, Woden, ACT, 1998)

Cadogan, T. (ed.), *Lewis' Cork: A Topographical Dictionary of the*

Parishes, Towns and Villages of Cork City and County (The Collins Press, Cork, 1998)

Campbell, C., *The Intolerable Hulks: British Shipboard Confinement, 1776–1857* (Heritage Books, Bowie, MD, 1994)

Clarke, M., *For the Term of His Natural Life* (The University of Adelaide Library, 2001)

Costello, C., *Botany Bay: The Story of the Convicts Transported from Ireland to Australia 1791–1853* (Mercier Press, Cork and Dublin, 1987)

Crocombe, A., *Convicts in Australia: A Workforce of Prisoners* (Echidna Books, Carlton, Vic., 2006)

Crowley, T. M., *A Drift of 'Derwent Ducks': Lives of the 200 Female Irish Convicts Transported on the Australasia from Dublin to Hobart in 1849* (Research Tasmania, Hobart, 2005)

Cunningham, P., *Two Years in New South Wales* (Angus and Robertson, Sydney, 1926)

Damousi, J., *Depraved and Disorderly: Female Convicts, Sexuality and Gender in Colonial Australia* (Cambridge University Press, Cambridge, 1997)

Dana, R. H., *Two Years Before the Mast* (World Public Library, 2010)

Daniels, K., *Convict Women* (Allen & Unwin, St Leonards, NSW, 1998)

Dunderdale, G. and Project Gutenberg Australia, *The Book of the Bush* (Project Gutenberg Australia, [Sl], 2000)

Gough, J., 'The Ranger: Seeking the Hidden Figure of History', in Gough, J., Knights, M., Hoffie, P. and Greeno, L., *The Ranger* (South Australian School of Art Gallery, University of South Australia, Adelaide, South Australia, 2007)

Hawkings, D. T., *Bound for Australia* (Library of Australian History, Sydney, 1988)

Henderson, J., *Observations on the Colonies of New South Wales and Van Diemen's Land 1831–32* (Libraries Board of South Australia, Adelaide, 1965)

Hicks, S., *What was the Voyage really like? A Brief Guide to Researching Convict and Immigrant Voyages to Australia and New Zealand* (Unlock the Past, Modbury, South Australia, 2010)

Horsburgh, J., *The India Directory* 3rd edition (Author, London, 1826)

Hughes, R., *The Fatal Shore: A History of the Transportation of Convicts to Australia, 1787–1868* (Collins Harvill, London, 1987)

Johnson, W., *The English Prison Hulks* (C. Johnson, London, 1957)

Kelly, F., *A History of Kilmainham Gaol: The Dismal House of Little Ease* (Mercier Press, Cork, 1988)

Layson, J. F., *Memorable Shipwrecks and Seafaring Adventures of the Nineteenth Century* (John G. Murdoch, London, 1880)

Lewis, S. D., *A Topographical Dictionary of Ireland* (S. Lewis and Co., London, 1837)

Mawer, G. A., *Most Perfectly Safe: The Convict Shipwreck Disasters of 1833–42* (Allen & Unwin, St Leonards, NSW, 1997)

Mayberry, P., *Irish Convicts to New South Wales* [online database], http://members.pcug.org.au/~ppmay

McIntyre, P., *Free Passage: The Reunion of Irish Convicts and their Families in Australia, 1788–1852* (Irish Academic Press, Dublin, 2011)

McMahon, A., *Convicts at Sea: The Voyages of the Irish Convict Transports to Van Diemen's Land, 1840–1853* (Anne McMahon, Hobart, Tasmania, 2011)

Melville, H., *Brisbane Convicts of Van Diemen's Land* (Australian Publishing, Brisbane, 1970)

Nash, M., *A Survey of Shipwrecks in Tasmanian Waters* (Dept. of Parks, Wildlife and Heritage, Hobart, Tasmania, 1990)

The Wreck of the *Neva*

O'Byrne, W. R., *A Naval Biographical Dictionary Compromising the Life and Services of Every Living Officer in Her Majesty's Navy, from the Rank of Admiral of the Fleet to that of Lieutenant, inclusive* (J. Murray, London, 1849)

O'Donnell, R., *Robert Emmet and the Rising of 1803* (Irish Academic Press, Dublin, 2003)

O'Sullivan, N., *Every Dark Hour: A History of Kilmainham Gaol* (Liberties Press, Dublin, 2007)

Oxley, D., *Convict Maids: The Forced Migration of Women to Australia* (Cambridge University Press, Cambridge and New York, 1996)

Parsons, R., *Ships of Australia and New Zealand before 1850 – Part Two* (Privately Published, Magill, South Australia, 1983)

Price, J. W. and Fulton, P. J., *The Minerva Journal of John Washington Price: A Voyage from Cork, Ireland to Sydney, New South Wales, 1798–1800* (Melbourne University Press, Melbourne, Victoria, 2000)

Reece, B., *The Origins of Irish Convict Transportation to New South Wales* (Palgrave, Houndmills, Basingstoke, Hampshire; New York, 2001)

Rees, S., *The Floating Brothel: The Extraordinary Story of the* Lady Juliana *and its Cargo of Female Convicts Bound for Botany Bay* (SCB edition, Hodder Headline Australia, Sydney, 2001)

Robinson, P., *The Women of Botany Bay: A Reinterpretation of the Role of Women in the Origins of Australian Society* (Macquarie Library, New South Wales, 1988).

Robson, L. L., *The Convict Settlers of Australia: An Enquiry into the Origin and Character of the Convicts Transported to New South Wales and Van Diemen's Land 1787–1852* (Melbourne University Press, Melbourne, 1965)

Select Bibliography

Robson, L. L., *A History of Tasmania. Volume 1. Van Diemen's Land from the Earliest Times to 1855* (Oxford University Press, Melbourne, 1983)

Shaw, A. G. L., *Convicts and the Colonies: A Study of Penal Transportation from Great Britain and Ireland to Australia and Other Parts of the British Empire* (Faber & Faber, London, 1966)

Shearer, J. D., *Bound for Botany Bay: Impressions of Transportation and Convict Life* (Summit Books, Sydney, 1976)

Smith, B., *A Cargo of Women: Susannah Watson and the Convicts of the* Princess Royal (Allen & Unwin, Crows Nest, NSW, 2008)

Smith, B., *Australia's Birth Stain: The Startling Legacy of the Convict Era* (Allen & Unwin, Crows Nest, NSW, 2008)

Statistical Returns of Van Diemen's Land from 1824 to 1839 (second edition, Hobart, 1839)

Stone, G., *Beautiful Bodies: The Doomed Voyage of the Convict Ship* Amphitrite *and her Cargo of Infamous Damned Whores* (Macmillan, Sydney, 2009)

Stone, P., *Encyclopedia of Australian Shipwrecks: And Other Maritime Incidents, Including Vessels Lost Overseas, Merchant Ships Lost at War, and Those Lost on Inland Waters, Together with a Bibliography of Vessel Entries* (Oceans Enterprises, Victoria, 2006), partly reproduced at http://oceans1.customer.netspace.net.au/easw.html

Swiss, D. J., *The Tin Ticket: The Heroic Journey of Australia's Convict Women* (Berkley Books, New York, 2010)

Tardif, P., *Notorious Strumpets and Dangerous Girls: Convict Women in Van Diemen's Land, 1803–1829* (Angus & Robertson, North Ryde, NSW, 1990)

Walker, D., *Beacons of Hope: An Early History of Cape Otway and King Island Lighthouses* (Deakin University Press, Warrnambool, Victoria, 1991)

The Wreck of the *Neva*

Williams, J. and Davis, R. P., *Ordered to the Island: Irish Convicts and Van Diemen's Land* (Crossing Press, Sydney, 1994)

SELECTED JOURNAL ARTICLES

Blair, S., 'The Felonry and the Free? Divisions in Colonial Society in the Penal Era', *Labour History*, No. 45 (Nov., 1983), pp. 1–16

Byrne, P. J., 'A Colonial Female Economy: Sydney, Australia', *Social History*, Vol. 24, No. 3 (Oct., 1999), pp. 287–93

Conlin, E. and Source, C., '"Doing Trade": A Sexual Economy of Nineteenth-Century Australian Female Convict Prisons', *World Archaeology*, Vol. 32, No. 2, 'Queer Archaeologies' (Oct., 2000), pp. 209–21

Cork Historical and Archaeological Society Journal, Vol. 93 (1988)

Damousi, J. S., 'Chaos and Order: Gender, Space and Sexuality on Female Convict Ships', *Australian Historical Studies*, Vol. 26, No. 104 (Apr., 1995), pp. 351–72

Damousi, J., '"Depravity and Disorder": The Sexuality of Convict Women', *Labour History*, No. 68 (May, 1995), pp. 30–45

Foxhall, Katherine, 'From Convicts to Colonists: The Health of Prisoners and the Voyage to Australia, 1823–53', *The Journal of Imperial and Commonwealth History*, Vol. 39, No. 1 (2011), pp. 1–19

Lohan, R., 'Sources in the National Archives for Research into the Transportation of Irish Convicts to Australia (1791–1853)', *Journal of the Irish Society for Archives*, Dublin (Spring, 1996), pp. 13–28

Middle Parish Chronicle, Vol. 1, No. 8 (July 1988)

Oxley, D., 'Living Standards of Women in Pre-famine Ireland', *Social Science History*, Vol. 28, No. 2 (Summer 2004), pp. 271–96

Rynne, C., 'An Archaeological Survey of Elizabeth Fort', *Cork Historical and Archaeological Society Journal*, Vol. 109 (2004)

Select Bibliography

Sullivan, C. W., 'Reconsidering the Convict Ships', *New Hibernia Review*, Vol. 12, No. 4 (Geimhreadh/Winter 2008), pp. 101–16

Williams, J., 'Irish Female Convicts and Tasmania', *Labour History*, No. 44 (May 1983)

Index